Windows NT 4

Answers!
Certified Tech Support

Barrie Sosinsky

Osborne **McGraw-Hill**

Berkeley • New York • St. Louis • San Francisco
Auckland • Bogotá • Hamburg • London
Madrid • Mexico City • Milan • Montreal
New Delhi • Panama City • Paris • São Paulo
Singapore • Sydney • Tokyo • Toronto

Osborne/**McGraw-Hill**
2600 Tenth Street
Berkeley, California 94710
U.S.A.

For information on translations or book distributors outside the U.S.A., or to arrange bulk purchase discounts for sales promotions, premiums, or fund-raisers, please contact Osborne/**McGraw-Hill** at the above address.

Windows NT 4 Answers!
Certified Tech Support

1234567890 DOC DOC 901987654321098

ISBN 0-07-882381-1

Publisher
Brandon A. Nordin

Copy Editor
Gary Morris

Editor-in-Chief
Scott Rogers

Proofreader
Pat Mannion

Acquisitions Editor
Joanne Cuthbertson

Indexer
Valerie Robbins

Project Editor
Claire Splan

Computer Designers
Mickey Galicia
Peter Hancik

Editorial Assistant
Gordon Hurd

Cover Design
Matt Nielsen

Technical Editor
Jeff Bankston

This book is dedicated to my son,
Joseph Julien Sosinsky,
who arrived just prior to my
starting the project.

About the Author . . .

Barrie Sosinsky is the Laboratory Director at *BackOffice Magazine*, a PennWell publication located in Nashua, NH. He is the best-selling author of over 25 computer books on topics as diverse as the Windows and Macintosh operating systems, databases, and the Internet. Over the past 12 years his consulting firm, Killer Apps in Medfield, MA, has worked with clients at major institutions on a variety of projects ranging from custom software design to documentation and training.

Contents

Acknowledgments

The author wishes to thank Joanne Cuthbertson for the opportunity to do this project, for her input and advice as the project proceeded. Gordon Hurd shepherded this book through product, and Gary Morris copyedited the manuscript.

Special thanks also go to Jeff Bankston, my technical editor, who has taken time from his busy schedule as an author and consultant to work on this project with me. I also wish to thank the folks at Stream International who tech edited the manuscript and provided many helpful corrections and technical insight.

Introduction

Windows NT is what Windows became when it grew up. Corporations use Windows NT Server to guard and manage their family jewels, programmers race around with Windows NT Workstation to provide themselves with crash protection, and you can use the power of Windows NT in your office or home. Windows NT, so dubbed as "New Technology," is the result of hundreds of man years of research at Microsoft and millions of man years of testing in the public domain. It is a powerful, yet complex operating system containing millions of lines of code. Since Windows NT runs your computer and all of the applications that you run on it, problems you have with Windows NT and any necessary troubleshooting you might have to do affects your computing in a fundamental way.

There are many books that have appeared on Windows NT over the past three years. They tend to be large volumes filled with complete explanations of the technology employed by this operating system. When you have a problem that you need to solve quickly, working your way through our competitors' books is a painful experience.

The book you hold in your hand offers a very different approach. This book provides you with 400 of the most commonly asked questions that are posed to Stream International, Microsoft's certified technical support contractor. These are real-world questions posed by users to expert support professionals every day.

If you have a problem, you can dive right into any of the 15 chapters in this book and find an answer to your particular problem of the moment. Questions and their answers are organized around topic areas: installation, multimedia, the file system, and so forth. Each chapter contains several topics that group individual questions together with related questions. At the start of each chapter is an "@ a Glance" section that summarizes each of the topic areas within a chapter. You can also consult the index to find answers to questions on a topic that might appear in one or more chapters, or to find related questions throughout the book.

You can think of this book as a friend you call on at 3 AM when your printer stops working, or the substitute to an expensive technical support phone call. This book is often cheaper, faster, and more accurate than the answers you might get in either of those cases, and it rewards you with answers again and again.

CONVENTIONS USED IN THIS BOOK

Windows NT 4 Answers uses several conventions designed to make it easier to read and find information on a particular topic or area. Among the conventions you will see are:

⇨ **Bold type**, which is used for text that you enter from your keyboard.

⇨ *Italic type*, which emphasizes certain important words or phrases that you need to know.

⇨ SMALL CAPITAL LETTERS, which are used to differentiate the keys on your keyboard. For example, you will see the words SHIFT and ENTER when those keys need to be pressed or are discussed.

⇨ Underlined letters appear in words that are commands on a menu or words in a dialog box. When underlined, these letters are accelerator keys. For example, the underlined letters in the phrase "Open in the File menu" would indicate that you could press the ALT key and the F key simultaneously to open the File menu, and then press the O key to give the Open command. In dialog boxes, a word like Normal style next to a check box or on a button would indicate that you press ALT and the underlined letter key to activate that check box or button.

For the most part, this book follows the standard conventions that appear in Microsoft's documentation and online help system for its Windows products. If any of the preceding techniques or operations are unfamiliar to you, you should consult your Window NT software manual's introduction for a fuller explanation of Microsoft's conventions.

You will find that this book presents a lot of information in a very compact form. Much of the discussion presents procedures for doing one thing or another, mostly taking corrective action. Therefore, this book contains many step-by-step procedures. Read the procedure in full before attempting the operation.

Embedded in the text are Notes, Tips, and Warnings. These emphasize an interesting related fact that is not required by a procedure but is of value, or draw your attention to something in the procedure that might cause you difficulty. You should pay particular attention to Warnings.

Since this book is meant to be very hands-on and direct, there isn't a lot of explanation with each question. When an overview of a particular area is necessary to understand the questions in a particular topic area of a chapter, you will find a sidebar containing that explanation.

NT MARCHES ON...

This book describes Windows NT Server 4 and Windows NT Workstation 4, up to Service Pack 3 (for Server). For the most part, answers that apply to the server version of the operating system also apply to the workstation version. We have attempted here to answer each question as if either operating system has this problem and requires this particular solution. When there is a difference between the two operating systems, we will generally state it.

Many questions will apply equally well to earlier versions of this operating system, particularly Windows Server and Workstation 3.5*x*. The interface changes substantially between these two versions, but many of the internal architectural features are identical.

Microsoft maintains an area of their Web site for Windows NT developments. You should browse **http://www.microsoft.com/ ntserver** for recent developments, updates, and upgrades. Other links mentioned in this book tell you where to find particular resources such as the Hardware Compatibility List, service packs, and so forth.

At the time of this writing, Windows NT Server 5 and Windows NT Workstation 5 are in early beta. Their release is at least a year away, slated for a fourth quarter 1998 introduction. Many of the features in these betas are either incomplete, not functional, or not even included in the versions we have seen. Therefore, Windows NT Server and Workstation version 4 is one of the longer lived versions of a major operating system that we have seen in recent years. Chances are good, therefore, that you will be able to continue to use this book for some time to come.

chapter

1 **A**nswers!

The Top Ten
FAQs

Answer Topics!

Sharing a folder with other people

Finding the latest version of the Windows NT
  Hardware Compatibility List

Getting more details in Explorer view

Restarting after a DOS application crashes

Changing the default printer

Pressing the SPACEBAR to invoke the "last
  known good" configuration

Tips for creating a user account

Recovering a deleted file

The minimum hardware requirements for NT
  Workstation and NT Server

Terminating an unresponsive application

The Top Ten FAQS @ a Glance

When you install a new operating system, it affects the way your entire computer operates. Windows NT controls essential functions like file storage and retrieval, printing, communications, and so forth. Most importantly, Windows NT controls how all of the applications that run on it "look and feel." So the questions you have regarding Windows NT take on added significance because the operating system is so basic and vital to your everyday computing needs. Among the Windows NT questions collected by Stream International, callers seeking help repeatedly requested answers to the following.

 ## 1. How do you share a folder with other people?

To share a folder with others:

1. Locate the folder to share, right-click it, and choose Sharing from the shortcut menu.

2. Click the Sharing tab and click the Shared As radio button.

3. Change the name and add comments to make the share's purpose obvious (optional).

4. Specify the number of users to allow to connect to the share at one time.

5. Next, click the Permissions button, click Add to add people or groups to the list, and then change the Type of Access to the folder.

See Chapter 5, "Working with Folders," for more information on creating and managing shares.

 ## 2. Where can I obtain the latest version of the Windows NT Hardware Compatibility List?

It's available from Microsoft on the World Wide Web at http://www.microsoft.com/isapi/hwtest/hsearchn4.idc. Versions for Win95, NT3.51, and 4.0 are available and can be viewed or downloaded. Chapter 2, "The Hardware Compatibility List" contains more information on this topic.

? 3. I want to get more details in my Explorer view. How can I do this?

To see more details:

1. Open the Windows NT Explorer.

2. Select the Options command from the View menu.

3. Click the Show all files radio button to see system files.

4. Check the Display the full path in the title bar and the Include description bar for right and left panes checkboxes.

5. Click the OK button.

6. Select the Details command from the View menu.

Chapter 6, "Using the Windows NT Explorer," describes this topic in more detail.

? 4. Do I have to reboot my machine if a DOS application crashes?

Not usually. Windows NT runs each DOS Application in a separate VDM (Virtual DOS Machine). If a DOS application crashes, all you need to do is close the current DOS session and start another one. This will create a new address space for the program to run in. This Windows NT feature allows multiple DOS programs to be run at the same time independent of one another. Chapter 3, "Running Programs," contains answers to several questions in this area.

? 5. How do you change the default printer?

Select the Printers command from the Settings submenu on the Start menu. Right-click the default printer and click on the Set As Default command in the shortcut menu to put a check mark on it.

? 6. What does "Press spacebar to invoke last known good" mean?

When you successfully log on to a Windows NT Server or Workstation, a small copy of your system registry is stored on your hard drive. After you make a change to your system (Device Driver, Network Adapter, etc.), your machine may not restart properly, or some other problem may exist that could prevent you from logging on. You can restart the computer and invoke the "Last Known Good" configuration by pressing the SPACEBAR when prompted. Keep in mind that this "Last known good" information is updated *every time* you log on and may not help you in some circumstances.

7. What are some good tips to remember when creating a user account?

Windows NT gives you several tools to implement your desired level of security with. Keep in mind that Windows NT is only as secure as YOU make it. Here are some suggestions for you to consider:

1. *Think "Global."* It is a general rule of thumb to add users to Global Groups. You would then add Global Groups to the Local Groups when needed. This allows for the central administration of a *group* of people rather than the tedious task of managing many single accounts.

2. *Create user templates whenever possible.* There is no need to create a new account over and over again every time a user account is needed in a domain. Create the first account for a specific purpose such as "Finance, Management, Etc.", assign the rights and groups you wish the account to have, and then save the account with a name that best suits that type of account. Remember to add an underscore (_) to the beginning of the account name so that it comes up first on your user list: for example, _Finance. When it is time to add a new user to your domain, make a copy of the template and then change the name and user information as needed.

3. *Standardize your account structure.* Using the same format when creating accounts can make administrating a domain a lot easier. Try to add a method to your madness when creating an account. Some companies prefer to use the first letter of a person's first name and then their last name (Jtest). Other companies prefer just a user's first and last name (JoeTest). Still others use an employee number (1040674). The point here is to think about what you want *before* you create your accounts. Use the same style (uppercase, lowercase, etc.) whenever possible.

4. *Disable or rename the built-in Administrator Account.* Because all Windows NT Servers ship with a default Administrator Account,

it is best to rename or disable it to thwart a possible breach in security.

5. *Never delete a user account.* More than once you will find that an employee may resign from your company or move from one domain to another. You would be surprised how many times they may actually come back! It is a good practice to disable a user's account rather than delete it. If the user will *never* come back, you can always rename the account and reuse it.

6. *Do not enable the Guest Account.* By default, Windows NT 4.0 ships with the Guest Account disabled. This provides for a secure environment. Do not enable the built-in Guest Account unless you have to.

7. *Always back up your User Accounts Database!* There is a utility called RDISK.EXE that you will find very useful. When executed with the /S parameter, it will back up the majority of your system's Registry. RDISK.EXE can be found in your \Winnt\System32 directory.

8. *Only assign users to groups they should be in.* There is no need to assign a secretary to your Global Administrators group. This could result in severe network security problems.

9. *Create a test account.* Chances are you will have administrator privileges throughout the network. A user may experience a problem that only affects accounts in a certain group. Use the test account for your testing. Nothing is more embarrassing than locking yourself out of your own network!

❓ 8. Can I recover a deleted file?

For security reasons, there is no way to recover deleted files in NT 3.51. In NT 4.0, double-click on the Recycle Bin on the Desktop. Chapter 6, "Recovering Deleted Files," covers this topic in detail.

❓ 9. What are the minimum hardware requirements for NT Workstation and NT Server?

⇨ For Windows NT Workstation 4.0: 486 DX/33 or Higher Processor, 12MB of RAM, and 120MB of free disk space.

⇨ For Windows NT Server 4: : 486 DX/33 or Higher Processor, 16MB of RAM, and 120MB of free disk space.

These are minimum configurations (as published by Microsoft) to get the machine off the ground but before anything realistically can be done. More realistic configurations are Pentium computers with 24MB and 32MB of RAM, respectively. Installing 64MB ram in the Workstation and 96MB in the Server is optimal. This question is covered in much more detail in the next chapter.

 10. I am running several applications on our NT Workstation and one of them stops responding. What is the best way to terminate the unresponsive app?

Use Task Manger to terminate the application. Right-click on the taskbar and choose Task Manager from the menu. In Task Manager, select the program (via the Applications tab) that has frozen and then select End Task.

chapter

2 **A**nswers!

Installing
Windows NT 4

Answer Topics!

Installing Windows NT 4
@ a Glance

⇨ Some careful **planning** can speed up your installation of Windows NT and allow you to obtain the specific configuration you require. Among the things you should know are which partition you will install the operating system on or upgrade to and which file system you want. You should also know your computer type and any associated hardware settings prior to installation.

⇨ Microsoft publishes a **Hardware Compatibility List** (HCL) with a listing of computers and peripheral devices that are tested and validated as compatible with Windows NT. The appearance of a component on this list indicates that the vendor has passed the Microsoft certification test for Windows NT. If a component doesn't appear on the list, it still may be compatible but hasn't been certified.

⇨ The **installation process** proceeds in stages through a thorough examination of your disks, the amount of free space, and other important factors. Setup installs the necessary files to boot your computer and then continues from the text mode portion to the graphical portion of the installation.

⇨ There are three ways you can install Windows NT using the Setup program. You can install locally using the Setup disks or by creating a set of boot floppies. You can also perform a **network installation**. These installations can be automated.

⇨ Setup lets you perform four different types of installations: typical, laptop, compact, and a **custom installation**. You can select the options you wish installed, as not all options are installed for each of these installation types.

⇨ Setup generally does a very good job of installing Windows NT. Still, it is possible to experience **installation problems**. These problems arise when you enter incorrect settings or have a hardware conflict. Installation can also fail when there isn't sufficient free space to copy the files or when your CD-ROM drive cannot be auto-detected. These and several other errors are described.

⇨ There are some issue that don't arise for **workstation vs. server installations**. You can create a domain controller on a server, and that server then must belong to that particular domain. If you wish to change the server's domain, you need to reinstall Windows NT. Also, a server allows you to perform a network installation and even perform a customized and unattended installation.

PLANNING YOUR INSTALLATION

? Which file system should I use for an installation: FAT or NTFS?

Setup is going to ask you to specify which partition (or volume) is going to be used as a boot partition, and which is going to be used for the system partition. The boot partition may be located on either a primary or an extended partition. The boot partition contains the Windows NT installation directory (/WINNT) as well as all of the Windows NT operating system files. The system partition is located on the active primary partition on the first partition of the first hard drive on your computer. This partition contains the files necessary for booting your computer, including the ones copied to your NT boot floppy disk: NTLDR, NTDETECT.COM, BOOT.INI, and either BOOTSECT.DOS or NTBOOTDD.SYS. Many installations put the system partition and boot partition on the same partition.

In general, NTFS is preferred to FAT for most installations. NTFS allows you to use the more powerful security features of that file system. Chapter 5 describes these file systems in more detail, as well as other aspects of the file systems that NT supports. Converting from FAT to NTFS is relatively easy, but the reverse procedure is more difficult, should you decide to make the change.

? I'm a busy person. How long will a Windows NT installation require?

There is no standard answer to this question. An installation depends significantly on the speed of your computer and on the options that you required. A standard installation on a low-end Pentium computer may take an hour, whereas an installation on a DEC Alpha may finish in as little as 15 minutes. Since some settings require thoughtful consideration, prior experience with the installation speeds up the process.

? What are the minimum requirements for installing Windows NT Workstation or Server?

Table 2-1 lists the minimum requirements for Windows NT Version 4.0 as described by Microsoft. This table also lists a more reasonable setup for average client and network demands for workstation and server, respectively.

Table 2-1 lists some of the common formats for data copied to the Clipboard.

 ## What settings do I need to know prior to installation of Windows NT?

Unless you are using a self-configuring bus like PCI, you will need to know what your hardware settings are. A chart of devices and their IRQs, DMA channels, and I/O port addresses will be invaluable when you are running the Windows NT Setup program. If you install a network adapter using the wrong settings, chances are that you will not be able to connect to your network should the installation complete itself.

Table 2-1. Minimum and Average Requirements for Windows NT Workstation and Server

Component	Workstation Minimum	Workstation Average	Server Minimum	Server Average
CPU	486/33	Pentium >90MHz	486/33	Pentium >100MHz
RAM	12MB	24MB	16MB	32MB[1]
Hard Drive	500MB[2]	1GB	500MB[3]	1GB
Display	VGA or better	VGA or better	VGA or better	VGA or better
Floppy disk drive	3.5"	3.5"	3.5"	3.5"
CD-ROM	Required /Optional[4]	Required	Required	Required
Network interface card	Required /Optional[5]	Required	Required	Required
Mouse	Recommended	Recommended	Recommended	Recommended

[1] Add additional RAM (and disk space) for every application that you have running on Windows NT Sever.

[2] Windows NT Workstation installs 117MB of files for a typical installation.

[3] Windows NT Server installs 124MB of files for a typical installation.

[4] A stand-alone workstation would require a CD-ROM drive. You can do a network installation for workstation and server. It is assumed that the server is networked, and that you would want to do a local installation of the operating system.

[5] An NIC would not be required for a stand-alone workstation. All other configurations are proposed to be networked computers.

What licensing type should I choose, and how do I change it once I've installed Windows NT?

Windows NT provides either a per-server or per-seat licensing mode when you install Windows NT Server 4. You will be asked to choose from the dialog box during the installation. Most small networks use a per-server licensing assignment, and switch over to per-seat as the network grows. Microsoft allows a *one-time-only switch* between these two modes without penalty.

To change licensing modes after installation on Windows NT Server:

1. Select the Control Panels command from the Settings submenu on the Start menu.

2. Double-click on the Licensing dialog box.

3. In the Choose Licensing Mode dialog box shown in Figure 2-1, select the product you wish to alter from the Product list box; then click on the Per Server radio button to switch from per-seat to per-server mode.

4. Click on the Add Licensing button.

5. In the New Client Access License dialog box shown in Figure 2-2, enter the number of licenses that you require in the Quantity spinner.

6. Click the OK button.

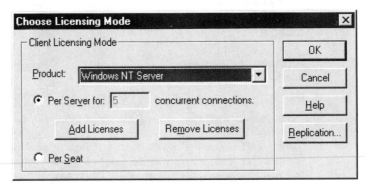

Figure 2-1.   The Choose Licensing Mode dialog box

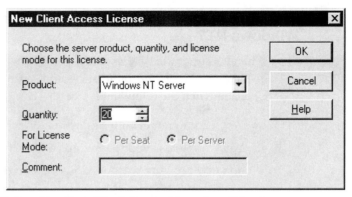

Figure 2-2.   The New Client Access Licensing dialog box

7. Click on the I agree that… checkbox in the licensing agreement dialog box (Figure 2-3) that appears.

8. Click OK to establish your per-seat licence.

Note: *A client access license for software like SQL Server is separate from the desktop operating system software that you purchase. Each server application that you run may require its own set of separate licenses.*

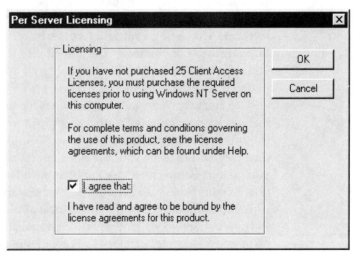

Figure 2-3.   The Licensing Agreement dialog box

? What are the advantages of upgrading vs. installing Windows NT?

When you upgrade Windows NT, you overwrite your previous installation. All of your preferences and settings are upgraded. Upgrade when the following is true:

⇨ You want to retain your desktop settings

⇨ You want to use your passwords and accounts

⇨ You don't require your previous version of Windows NT

When you install Windows NT, you leave your previous version of Windows intact. Install when the following is true:

⇨ You need to retain the ability to boot to your previous operating system

⇨ You are installing Windows NT on many computers, and you want the computers to be configured the same way

? When I upgrade my version of Windows, where should I locate the new files?

Windows NT Setup will detect a previous version of Windows, and it will ask if you really want to upgrade the operating system. In Windows 95, none of the Windows 95 registry settings will be carried forward. All existing applications must be reinstalled after the upgrade to NT. If you locate the new files in the same directory as your previous version of Windows, then all application and user preferences will be upgraded. Windows NT will also ask you if you wish to create an uninstall disk, which is a good safeguard. This method works properly for upgrading Windows NT 3.*x*.

It is preferable to install Windows NT into its own separate directory, and to leave your previous operating system intact. When you do that, Setup creates a dual-boot installation that allows you to boot to your previous operating system at startup. This can be invaluable should you find that a critical application or service fails in the new version of Windows NT. The downside to installing Windows NT 4 into a separate directory is that you will be required to install all of your applications and reconfigure all of your user preferences. If you have Windows 95 and OS/2 installed on your computer, you will have to install Windows NT 4 into a different directory. You cannot install over these operating systems.

THE HARDWARE COMPATIBILITY LIST

 I want to add a CD-ROM drive or some other component to my system. What is the best way to determine that the component will be supported by Windows NT?

Microsoft publishes a list of compatible computers, devices, and other hardware called the Hardware Compatibility List (HCL). Each operating system has an extensive list of hardware that has been tested and found to operate correctly with that specific version of the operating system. That is, there is an HCL for Windows NT 4 and one for Windows NT 3.51, but there aren't separate HCLs for server and workstation versions of the operating system.

Microsoft maintains a certification program for vendors that enable them to be listed. For example, a video board is listed as being Windows NT Workstation 4 compatible if it can be installed in standard computers and has a device driver that is also compatible with the operating system.

You can obtain the Hardware Compatibility List by searching the Microsoft Web site (http://www.microsoft.com/hwtest/hcl/) for it. The latest version of this list is available in both searchable and downloadable form as a text file or as an online help (.HLP) file. For example, you will find the server version at http://www.microsoft.com/ntserver/hcl/hclintro.htm; and you can also access the list at http://www.microsoft.com/ntworkstation/.

 Note: The absence of a device from the HCL doesn't necessarily mean that Windows NT isn't supported. It may just mean that the component is too new, or that the vendor has not sought or obtained certification.

Products that have passed the certification program often carry the Windows NT logo on the box. You can also contact the manufacturer to determine if their device is compatible with Windows NT, or search their Web site or BBS for this information.

If you already have Windows NT installed on your computer, one easy way to determine device compatibility with Windows NT is to see if there is a driver in the system for that manufacturer or model. This method isn't foolproof, and it won't always get you the latest version of a specific driver, but it will tell you if the model was supported at the time your disks were manufactured. Inclusion makes the purchase of the device a good bet.

❓ What's on the HCL?

The HCL lists the following components:

- ⇨ Disk controller cards and hard drives
- ⇨ Hardware security hosts
- ⇨ ISDN host adapters
- ⇨ Keyboards
- ⇨ Modems
- ⇨ Multiport serial adapters
- ⇨ Network adapters
- ⇨ Non-SCSI CD-ROM drives and tape drives

Note: *The hardware listed (other than computer systems themselves) in the HCL applies to the Intel platform. If you are purchasing a MIPS or DEC Alpha computer, then make sure the hardware you are purchasing conforms to those platforms.*

- ⇨ PCMCIA cards for laptops
- ⇨ Pointing devices
- ⇨ PowerPC computers and hardware
- ⇨ Printers
- ⇨ Processor upgrades
- ⇨ RAID systems
- ⇨ SCSI CD-ROM drives, tape drives, removable media, and scanners
- ⇨ SCSI controllers or host adapters; as well as Wide SCSI
- ⇨ Sound boards
- ⇨ Storage cabinets
- ⇨ Third-party remote access servers
- ⇨ Uninterruptible Power Supply (UPS) devices
- ⇨ Video or graphics display and capture cards
- ⇨ X86, MIPS RISC, and Digital Alpha AXP RISC computers for single and multiprocessor systems.

Note: *Some computers listed on the HCL are certified for NT Workstation and aren't necessarily qualified for use as a server platform. Be careful when selecting a computer based on its appearance on the HCL, and always check with the vendor for their recommendation. You should also note that Windows NT will not support the MIPS platform in the future.*

THE INSTALLATION PROCESS

How Does the Installation Process Work?

Windows NT installation proceeds through several phases, and varies somewhat depending on whether you install the software using the installation disk or by using the WINNT.EXE program. Prior to files being copied to disk, the Setup program runs CHKDSK to examine your system after which your computer is rebooted.

In the precopy phase of the installation when WINNT.EXE or WINNT32.EXE is used, Setup creates a set of floppy disks. These disks are similar to the diskettes used in a CD-ROM installation and point to the files on your hard drive where the required files are stored. The WIN_NT$.~1s folder is created and installation files are copied from the source disk or folder into that temporary folder, which is deleted after the installation. After the files are copied, your computer is rebooted.

The second part of the installation is called Phase 0. When you boot with the Setup Boot Disk or reboot using the WINNT.EXE /B command, you enter this part of the installation. Here you confirm the detected hardware and drivers, or specify the ones that are appropriate to your system. You are also asked to agree to the Windows NT Licensing Agreement. You choose an installation directory, either a new directory for an installation or an existing directory of your operating system for an upgrade.

Phase 0 continues. You are then asked to verify your hardware and software and select the partition containing the installation, as well as the file system you wish to use. Then your computer examines your hard drive using CHKDSK to see if there is a problem. After all of the steps in Phase 0, your computer reboots.

Phase 1 begins when the NT Setup Wizard appears. This wizard collects username, CD key number, Licensing mode, your computer name, a server type (for server installation), a password for the Administrator account, and whether to create an Emergency Repair Disk. A screen appears allowing you to select any optional components. This ends Phase 1.

The next part of the installation is Phase 2. Here you specify if your computer is connected to a network, whether to install IIS, and information about your network adapter and any protocols you want installed. After you verify your network settings you enter domain or workgroup information. Phase 2 is bypassed when you specify that the computer isn't on a network.

Phase 3 completes IIS installation by having you enter specific information. You also enter date, time, and time zones. A test is done for your video settings. If you specified that an ERD should be created, it is done at this stage. You remove the CD-ROM disk (for that type of installation) and you reboot your computer. The last reboot completes the Windows NT installation process and you see the Windows NT desktop appear after you enter your username and password into the login dialog box that appears.

I've changed my mind and I want to delete Windows NT from my system. How do I do that?

You can remove Windows NT from a FAT partition easily when you have a dual-boot configuration and either MS-DOS, Windows 95, or another version of Windows NT installed.

To remove Windows NT from a FAT partition:

1. Boot your computer to MS-DOS (or Windows 95) using a floppy disk with the SYS.COM utility on it.

2. Enter SYS C: at the Command Prompt and press the ENTER key. This replaces the Windows NT boot sector with the boot sector of MS-DOS or Windows 95.

3. Remove the floppy disk from your computer and reboot.

4. Find and delete the following files in the root directory of the Windows NT partition: PAGEFILE.SYS, NTLDR, BOOT.INI, NTDETECT.COM, BOOTSECT.DOS, and NTBOOTDD.SYS. These

files are hidden read-only system files, so you may need to view all files in the Windows 95 Explorer or in DOS to find them.

5. Delete the Windows NT installation folder, which is usually \WINNT.

6. Delete the \Program Files\Windows NT folder to complete the deinstallation.

To remove Windows NT from an NTFS partition, you must delete the entire partition. No other operating system will run on an NTFS partition. You can delete it using the FDISK utility of MS-DOS, or by running Setup and deleting the partition when you get to the disk partition information section in Setup. Alternatively, get the utility DELPART.EXE from CompuServe. Search for the filename ELPRT.EXE. The latter two methods will also allow you to delete an NTFS extended partition.

 When I run the Windows NT Setup program, it posts a message that I don't have enough disk space to proceed. What should I do?

As part of the installation, the Windows NT Setup program examines the partition that you specify Windows NT to be installed on. It checks the options you've selected (standard installation or the components of a custom installation) for the amount of free space required. It then checks your file system to determine if sufficient disk space exists to copy the files to your disk. When there isn't adequate free space, the installation will stop and post an error message. You will need to take corrective action in order to proceed.

The Setup program is both smart and stupid. It protects your files in the Recycle Bin by not deleting them, which is wise. However, it leaves any number of TEMP files scattered about your disk that could be safely deleted.

To free up some room on your disk, consider doing any of the following:

⇨ Empty your Recycle Bin.

⇨ Delete any system dump files generated. The MEMORY.DMP file is the exact size of the amount of installed RAM in the computer. USER.DMP varies in size.

➪   Delete any TEMP files that you find in the various locations that they are stored in, when you are sure that they are no longer needed.

 Note: *Typical locations for temp files are the print cache folder, your Internet cache folders, temp files in the \WINNT and \WINNT\SYSTEM directories, and so forth.*

 Tip: *One way to hunt down temp files where they live and kill them is to use the Find function on your desktop. Do a search for *.TMP, and then stand back as a long list of files are returned.*

➪   Uninstall programs you no longer use.

➪   Compress any files that you use infrequently.

➪   Change the size of the system partition that you wish to use for your installation from within the Disk Administrator.

➪   Create a new partition with more free space to allow for the installation.

➪   Compress your NTFS partition to make more room.

A short word about temporary files is in order. Generally speaking, any TEMP file that is required is locked by the program that requires it. Be very careful about deleting any temporary file that the operating system posts a message about. Also, some TEMP files are stored by programs like Microsoft Word to recover from a crash. But as a general rule, it's a good idea to do house cleaning every so often.

❓ Installation stalls when it attempts to detect my hard disk drive(s). What should I do?

Some drives and other mass-storage devices cannot be automatically detected during setup. In some cases, installation will lock up your computer. If this is the case, force a manual reboot and reinitiate the Setup program. When you reach the step for hard drive detection, select the device by type using the manual detection method.

I chose not to install the Internet Information Server, but I've changed my mind. How do I install IIS at a later date?

The easiest way to do this is to double-click on the icon labeled Install Internet Information Server that appears on your desktop after installation. If that file is deleted, perhaps you can find the shortcut in your Recycle Bin.

IIS is copied into the INETSVR directory within Windows NT SYSTEM32 directory. Launch the SETUP.EXE program in that folder to install IIS on your machine.

I've noticed that the current version of the operating system has changed and/or that Microsoft has advertised a service pack for the operating system. Are these worth installing?

A minor operating system upgrade during the lifetime of a major version is called a slipstream release. As Microsoft fixes problems and adds minor enhancements or features it creates a new "build" of the software. From time to time these builds are released to manufacturing and included with new product. You can also purchase a slipstream release.

Microsoft also creates what they call *service packs.* A service pack is a self-running program that modifies your operating system and updates it. You may find that, within the lifetime of an operating system version, from one to four service packs are released. For example, Windows NT Server 4.0 prior to the release of beta for Windows NT Server 5 had Service Pack 3 available.

You should try to install the latest service pack, as it generally solves a lot more problems than it creates. (It is not unknown for a service pack to create error conditions that didn't previously exist in your workstation's configuration.) You get the latest version of the operating system from Microsoft or can download any of the available service packs from the Microsoft Web site.

Tip: Be aware that a service pack is a large download—typically from 5MB to 30MB, with 10MB being about average. Although there are often many available Microsoft and contract mirror sites available to service the download, you may want to schedule your download for an off-peak time.

If your system is working satisfactorily and you are not experiencing any problems, or if you don't need the minor enhancement, then you don't need a service pack or a slipstream upgrade. Most often these upgrades solve many more problems than they create. In some instances, though, service packs can disrupt your configuration. If you are having problems with Windows NT, by all means upgrade. If your configuration is acceptable, the upgrading is a gamble—but generally a good one.

NETWORK INSTALLATIONS

? I can't join a domain during Setup. How do I correct this?

Unfortunately, this is one of the more common problems involved with installing Windows NT. The causes are many and varied. Always check your network cabling and network interface card to see that they are intact and joined properly. Then check your hardware and software settings to determine if they are correct. For example, entering the wrong subnet mask into your TCP/IP dialog box can give you this problem. Then check that you've entered the right administrator username and password in the correct case. Often the problem can be traced to the CAPS LOCK key being pressed by accident. Make sure you have used the correct settings with your NIC card.

? I want to install Windows NT, but I don't have a network adapter card. Is there a way to install network services and add the card later?

Yes. The easiest method that you can use is to select the MS Loopback Adapter from the network adapter list when Setup asks you for your network card. This adapter doesn't have any hardware, but is a fake adapter that allows you to configure network services (like TCP/IP) correctly. You can add your network card at a later time.

? How do I do a network installation, and why would I want to?

If your computer doesn't recognize your CD-ROM drive, you have a network PC (NetPC) that doesn't come with an appropriate disk drive, or your Windows NT boot disk isn't recognized, you might to install Windows NT across a network. You do this by establishing a network share for a CD-ROM drive, and running the Windows Setup program WINNT.EXE from the CD-ROM share. Some administrators create a shared folder and copy the installation files to that folder. An installation using WINNT.EXE will require 80MB of disk space.

When running WINNT.EXE, the command syntax is

```
WINNT [/S: /T: /I:inifile] {/B\ /C| /F| /OX| /O| /X}
```

The source /S: requires the location of the Windows NT files as a full path in either the \\servername\sharename[\path] or volume:\[path] form.

The other switches for this command are

⇨   B.   Floppyless installation

⇨   C.   Skip the free space check for the setup floppy boot disks

⇨   F.   Do not verify files that are copied.

⇨   O.   Create boot floppy disks only.

⇨   OX.   Create boot floppy disk for a floppy disk installation or a CD-ROM installation.

⇨   X.   Do not create setup boot floppy disks.

You can also install Windows NT from a previous installation on Windows NT Server or Workstation 4 using the WINN32.EXE program.

Some administrators copy the \i386 directory from the server CD-ROM to a shared folder on the server. About 80MB is required for the files in this folder. Then WINNT /B is run to install without using floppy disks. If you use this method to install Windows NT Server, you can change your configuration without requiring the installation CD-ROM.

After installation, network services don't start up properly. What is wrong?

First check and see if the settings for your network interface card and any installed protocols are properly set. Check that the IRQ, I/O Port, and transceiver settings are correct. Then check that your computer name is unique and that it has been added to the domain. When creating a PDC, make sure that the domain is unique.

CUSTOM INSTALLATIONS

? **Setup offers me four different types of installations. What are the differences?**

When you run Setup, you are offered the following four installation options:

⇨ *Typical.*   Most people opt for a typical installation on a desktop computer. This installation selects common components and allows you to choose additional ones in the Setup wizard.

⇨ *Portable.*   This installation installs special files meant for laptop computers, and a set of files that are popular in a mobile computing environment. You can select additional components during setup.

⇨ *Compact.*   This installation copies the minimal amount of files for computers where disk space is at a premium. When the list of optional components is shown, none are selected. You must select all of the components that you are interested in. The compact installation automates several steps in the installation setup process.

⇨ *Custom.*   The custom installation is very similar to the typical installation in terms of the options that are installed. Whereas the typical installation automates many steps in the process, a custom installation forces the user to select options and verify all selections before proceeding.

? **Some options don't appear to be installed in the typical installation. How do I install optional components?**

A custom installation lets you define what components you wish to have installed. A typical installation installs common components, but not all components that are available. For example, the typical installation doesn't install games.

In Setup, you can select additional components from a Select Components step. Among the options offered are the following:

⇨ Accessibility Options

⇨ Accessories

⇨ Communications

⇨ Games

⇨ Microsoft Exchange

⇨ Multimedia

To add an optional component group, click on the checkbox next to the name. Click the Details button to choose from two or more components in that category. Many common applications and applets like Microsoft Paint require specification. If a category is checked but grayed, some but not all of the available components in that category are selected for installation.

If you wish to install a component of Windows NT after you have installed the operating system, here's how to do it:

1. Select the Control Panels command from the Settings submenu of the Start menu.

2. Double-click on the Add/Remove Programs icon.

3. Click on the Windows NT Setup tab in the Add/Remove Program Properties dialog box, as shown in Figure 2-4.

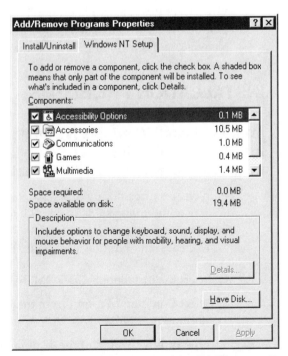

Figure 2-4.   The Windows NT Setup tab of the Add/Remove Programs control panel

4. Select the components that you want to install by checking the box next to their name.

5. Most components have multiple items that you might want to pick and choose from. To select a single component in a component group, select the component group and click on the Details button.

6. Select the component(s) you desire, and then click the OK button twice.

7. If Windows NT requests your installation disk, insert it into your CD-ROM drive and Setup will copy the appropriate files to your computer.

Most programs installed through the Add/Remove Programs control panel can be used without rebooting your computer. In its appearance and action, the Add/Remove Programs control panel is almost identical to the step in the Setup wizard described earlier.

Not all components in Windows NT are installed in this manner. Notably, network services are installed through the Network control panel. Those components include IPX/SPX, NetBEUI, TCP/IP, RAS, WINS, DHCP, and a host of others. Typically, you must reboot your computer when you install a network service. See Chapter 14, "Networking Issues," for more information.

INSTALLATION PROBLEMS

 I want to install Windows NT on another system, but I've lost the three Windows NT Setup floppy disks that the installation creates. How do I create a new set?

Setup creates three floppy disks that you need to use should there be a problem with your system, or should you need to reinstall the operating system.

To create new Windows NT Setup floppy disks:

1. Insert the installation CD-ROM disk into the drive.

2. Select Command Prompt from the Programs submenu of the Start menu.

3. Type **WINNT32 /OX** at the command prompt and press the ENTER key.

4. Enter the location of the Windows NT 4.0 files into the Windows NT 4.0 Upgrade/Installation dialog box. For example, enter **D:\I386** if that is your CD-ROM drive volume and processor type.

5. Click on the Continue button.

6. As Setup requests them, insert three blank formatted disks into your floppy disk drive. They become Setup disk 3, Setup disk 2, and the Windows NT Setup boot disk (Setup disk 1), respectively.

7. Type **EXIT** at the command prompt and press the ENTER key to close the window.

? I have the recommended free space, but the installation still fails due to lack of disk space. What's going on?

When Setup estimates the amount of space available on your hard drive, it bases its calculation on a 16KB sector size. If you have a large partition, you may be using 32KB or 64KB sectors, which would throw off the calculation. In that case, the solution is to create more free disk space by one of the methods mentioned in this chapter.

? My CD-ROM drive won't read my CD-ROM disk, but otherwise operates correctly. How do I get a new installation disk?

First try cleaning the back side of the CD-ROM with a moist cloth to remove dust or particles from the surface. If that doesn't solve your problem, you may have a defective CD-ROM disk. Manufacturing defects aren't common but they do happen; and you can damage a disk by scratching or otherwise mishandling it.

You will recognize a CD-ROM disk problem when you see a read error posted, or when the installation does not complete itself. You may not always be able to diagnose this problem easily.

To obtain a replacement CD-ROM, call Microsoft at (800) 426-9400. Have your registration number at hand, as the Microsoft sales and support staff will require it in order to process your request. New media requests for software under the warranty are generally sent without cost, or frequently for the cost of postage or a nominal disk charge if the warranty is expired. If you are requesting an upgrade in the operating system version as a slipstream upgrade, you may be charged postage and a small media fee.

? My installation doesn't boot, and the computer doesn't seem to recognize my SCSI disk drive. What should I do?

Windows NT does not properly recognize some SCSI device adapters. The key to getting a difficult SCSI drive to be recognized in the detection routine of Setup is to look for the ATAPI driver for an IDE-based CD-ROM drive. This problem is less common with the newer IDE interface. So if auto-detection doesn't detect an IDE CD-ROM, press the S key to see a list of SCSI devices, and then choose the ATAPI 1.2 driver.

If you are not able to boot a new Windows NT installation, you might want to try booting to a different operating system if you have a multiboot capability. Then start WINNT up using the Setup CD-ROM.

If you can't even get that far, and are unable to install Windows NT, you can try a network installation. Try contacting the SCSI device controller manufacturer to see if there is an upgrade in hardware or software available for your controller. (Some SCSI controllers are chips on your computer's motherboard.) If you are unable to resolve these problems, you may be forced to replace the adapter with one that is recommended on the Hardware Compatibility List.

? After installation I see a STOP error after I reboot. What do I do now?

The dreaded blue screen of death, aka a STOP error, can be caused by several different factors—most commonly a corrupt boot sector. This may be due to a boot sector virus, which can be repaired using the **FDISK /MBR** command using an MS-DOS boot disk. Many virus protection programs will repair this type of error. However, doing so renders the boot sector nonbootable by NT. You'll next have to use your repair diskette created during the installation to restore the NTLDR boot record.

After a new installation, you may get a STOP error if you have a hardware conflict where the same IRQ, I/O, or DMA address is shared by two or more devices. Resolving the conflict by reconfiguring your hardware will generally fix the problem.

WORKSTATION VS. SERVER INSTALLATIONS

? What happens when I create a domain controller?

When you install Windows NT Server, you are offered the opportunity to create either a primary domain controller, backup domain controller, or stand-alone server. If you create a domain controller, a copy of the security database is placed on that server and the server is bound to the domain that it joins. If you wish to switch the computer to another domain, you will need to reinstall Windows NT Server and re-create your working environment. A stand-alone server can join a domain and then be switched to another domain without another installation.

? How do I install Windows NT over a network in an unattended installation?

In order to run a network installation, you need to use the WINNT32.EXE program on the network share. This program takes the /U switch for an unattended installation. This switch requires that an answer file or script be specified in order to automate the installation.

You can create an answer file for each computer type or installation type you desire. The Setup Manager utility that is on the Windows NT Server CD-ROM in the SUPPPORT\DEPTOOLS\<COMPUTERTYPE> folder lets you create the appropriate text file containing the script.

To create an answer file:

1. Run the Setup Manager at the following location: SUPPORT\DEPTOOLS\I386\SETUPMGR on the Windows NT Server installation CD-ROM.

2. Click on General Setup.

3. Enter the information into the tabs specifying user information, computer role, install directory, display settings, time zone, and licensing mode.

4. Click the OK button.

5. Click the Network Setup tab and enter the information on the type of installation in the General section, the protocols required, and whether you wish to have IIS installed.

6. Click OK, and then click the Advanced Setup tab.

7. Enter whether you wish to reboot after installation, skip the Welcome wizard, and/or skip the Administrative Password wizard page, as well as use the current file system.

8. Click OK, and then Save.

9. Enter the name **Nts_source** in the Save as an Answer file dialog box.

10. Type **Unattend** in the File name box.

11. Click on Text Files (*.TXT) in the Save as type list box; then click Save and Exit to close the Windows NT Setup Manager utility.

12. Open the NTS_SOURCE\UNATTENDED.TXT file that you just created in Notepad.

13. Edit the following information: In the [unattended] section, add the line **OEMSkipEula=yes** to bypass the licensing agreement.

14. Edit the [network] section to add the line **CreateComputerAccount=Administrator, password** to bypass the credentials and password used to create the computer account.

If you are going to perform an unattended installation to two or more computers, you will need to create a Uniqueness Database File (UDF). This file specifies the differences between installations such as computer name, username, and so forth. The /UDF switch for WINNT and WINNT32 specifies the use of this file. You create a UDF file using any text editor.

The following is an example of a UDF text file:

```
; UDF file for three users
;
[UniqueIds]
u1 = UserData
u2 = UserData
u3 = UserData
[u1:UserData]
Fullname = "Joe Smith"
OrgName = "ABC Corp"
ComputerName = "Mandalay"
[u2:UserData]
Fullname = "Sam White"
OrgName = "ABC Corp"
ComputerName = "Rangoon"
[u2:UserData]
Fullname = "Al Green"
```

```
OrgName = "ABC Corp"
ComputerName = "Singapore"
```

Combining the use of both an unattended answer file and a UDF file, you would use the following command to run the installation, where the network share is the F: drive and contains the two text files UNATTENDED.TXT and UDFF1.TXT:

```
WINNT /S:F:\ /U: Unattended.txt /UDF:ID1, UDFF1.txt
```

chapter

3 **A**nswers!

Running Programs

Answer Topics!

Running Programs @ a Glance

⇨ The **Start menu** is highly configurable. You can add programs, folders, files, and other items to it by clicking and dragging them to the Start button. Your configuration of the Start menu is stored with your user profile in Windows NT.

⇨ You can **start programs** in several ways. The Programs submenu on the Start menu lets you launch programs that have been installed on your system. To open recently used files, select them from the Documents submenu. Another method you can use to start a program or open a file is to search for it with the Find command. The most common tool used to launch a program is the Run command on the Start menu. There you can enter a single command line, as you would in a DOS session.

⇨ When you run **MS-DOS programs**, the Command Prompt window automatically opens. Each Command Prompt window runs in its own virtual machine. You can configure the way an MS-DOS program runs in Windows NT, and the way the Command Prompt window appears. Windows NT comes with a variety of MS-DOS programs rewritten to run in a 32-bit environment.

⇨ **Menus and dialog boxes** are standard Windows interface elements. For the most part, they operate in Windows NT the same as they do in Windows 95. Both dialog boxes and menus have a number of features that allow you to move the focus to and select various controls in the dialog box or commands in the menu using either your mouse or keyboard.

⇨   Each program that you install will have a slightly different procedure for **installing and removing** components. Most programs use a program called either Install or Setup (INSTALL.EXE or SETUP.EXE) to control the installation procedure. You should use the Add/Remove Programs control panel to install or remove a program. Using this control panel ensures that all of the appropriate entries in the Windows NT Registry are either added or removed.

⇨   You can **run multiple programs** in Windows NT (multitask) and switch between them. Use either the buttons on your Taskbar or the Task Manager to switch between running programs and reverse your current foreground and background programs. Many processes run as services in Windows NT. Copy a program or a shortcut to the Startup menu to have a program start up automatically when you boot your computer. Open the Services control panel and configure startup and services there. Many services come with an administrative tool (found in the Administrative Tools folder) that lets you configure how those services run.

WORKING WITH THE START MENU

 How can I add options anywhere in my Start menu?

Use the Taskbar Properties dialog box:

1. Right-click on a blank area on the Taskbar and select the Properties command.

2. Click the Start Menu Programs tab; then click the Add button.

3. Click the Browse button; then select the program you desire from the Browse dialog box.

4. Click the Open button, or enter the path to the program file in the Command line text box.

5. Click the Next button; then from the Select Folder dialog box, select the folder you wish to place the item in.

6. Click the Next button; then name the item and click the Finish button.

How can I make several changes to my Start menu all at once?

Use the Advanced dialog box to alter the contents of the Start menu. The Advanced dialog box is accessed from the Start Menu tab of the Taskbar Properties dialog box. A more general procedure allows you to make wholesale changes to the Start menu:

1. Right-click on the Taskbar and select the Properties command.

2. In the Taskbar Properties dialog box (see Figure 3-1), click the Start Menu tab; or press CTRL-TAB to move to that tab.

3. Click the Add button to open a dialog box that lets you create a shortcut to your Start menu; or click the Remove button to open a different dialog box that allows you to select a shortcut to remove.

4. Click the Advanced button to open the Start Menu folder in the Windows Explorer, as shown in Figure 3-2.

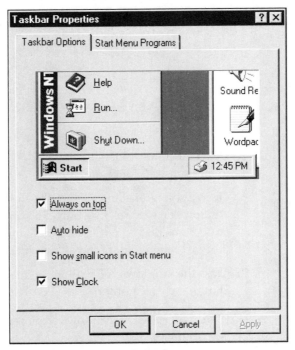

Figure 3-1.   The Taskbar Properties dialog box

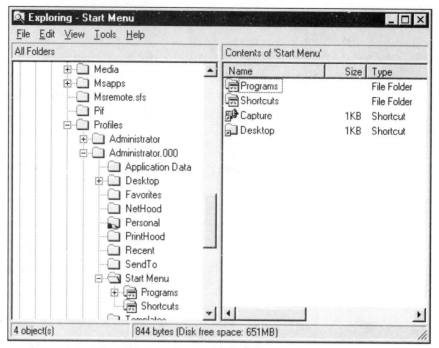

Figure 3-2.   The Windows Explorer shown open to the Start Menu folder

    Tip: *You can also right-click the Start button and select the Explore command to open the Windows NT Explorer to the Start Menu folder directly.*

5. Delete or create folders in the Windows Explorer, drag-and-drop items to these folders, and make whatever changes you wish.

6. Open a second instance of the Windows NT Explorer. This second window can serve as the source of your programs, folders, and other items that you drag into the Window NT Explorer open to the Start Menu folder (and all that it contains).

7. Close the Windows NT Explorer(s) to save your changes to the Start menu configuration.

When you close the Windows Explorer, your changes will appear on the Start menu.

? How do I add the Desktop folder to my Start menu?

You may find it valuable to add the Desktop folder to your Start menu. In Windows NT, that folder is located in the folder WINNT\ Profiles\<username>, where username is the name of the user account you logged in with. Add a shortcut for that folder to the Start Menu folder for the same username.

? Is there a really easy way to add programs to the top of my Start menu?

Use the drag-and-drop method to add a program to your shortcut menu:

1. Select the Windows NT Explorer command from the Programs submenu of the Start menu.

2. Double-click on the volume containing the program you wish to add in Windows NT Explorer; then double-click on the folder containing that program.

3. Locate the program file with the file type Application.

4. Right-click on the program file; then drag it over the Start menu and release the mouse button.

When you click the Start button, your program will appear above the Programs folder, as shown in Figure 3-3.

Actually, any shortcut, file, or folder can be used as the source of the drag-copy to the Start menu. If you see an item you want to add on your desktop or in an open folder, simply drag it to the Start button. Windows NT creates a shortcut of the item and places it into the Start Menu folder for your username's profile.

? My mouse isn't working. Can I start a program or file on the Start menu just using my keyboard?

To start a program on the Start menu with your keyboard:

1. Press the CTRL-ESC key to open the Start menu.

 Tip: *Some Windows keyboards contain a Windows key (usually found between the* CTRL *and* ALT *keys) that opens the Start menu.*

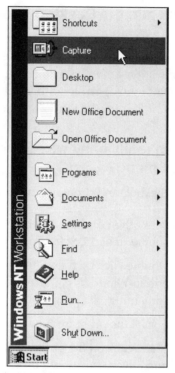

Figure 3-3.   The Start menu with a program added to it

2. Use the UP or DOWN ARROW key to move through the commands on the Start menu; or press the underlined letter key to select that item. For example, press R for the command Run.

3. If the item has a right-facing arrow, press the RIGHT ARROW key to move to the submenu.

4. Use the UP or DOWN ARROW key or the underlined letter in the item to highlight that item on your keyboard.

5. Press the ENTER key to launch your program or file, or open your selected folder.

How do I start a file I've used recently?

The Documents submenu of the Start menu stores up to 15 of your most recently used files in alphabetical order. To start a recently used file, select that file by name from the Documents submenu.

How do I clear the document list of files I've used recently?

If you want to flush the contents of the Documents folder:

1. Right-click on the Taskbar and select the Properties command.
2. Click the Start Menu Programs tab.
3. Click the Clear button in the Documents Menu section.
4. Click the OK button to return to your desktop.

STARTING PROGRAMS

How do I launch a program or file with my mouse from the desktop?

You can right-click an item on your desktop, in a folder, or in the Windows NT Explorer and open that file from anywhere. If the file is a program, you will see the Open command at the top of the shortcut menu. That command will start a program, or launch a data file that has a registered program associated with its file type. Files of this kind will display an appropriate file icon on your desktop or in the Windows NT Explorer.

Files that belong to a registered application will launch when you double-click or right-click them and select the Open command from the shortcut menu. If a file belongs to an unknown application, the Open With dialog box appears, allowing you to select which application will be used to open that file.

I know what my program is named and where it is located. How do I start it manually?

To start a program manually:

1. Click the Start menu and select the Run command; or press CTRL-ESC followed by the R key.
2. Enter the path and filename into the Open combo box of the Run dialog box (see Figure 3-4).

 Tip: *The Run dialog box maintains a history of previously entered commands. You can choose a previous file by selecting it from the drop-down list of the Open combo box.*

Figure 3-4.   The Run dialog box

3. Or, if you don't know the name of the program file or its path, click the <u>B</u>rowse button to view the Browse dialog box shown in Figure 3-5.

4. Locate the folder or disk in the Look <u>i</u>n list box, select the file in the file list box, and then click the <u>O</u>pen button.

5. Press the OK button in the Run dialog box to start the program.

 Note: *The Run dialog box is a single line processor. You can enter the same command into this dialog box with any parameters you desire that you would enter into a Command Prompt session.*

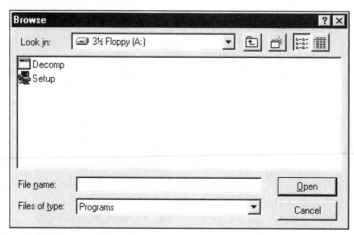

Figure 3-5.   The Browse dialog box

Tip: *You can enter an URL or UNC location into the Run command. Windows NT recognizes it as a Web address, launches your browser and attempts to locate the resource.*

? How do I start a program whose name I know but that I can't locate?

Use the Find command to search for the file. The Find command on the Start menu lets you search for files using a variety of search criteria. You can enter all or part of the filename; filter your search by file type, date created, or date modified; search by size; even search for character strings within files. Find can operate in the background, and returns matches to your search in the Find window.

To search for a file whose name (or other properties) you know:

1. Select the Files or Folders command on the Find submenu on the Start menu.

2. Enter the name of the file and the location you wish to search in the Named text box of the Find dialog box (see Figure 3-6).

   You can also search using wildcards: the ? symbol for any single character; or the * symbol for any character string.

3. In the list of matching files (see Figure 3-7), either double-click on a file to launch it, right-click on the file and select the Open command, or drag-and-drop the file to the application responsible for opening it.

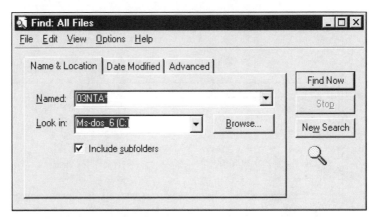

Figure 3-6.   The Find: All Files dialog box

? What happened to the Run command?

The Run command has appeared in Windows since version 3.*x* of the operating system. While it was once on the File menu of the Task Manager, it is now on the Start menu in both Windows NT and Windows 95. If you know the path and program name, you can use the Run command to start your program directly. The Run command also comes into play whenever you need to use Install or Setup programs to either install or remove programs from Windows NT. Many times the autoplay feature on a CD-ROM will fail, and you will need to manually start a component or program.

STARTING AND RUNNING MS-DOS PROGRAMS

? How do I configure a DOS program to run in a DOS session under Windows NT?

Windows NT allows you to set a number of properties that control how an MS-DOS-compatible program will run in a DOS session. These properties are set in the Property sheet of an MS-DOS program.

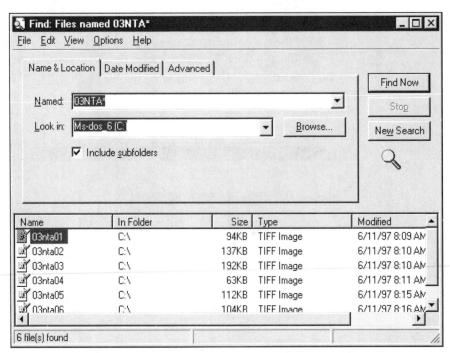

Figure 3-7.   A list of matching files found in Find command

To open the Property sheet of an MS-DOS program:

1. Right-click on the file, on a shortcut on your desktop, or in the Windows NT Explorer; then select the Properties command from the shortcut menu.

2. Or click on the file or shortcut and select the Properties command from the File menu.

In either case, the Properties sheet appears, as shown in Figure 3-8.

How do I change an MS-DOS program's attributes?

To change an MS-DOS program's attributes, click the General tab in the Properties sheet and set the Read-only or Hidden checkboxes on or off.

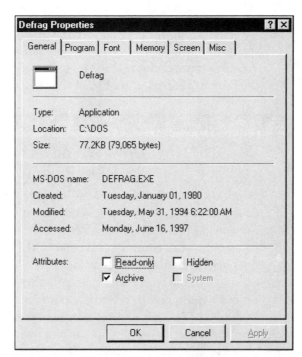

Figure 3-8.   The General tab of an MS-DOS program's Properties sheet

I've clicked on the Close box of a Command Prompt window and it won't close. How do I close a DOS session?

There are several ways to close an MS-DOS program running in a DOS box. Try any of the following methods:

⇨ Type **exit** or **quit** at the command prompt; then press the ENTER key. This is the most generally useful method for quitting a DOS program. If the configuration setting Close on exit described just above is set, then the DOS box may close automatically by itself.

⇨ Click the Close box (X) at the right of the Command Prompt window. If there is no program running inside the DOS box, the window and the session will generally close without a problem. If there is a program running, often Windows NT will ask you to exit the program before attempting to close the Command Prompt window.

⇨ Use the method described in the section "Recovering from a Crashed Program" at the end of this chapter to close a misbehaving MS-DOS program.

How do I have a DOS session close automatically when I exit a program?

If you want the DOS window to close automatically when you exit your program, click the Close on exit checkbox on the Program tab of the Properties sheet of that MS-DOS program.

How Does Windows NT Run MS-DOS Programs?

Windows NT will run most MS-DOS programs without error. It does this by creating a **virtual machine** in which a DOS program can run in protected memory, separate from any other programs running on your computer. You start an MS-DOS program by opening the command called Command Prompt on the Programs submenu of the Start menu. This program offers you a complete set of DOS commands rewritten to run in a 32-bit environment. Windows NT does not allow programs to directly access I/O (Input/Output or peripheral) devices directly. When a DOS program fails, this is usually the cause.

? How do I use command line switches for an MS-DOS program?

You can add command line switches to the path statement in the Run command to use that switch during a Command Prompt session.

To configure a DOS program so that it always uses a switch, click the Program tab (see Figure 3-9) and enter the command you wish to execute to run that MS-DOS program into the Cmd line text box. This command should include the path to the executable file as you would type it from the command prompt, and any switches, pipes, redirections, wildcards, or other parameters that you would enter.

Tip: *If you want Windows NT to prompt you for any parameters when it starts your DOS program up, put a question mark at the end of the entry in the Cmd line text box.*

You can also set the command environment that an MS-DOS program will run in by altering the parameters in the Windows NT PIF Settings dialog box. Click the Windows NT button on the Program

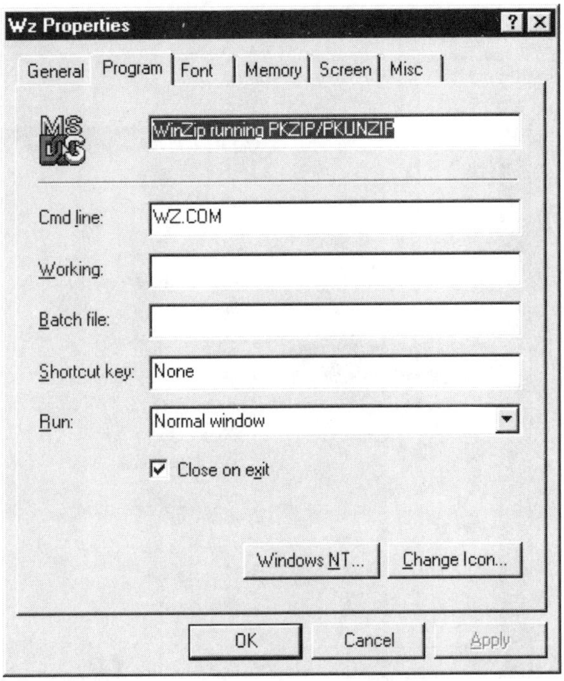

Figure 3-9.   The Program tab of an MS-DOS program's Properties sheet

tab of an MS-DOS program's Property sheet to view this dialog box shown here.

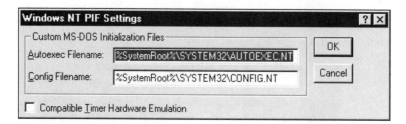

How do I run DOS programs in a DOS box in Windows NT?

To run a DOS program using the Command Prompt, select the Command Prompt command from the Programs submenu of the Start menu (see Figure 3-10). The Console or MS-DOS environment appears in a window on your screen, as shown in Figure 3-11. At the DOS prompt, change your directory to the one that contains the program

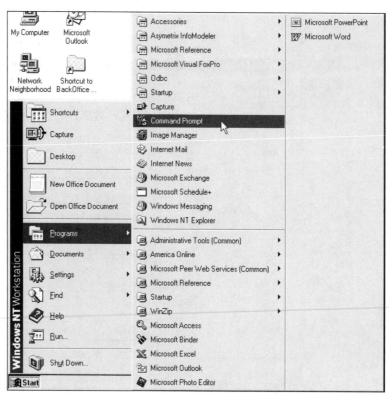

Figure 3-10.   The Command Prompt command on the Start menu

Figure 3-11.   The DOS window

you wish to run. Then type in the name of the program and press the
ENTER key. The code looks something like this:

```
C:\> CD C:\<target folder>
C:>\ <application name>
```

I like using DOS commands. What familiar commands are available?

The following are the important commands supported in the
Command Prompt environment.

⇨   ATTRIB.EXE (display or change file attributes)

⇨   DISKCOPY.COM (copy a diskette)

⇨   DOSKEY.COM (edit command lines and create macros)

⇨   FC.EXE (file compare)

⇨   FIND.EXE (locate text in a file)

⇨   FORMAT.COM (format a disk)

⇨   LABEL.EXE (add, remove, or change a disk label)

⇨   MORE.COM (display or print another screen)

⇨   MOVE.EXE (move one or more files)

⇨   SORT.EXE (sort input)

⇨   START.EXE (run a program)

⇨   SUBST.EXE (assign a drive letter to a path you specify)

⇨   XCOPY.EXE (copy directories and subdirectories)

? How do I get help for a DOS command from the command line?

Enter the following command at the command line, and press the ENTER key:

```
C:\> <command name> /?
```

? How can I use the online Help system?

1. Open the Help system by selecting the <u>H</u>elp command on the Start menu.

2. Click the Index tab and enter the command name in the "1 Type the first few letters of the word you're looking for" text box.

3. Double-click on the command name in the "2 Click the index entry you want, then click Display" list box (see Figure 3-12).

? I want my DOS program to have a more recognizable icon. How do I change an existing icon?

Click the Change Icon button found on the Program tab of the Properties sheet and select a button from the scrolling list box. Or click the Browse button to locate the icon file (.ICO) that you wish to be displayed whenever that program is browsed in a folder in Windows NT.

? How do I launch a DOS program directly?

When you install a DOS program, it isn't added to the Start menu in the same way that Windows programs are. Still, you can add a DOS program to your Start menu in the same way you would any other Windows program and have it appear like this. This topic was covered previously in this chapter.

When you select a DOS program from the Start menu, or double-click its icon or on a shortcut to that program on the desktop or in the Windows NT Explorer, most DOS programs will open correctly.

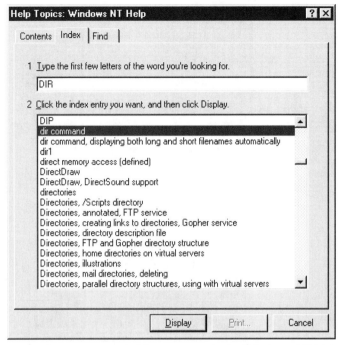

Figure 3-12.   Getting help on a DOS command in the Windows NT Help system

? I'm getting "out of memory" error messages when I run a DOS program. How do I change the memory allocation and type assigned to an MS-DOS program?

Click the Memory tab (see Figure 3-13) and change the various types of memory there:

⇨ Conventional memory

⇨ Expanded (EMS) memory

⇨ Extended (XMS) memory

⇨ MS-DOS protected-mode (DPMI memory)

If you change these settings, you may want to check the documentation that came with your MS-DOS application to find out how they should be set.

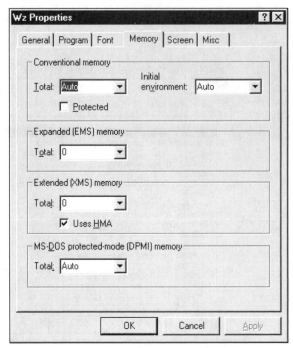

Figure 3-13.   The Memory tab of an MS-DOS program's Properties sheet

Tip: *For a problem MS-DOS program that crashes, check the Protected checkbox to ensure that the program runs inside the DOS box in protected memory. The DOS box itself runs in protected memory, but this setting offers some additional measure of protection.*

How do I modify the Command Prompt window?

You have control over several features that make the Command Prompt window easier to view and work with. Some of these properties are set as a default in the Console control panel; others are set for particular MS-DOS programs as part of their Properties sheet. When properties assigned in the Console control panel are also assigned in a particular program's Properties sheet, then the program's properties override the default condition while the program is running.

To set default properties in the Console control panel:

1. Click the Control Panel command on the Settings submenu of the Start menu.

2. Double-click the Console control panel icon, as shown here.

3. Click the option(s) you desire, and then click the OK button.

The Console control panel lets you change the cursor size—whether the Command Prompt opens in a <u>W</u>indow or F<u>u</u>ll screen—or the size of the memory assignment on the Options tab (see Figure 3-14).

Figure 3-15 shows you the Font tab of the Console control panel. It is very similar in appearance to the Font tab you see in a program's Properties sheet.

The Command Prompt window is hard to see on my laptop. How do I modify the colors in a window for an MS-DOS session?

Make your selections from the Colors tab of the Console control panel.

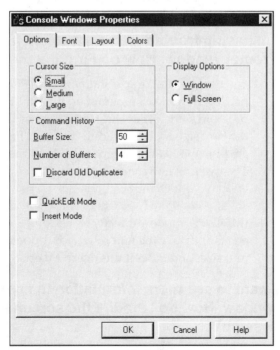

Figure 3-14.   The Options tab of the Console control panel

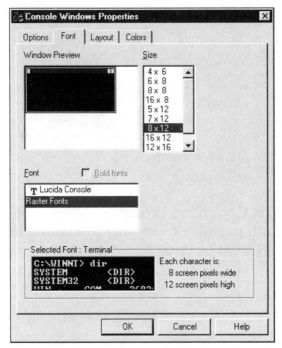

Figure 3-15.   The Font tab of the Console control panel

？ I'm having trouble reading the font in the Command Prompt window. How do I modify the font?

You can change the size and type of the font used in the window for a particular MS-DOS program on the Font tab of the MS-DOS program's Properties sheet, as shown in Figure 3-16. The TT icon in the Font size list box indicates the use of a TrueType font. Other fonts are bitmapped and designed to display best at different resolutions. The two preview panels in the middle of the Font tab show you the effect of your changes.

If you set the Font size to Auto, you can resize the Console (MS-DOS) window directly by clicking and dragging the window edges and have the font resize appropriately. Experiment with other font sizes and types if this doesn't work

？ I want to see more information in my Command Prompt window. How do I modify the screen size for an MS-DOS session?

If the window is on your screen, click-and-drag the border as you would any other window. Toggle the window between its normal size

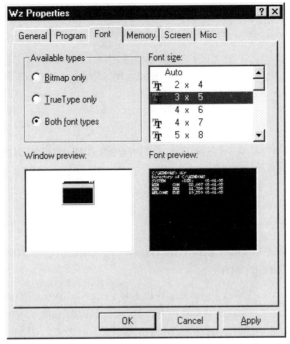

Figure 3-16.   The Font tab of an MS-DOS program's Properties sheet

and full screen by double-clicking on the Title bar, as you would any other Windows window.

To change the default size of the MS-DOS window, click the Layout tab of the Console control panel and select a window size there. You can also set the default position that the window appears at on your screen when the session starts.

? The Command Prompt window occupies my whole screen. How do I switch to a normal window or to another program?

MS-DOS programs normally run in a standard window that you can activate when you click on it. You can also use the ALT-TAB keystroke to make this session run in the foreground or background. If you want your MS-DOS program to run full screen, select Maximized from the Run list box on the Programs tab of the MS-DOS Properties sheet. Set this attribute to Minimized to have the program run as a task on the Taskbar. You can still use the ALT-TAB keystroke to move the focus to or away from a DOS session in either of these other states. You should be aware that many DOS programs will ignore this setting.

? I want an easy way to launch a DOS program. How do I assign a shortcut key to do this?

Enter the keystroke into the Shortcut key text box on the Program tab of the MS-DOS program's Property sheet. Make sure that you close the Properties sheet and test the keystroke. Many MS-DOS programs will not accept a shortcut key.

? How do I switch between a windowed and a full-screen DOS session?

Press ALT-ENTER. Press them again to return to the window's previous state.

? How do I set the working directory for an MS-DOS program?

Enter the path to the directory into the Working text box in the Program tab of the MS-DOS program's Property sheet. When you start an MS-DOS program, the program switches the location of the command prompt to that directory. This can be useful in accessing important files, or saving files conveniently to that location.

? My DOS program requires a special working environment. How do I specify that during startup?

You can enter AUTOEXEC.BAT and CONFIG.SYS files that DOS uses when it starts up to configure its working environment. If you make changes to the PIF settings, you should have a good reason for doing so and should understand the implications of those changes.

USING MENUS AND DIALOG BOXES

? How do I use menus?

To activate a menu command using the mouse:

1. Click your mouse pointer on the menu pad (the menu name) in the menu bar.

2. Drag your pointer down to the command name and release the mouse button.

3. For a command with a hierarchical submenu (with a right-facing arrow), drag the pointer to the right when the command is highlighted and select the command on the submenu you need.

4. For a command with an ellipsis, make your selection from the dialog box that appears.

All of the menu names in the pads in the menu bar, and the commands in the menus, contain underlined characters. These characters are accelerator keys, or *hot keys*.

To activate a menu pad with your keyboard:

⇨ Press ALT and the underlined character or letter for that menu pad. You can move to another menu pad using the RIGHT or LEFT ARROW key.

To select a command on an open menu:

⇨ Press the accelerator key for that command; or use the UP and DOWN ARROW keys to highlight the command, and then press the ENTER key.

⇨ If the command is on a submenu, press the RIGHT ARROW key to highlight that command, and then press ENTER.

⇨ If the command has a hot-key combination (CTRL-Q for Quit, for example), then that keystroke will give the command without your having to open and work with the menu.

❓ I'm stuck on a menu, even though I've been working in a program. How do I escape?

If your menus start to act weird, chances are that you've accidentally pressed the ALT key. In order to close a highlighted menu command, press the ESC (Escape) key. To close a highlighted command and a selected menu pad (both), press the ESC key twice.

❓ How do I access the special menus of applications and windows?

Two special menus do not have underlined accelerator keys. They are an application menu and a window menu.

To activate an application menu:

⇨ Press ALT-SPACEBAR.

To activate a document window menu:

⇨   Press ALT-Hyphen.

What shortcuts exist that I can use in dialog boxes?

Dialog boxes appear as the result of program execution, or from operating system functions. All dialog boxes have certain features that you can take advantage of:

⇨   Dialog boxes have *default actions*. Typically, this is a command button that is shadowed to indicate the action, and the button is active when the dialog box opens. Press the ENTER key to initiate this action.

⇨   Dialog boxes have a *Tab order*. Press the TAB key to move from control (text box, list box, etc.) to command buttons through the Tab order. Use SHIFT-TAB to move backwards through the Tab order.

⇨   You can *dismiss a dialog box using the ESC key*.

⇨   Some features in dialog boxes show an underlined letter or accelerator key. Press ALT-<Letter> to move to that control in the dialog box.

Where do shortcut menus appear?

Shortcut menus appear throughout Windows NT, in the interface and in programs. The best way to discover these valuable shortcuts is to right-click in different parts of your screen. If Windows or that application has a shortcut menu for that feature, it will pop up and display a context-sensitive set of menu commands. You can select a command from a shortcut menu by using either your mouse or your keyboard. Press ESC to close a shortcut menu.

Unfortunately, in the current version of Windows NT there is no clue where a shortcut menu is supported, or what commands will be displayed. These need to be discovered by trial through use.

INSTALLING AND REMOVING PROGRAMS

How do I install a program in Windows NT?

To install a program:

1. Select the Control Panel command from the Settings menu of the Start menu.

Add/Remove
Programs

2. Double-click on the Add/Remove Programs control panel icon, shown here.

3. Click the Install/Uninstall tab (see Figure 3-17), and then the Install button.

   Windows NT will search for Setup on your floppy disk drive, and then on your CD-ROM drive. If it is unable to locate the installer, you may be asked to specify its location.

4. Confirm the choice of the installation program.

Note: *You can also start an installation by double-clicking on the Setup or Install program on your drive's window, or by specifying it in the Run command. If the installation is written properly, it will write its changes to the Windows NT Registry even if you don't install the program using the Add/Remove Programs control panel as described. Still, the control panel is the recommended installation method.*

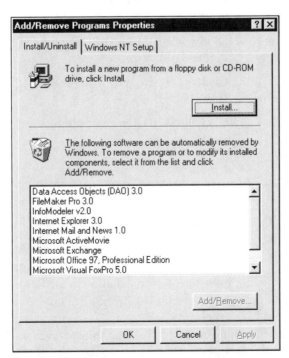

Figure 3-17.   The Install/Uninstall tab

If you want to install programs that are part of your Windows NT installation, then use the Windows Setup tab to select the components you wish to add. Be sure to have your installation disk available before proceeding.

If you install a service in Windows NT, that service may install the components required as part of its installation routine.

❓ How do I remove a program?

Removing an installed program is more problematic in Windows than installing it is. Whereas using the Add/Remove Programs control panel is not mandatory when installing a program, you will run into difficulties with orphaned registry entries, shortcut menu commands that don't function, and other problems if you don't use the control panel. If you remove a program library (.DLL) file that is shared and is used by other applications, simply deleting the program in the Windows NT Explorer is asking for trouble.

To remove a program:

1. Select the Control Panel command from the Settings menu of the Start menu.

2. Double-click on the Add/Remove Programs control panel (see Figure 3-18).

3. Click on the program you wish to remove in the Install/ Uninstall tab.

4. Click the Add/Remove button.

Warning: *Do not remove programs in Windows NT by simply deleting them or by dragging the folders that contain those programs to the Recycle Bin.*

If you don't see the program you want to remove in the list of programs, then the installer for that program did not enter the components of its installation in the Registry. In that case you can delete program files directly from the Windows NT Explorer, or directly from the desktop. Remember that when you delete a shortcut, you leave the file that it points to on disk. When you delete the actual program or folder, you are deleting the file itself.

RUNNING MULTIPLE PROGRAMS

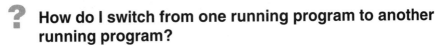 **How do I switch from one running program to another running program?**

There are several methods for changing the focus from one program open in memory to another. The most common methods are the following:

⇨ Click the button for that program on the Taskbar. This should bring the focus to the program and switch it from background to foreground processing.

⇨ Press ALT-TAB to view the "Cool Switch." Continue pressing it to cycle through the icons for the programs and folders that are open on the Taskbar. When the program or folder you wish to view is outlined in the Cool Switch, shown here, release the ALT key and Windows NT will move the focus to that program.

⇨ Click on any part of a window that is managed by the program you wish to switch to. Windows NT opens the rest of that window to view and brings any other window managed by that application to the view. The application also becomes the foreground-processed application.

⇨ Use the Switch To button in the Task Manager as follows:

1. Right-click on the Taskbar and select the Task Manager command from the context-sensitive menu.

   2. Click the Applications tab in the Task Manager.

   3. Select the application you want to switch to in the Task list box.

   4. Click the Switch To button.

   5. Close the Close button at the right side of the Task Manager's Title bar.

   The Task Manager is shown and described in the last topic in this chapter.

How Does Multitasking Work?

It is one of the great strengths of the Windows NT operating system that it allows you to multitask programs, running each in its own protected memory space. You can start and stop applications and services at any time, even when another application is being started or stopped concurrently.

The operating system prioritizes its tasks so that programs with the highest priority get more attention from the processor(s) than those with lower priority. An application that is running in the foreground gets a higher priority and is processed more quickly than one running in the background. Typically, printing and communications processes are run in the background.

Processes are managed through a system of *threads*. A thread is a task scheduled for execution. Windows NT gives you fine control over the management of threads, and lets you assign different priorities to different tasks. Typically, changing thread priorities is an advanced topic for most applications. Most applications and services are run using their default priorities.

If a program manages a window, that program will have a button appear in the Taskbar, which is typically found at the bottom of your screen (you can move the Taskbar elsewhere or minimize it from view). If a program runs as a service on Windows NT, that service will be viewable and controllable in the Service Manager control panel. Many services also come with utilities that appear in the Administrative Tools folder found on the Programs submenu of the Start menu. These utilities let you start, stop, pause, and configure the services.

❓ How do I manage and configure a service using a utility?

Not all services provide an administrative tool. Those that do generally install their utility in the Administrative Tools folder in the Programs submenu of the Start menu. These utilities usually show the various servers and processes running for that particular service. Commands that start, stop, and pause the service are typically found in the menu commands of that utility and the buttons contained in the interface. Most often you will see which computer and user are running that service. An example of this type of tool is the Remote Access Admin utility that installs when you install the Remote Access Service on either Windows NT Workstation or Server.

❓ How do I use the Services control panel to manage and configure a service that has no associated utility?

To start, stop, and configure a service running on either Windows NT Workstation or Server:

1. Select the Control Panel command from the Settings submenu of the Start menu.

2. Double-click the Services control panel icon, shown here.

What Is a Service Running on Windows NT?

Services are programs running on Windows NT that don't display a window, don't show a button on the Taskbar, and don't appear in the Cool Switch. Typically, they are processes that provide network, communication, or other services. Some of these services provide configurable control panels; others offer a special administration tool for that service in the Administration Tools folder of the Programs submenu. All of these services running on Windows NT appear in the Service control panel. Only the Services control panel offers a general control that applies to all services on both Windows NT Workstation and Server.

3. Highlight a service in the Services list box, as shown in Figure 3-18.

4. Click the Start, Stop, or Pause button, as desired.

Depending on whether the service is running or stopped, different buttons will be enabled.

RECOVERING FROM A CRASHED PROGRAM

What are some of the symptoms I will see when a program crashes?

When a program stops executing, you may see any of several different problems:

⇨ Your input devices fail to operate correctly: your pointer is frozen, you can't enter characters or keystrokes from your keyboard, and so on.

⇨ Output to output devices ceases. Your printer stops printing, for example.

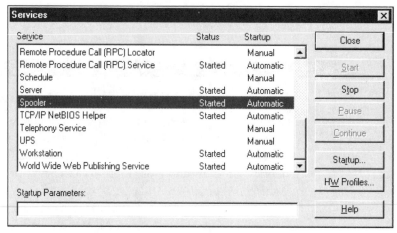

Figure 3-18.   A service selected in the Services control panel

⇨ Communications stop with a communication service.

⇨ You can't switch to another application.

In many cases, you might not even notice a problem with any other application. The offending program ceases to operate and function without affecting other programs or your computer.

? How do I close out a crashed session?

There are instances when a crashed program dramatically affects your Windows NT Workstation or Server's performance. This doesn't happen often with Windows NT, because the operating system usually doesn't give access to sensitive computer functions to applications. When you see this type of behavior, it most often indicates an operating system component malfunction. For a situation like this, you will want to use the NT Security dialog box to close and end your session.

To close a session using the Windows NT Security dialog box:

1. Press CTRL-ALT-DEL.

2. In the Windows NT Security dialog box shown in Figure 3-19, click either the Logoff or Shutdown button.

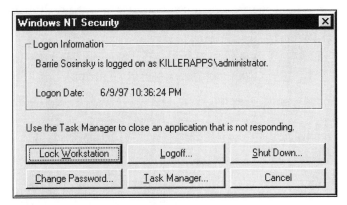

Figure 3-19.   The Windows NT Security dialog box

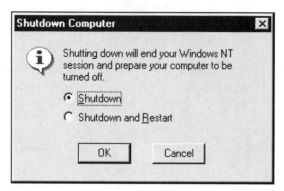

Figure 3-20.   The Shutdown Windows dialog box

3. Make a selection in the Shutdown Windows dialog box shown in Figure 3-20.

   Logoff closes your programs and logs you out of the networked processes that your workstation or server is using. Shutdown logs you off and turns off all of your computer's hardware. You can also choose to restart your computer in the Shutdown Windows dialog box. In that case, your computer does a warm reboot.

? How do I close out a crashed program using the Task Manager?

The first tool you should use to end a malfunctioning program is the Task Manager:

1. Right-click on the Taskbar and select the Task Manager command from the context-sensitive menu.

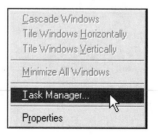

Note: *You can also get to the Task Manager by clicking the Task Manager button in the Windows NT Security dialog box, as described in the next section.*

2. Click the Applications tab in the Task Manager, as shown in Figure 3-21.

3. Select the program in the Task list box.

4. Click the <u>E</u>nd Task button.

To close a service using the Task Manager:

1. Click the Process tab in the Task Manager.

2. Click the service in the Service list box, as shown in Figure 3-22.

3. Click the <u>E</u>nd Process button.

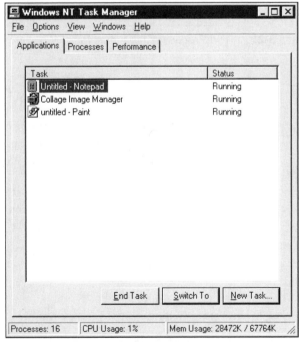

Figure 3-21.   The Applications tab of the Task Manager

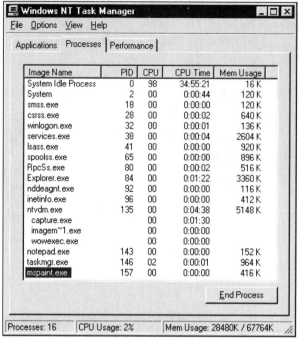

Figure 3-22.   The Processes tab in the Task Manager

 Tip: *Most often you can close out a malfunctioning program in Windows NT and continue working without delay. It is almost always a good idea to immediately save your work, close your other program, and reboot your computer to be safe.*

chapter

4 **A**nswers!

Customizing Your Desktop

Answer Topics!

Customizing Your Desktop
@ A Glance

⇨   The **Taskbar** contains the Start button with the Start menu, and buttons for any open file or any open folder. The Taskbar is highly configurable and can be docked to any side or minimized when not in use. It is also a command bar that appears by default at the bottom of your screen. The Start button always appears at the right of the Taskbar when it is in a horizontal position and at the top when it is in a vertical position. Any open programs or folders display a button on the Taskbar.

⇨   You **change the way your desktop looks** through control panel settings. The entire set of Desktop properties that you select is saved to your user profile and restored when you log onto Windows NT with your username and password. Administrators have the ability to control users' desktops, and that ability and the changes you can make to the desktop in future versions of Windows NT will be even more tightly controlled. Many important desktop settings are contained on the tabs of the Display control panel.

⇨   You can **change the display properties of** the desktop. The Display control panel also allows you to change your monitor type, screen resolution, and the number of colors you can see, as well as turn a screen saver on or off.

⇨   A folder in the Windows NT desktop represents a directory in the Windows NT file system. Each of the folders that you open on your desktop contains icons for its contents in a particular view. You can alter the way those icons are organized in the window and the way they look by **changing folder views**.

⇨   Several **icons** appear on your desktop that offer special services. The My Computer icon lets you view your computer's drives, the control panels, and your printers. The Recycle Bin is a folder for files to be deleted. Other icons let you launch your browser, synchronize files used on your laptop, and so forth.

⇨   **Control panels** are small programs or applets that let you change configuration settings in the Windows NT Registry. Many configuration tasks are accomplished in the control panels.

⇨   You can **make programs launch at startup**. The Startup folder is where you copy programs or place shortcuts to programs that you want to launch when you boot your computer. The Startup folder is stored with your user profile. A *service* is a process running on Windows NT. You don't see a button on the Taskbar for a service. To view and configure services running on Windows NT, you must open the Services control panel.

WORKING WITH THE TASKBAR

I need to use the bottom of my screen. How do I move the Taskbar to another edge of the screen?

To dock the Taskbar to another edge of your screen, click on a blank portion of the Taskbar and drag it to the top, right, left, or bottom edge of your screen.

Windows NT remembers the location of the Taskbar from your last session as part of your user profile, and returns it to view in that location.

Is there some way to make the Taskbar act as if it were a normal window?

Use the Always on top setting in the Taskbar Properties dialog box. This feature keeps the Taskbar in view regardless of what applications or folders are open on your desktop. It is on by default. If you set this property to off, the Taskbar is treated like another application window. It is hidden when you run another application full screen.

How do I change Taskbar options?

You can control several features of the Taskbar in the Taskbar's Properties dialog box. Right-click on the Taskbar and select the Properties command to view the Taskbar Properties dialog box shown in Figure 4-1; or select the Taskbar command from the Settings submenu of the Start menu to view this dialog box.

How do I see small icons on the Taskbar?

Select the Show small icons in menu option in the Taskbar Properties dialog box. This reduces the size of the icons in the Start menu.

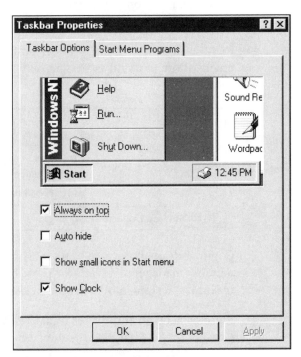

Figure 4-1.   The Taskbar Properties dialog box

What shortcuts are available on the Taskbar?

The Taskbar shows three different shortcut menus depending on where you right-click on it:

⇨   Right-click on the Start button to view the shortcuts associated with the Start menu, as shown here.

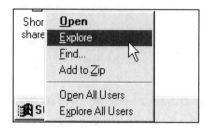

The Start Menu shortcut menu lets you open the Start Menu folder with the Open command. Folders you see on this menu contain shortcuts to all of your installed programs. You can use the Explore command to open the Start Menu folder in Explore view. The Find command opens the Find utility to search for a file in the Start Menu folder (by default).

⇨   Right-click on a program or folder button on the Taskbar to open a shortcut menu associated with that program or folder, as shown here.

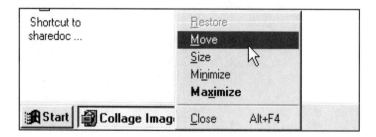

Commands on a program or folder shortcut menu provide window management features. These include the minimize, maximize, restore, move, size, and close commands.

⇨   Right-click on an empty area of the Taskbar to display the shortcut menu of the Taskbar itself, as shown here.

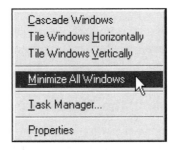

Commands on the Taskbar's shortcut menu let you change window properties for all open application and folder windows. Most importantly, the Properties command lets you configure the Taskbar and gives you access to properties of the Start menu.

Is there some way to make the Taskbar disappear when I don't need it?

Set the Auto-hide property to on in the Taskbar Properties dialog box. This is a neat feature that most people don't discover and don't use. If you select Auto-hide, the Taskbar disappears when you are not using it. Move your pointer over the edge of the screen where the Taskbar should be to have it reappear.

How do I remove the Taskbar from view?

To minimize the Taskbar, move your pointer over the border of the Taskbar until it becomes a double-headed arrow. Then click-and-drag the Taskbar to the edge of your screen.

To return the Taskbar from view, or to make the Taskbar wider, move your pointer over the edge of the Taskbar, and then click-and-drag it to the size you desire.

What do the status indicators on the left side of the Taskbar indicate?

The very right side of the Taskbar contains several status indicators. These indicators are for programs or services (typically control panel applets) that are running on Windows NT. You may see a clock there, a modem icon indicating modem status, a sound icon, and other icons. Only the clock icon is controlled in the Taskbar Properties dialog box. Other icons are added by particular programs. If you move your pointer over these indicators, their name and condition appear in a Tooltip. If you double-click on the indicator, the applet responsible for configuring them appears.

The time in the Taskbar is wrong. How do I correct it?

Double-click on the time to open the Date/Time control panel. Click on the hour, minute, second, or AM/PM indicator and use the spinner to change to the correct time. Click the Apply button to set the time, or close the Date/Time control panel.

How do I make the clock in the Taskbar disappear?

Click on the Show Clock checkbox in the Taskbar Properties dialog box off. When enabled (by default) the clock appears in the status area of the Taskbar. The Date/Time control panel controls what you see in the clock.

CHANGING THE LOOK OF YOUR DESKTOP

How do I change the appearance of specific interface items on my desktop?

Your desktop color and the color and fonts of items in the interface on your desktop are controlled on the Appearance tab of the Display control panel, as shown in Figure 4-2.

To change an element of the desktop:

1. Click on that item in the top pane of the Appearance tab. The item type appears in the Item list box below.

2. Select the color you desire from the color palette by clicking on the Color sample and dragging to the color you want.

3. Select the font and style you want from the Font list box, the Size combo box, the Color palette, and the style buttons.

4. Click the Apply button to effect your changes, or click the OK button to close the Display control panel.

Windows can save all of your appearance settings as a set to a file that is called a *scheme*. You can then recall a set of settings one group at

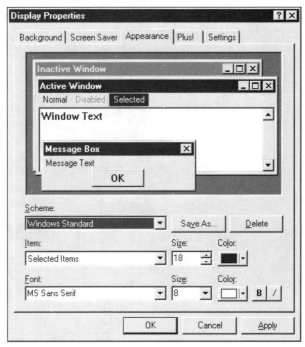

Figure 4-2.   The Appearance tab

a time. Use the Save As button to save a scheme, and select that scheme by name from the Scheme list box.

Tip: *Schemes can be useful when you need your system to appear a certain way from time to time. For this book I created a scheme that is used for taking screen shots and having them convert best to grayscale. When I want to return to my standard desktop, I select the Windows Standard scheme.*

I'm having trouble seeing items on my desktop. How do I change the background?

The background of your desktop is set on the Background tab of the Display control panel.

To open the Background tab:

⇨   Right-click on the desktop and select the Properties command; then click on the Background tab as shown in Figure 4-3.

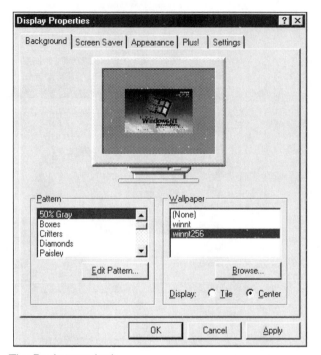

Figure 4-3.   The Background tab

As an alternative, you can double-click the Display icon in the Control Panel folder to open the Display control panel. Then choose a background from the Background tab, as described above.

You can put a picture on your screen (a .BMP or Microsoft Paint file) as wallpaper, and apply a pattern to that picture. Windows comes with a number of small .BMP files for you to choose from. You can center the picture; or you can tile your screen with it, which repeats the picture like a mosaic.

? Where do I find the files that are displayed on my desktop?

If you have used Windows 95 for some time, you may have gotten used to finding items in the Desktop folder in the location:

```
<root directory>\Windows\Desktop
```

In Windows NT, your Desktop folder is no longer located in that folder. Desktops are stored as part of a user profile. To find your Desktop folder, search along the following path:

```
<root directory>\WINNT\Profiles\<Username>\Desktop
```

Note: *Depending on how your administrator has set up your workstation or server, you may not have access to browse the Desktop folder in your profile or in any other user's profile.*

WORKING WITH DISPLAY PROPERTIES

How do I change the colors I see on my desktop?

The number of colors you can see on your monitor can also be changed on the Settings tab of the Display control panel. Color depth is a function of your monitor type, your graphics card, and your display driver. Depending on the capabilities of these three items, you can often change your color depth and resolution. One display characteristic is often related to another. If you increase your display resolution, you may need to decrease the number of colors you display, and vice versa.

To change the number of colors displayed on your screen, select the color depth from the Color palette list box on the Settings tab.

How do I change the fonts I see on my screen?

Make a selection from the Font Size section in the Settings tab of the Display control panel.

How do I change my monitor's resolution?

The resolution of a monitor is the number of pixels or picture elements that a screen will show. The greater the resolution on your screen, the more features of your desktop will appear. At greater resolution windows appear smaller, and you can fit more of them in the available area. Windows lets you select from standard resolutions such as: 640 x 480 pixels, 800 x 600 pixels, 1024 x 800 pixels, and so forth. The type of display, your graphics card, and the display driver you are using determine what resolution(s) your monitor or display is capable of.

To change your display resolution:

1. Right-click on the desktop and select the Properties command.

2. Click the Settings tab, as shown in Figure 4-4.

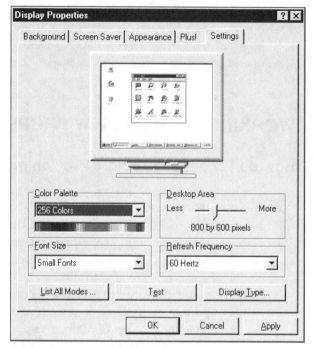

Figure 4-4.   The Settings tab of the Display control panel

3. Click-and-drag on the Desktop Area slider to change to the resolution you need. You may need to adjust the Refresh Frequency for higher resolutions.

4. Click the Apply button to see if the resolution can be changed successfully.

How do I turn a screen saver on or off?

A *screen saver* is a small program that runs whenever Windows NT detects a certain period of inactivity. Inactivity is generally associated with a lack of keyboard input or mouse movement. Processes such as communication and printing can be going on in the background and you can still have the screen saver startup.

The purpose of a screen saver is to prevent your monitor from having the image displayed on it burned into the phosphor coating. New monitors rarely have this problem. Still, screen savers are both useful and fun.

You can set a password for your screen saver to lock out the computer to other users. If you forget the password, just reboot the system and change it.

To turn a screen saver on or off:

1. Open the Display control panel (the Properties dialog box) and click on the Screen Saver tab, as shown in Figure 4-5.

2. Select the screen saver picture and animation from the Screen Saver list box.

3. Click on the Password Protected checkbox to enable that feature, and then click the Change button to enter your password (if desired).

4. Click the Apply button.

❓ Can I use Windows 95 themes with Windows NT?

Desktop Themes from the Windows 95 Plus Pack can be used with Windows NT. Several of them now ship with Windows NT. Themes

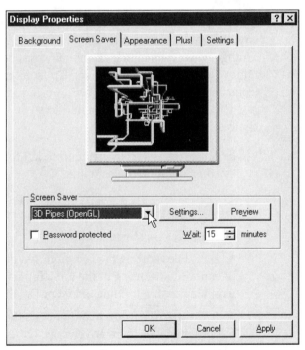

Figure 4-5.   The Screen Saver tab of the Display control panel

include desktop backgrounds, sounds, wallpaper, cursors, icons, and fonts. They are found in the WINNT folder, and you can select and install them using the Desktop Themes control panel.

CHANGING FOLDER VIEWS

❓ What is the Desktop?

The Desktop itself is a folder, but one that doesn't show any window interface elements. The Desktop folder is saved inside each user profile, and is reestablished when you log onto Windows NT for that user account.

To view your Desktop folder, open the Windows NT Explorer and select the Desktop folder at:

```
<root>\WINNT\profiles\username\Desktop
```

❓ How do I arrange the way icons are organized in a window?

If your view is a large or small icon view, you can move the icons anywhere you wish in a folder's window. The View menu lets you arrange your icons in one of several ways, depending on your current folder view. You can use the Line Up Icons command to place the icons in the window at the nearest position on an invisible grid.

The Arrange Icons submenu offers you the following additional choices:

- ⇨ *by Name.* Icons sort by name from left to right across a row, starting again on the next line.

- ⇨ *by Type.* Files sort by file type. This is particularly useful in Detail view where the file type is shown as a column in the window.

- ⇨ *by Size.* Files sort by file size.

- ⇨ *by Date.* Files sort by the last modified date and time with the last one modified coming at the top left position in a Large or Small Icon view or the top line of List or Detail view.

- ⇨ *Auto Arrange.* This command re-sorts the icons or names in a folder whenever there is a change. Other commands need to be reissued in order for this to occur.

Figure 4-6 shows you the View submenu of a folder's window shortcut menu.

These view commands are available in the Windows NT Explorer, with the exception of the Auto Arrange command. In either a desktop or Windows NT Explorer view of your folder, use the Refresh command on the View menu to see the most up-to-date information about a folder's contents.

 Tip: *If you are in Detail view or viewing a folder in the Windows NT Explorer, you can click on a column header to sort by that detail type. Click on the column header again to sort in the opposite direction.*

How do I change the view of my folder?

To change the view of a folder:

⇨ Select the Large Icon, Small Icon, List, or Details command from the View menu.

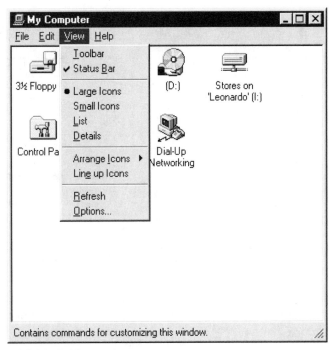

Figure 4-6.   A folder's View submenu

⇨ Or right-click on the window and select these commands from the
    View submenu on the shortcut menu, as shown in Figure 4-7.

There are four possible views that you can select for a folder:

⇨ *Large Icon.*   You see only large icons and the filenames in the
    folder window. In this view you can put the icons wherever you
    want in the window.

⇨ *Small Icon.*   You see small icons only in the folder window, along
    with their filenames. In this view you can move the icons
    anywhere you wish in the window.

⇨ *List.*   You see small icons arranged in stacked columns, with
    their filenames. You can't control where the icons are stacked
    in this view.

⇨ *Details.*   You see a display of the files in a view similar to the one
    you see in the Windows NT Explorer. In addition to the filename,
    you see the size, type, and date last modified in additional columns.

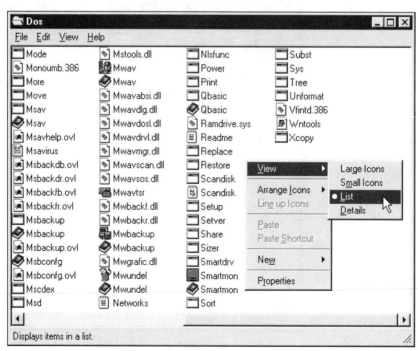

Figure 4-7.   A window's shortcut menu

How do I open a folder without showing the parent folder?

To have a folder open within another folder by simply replacing the contents of the parent folder:

1. Select the Options command on the View menu of the folder.

2. Click the Folder tab, as shown in Figure 4-8.

3. Click on the Browse folders by using a single window radio button.

4. Click the OK button.

The default behavior is to have folders open as a nested set of folders. Windows remembers your setting for each folder that you set an option for.

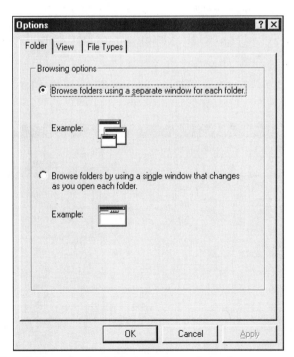

Figure 4-8.   The Folder tab of a folder's Options dialog box

How do I view a folder with a toolbar and a status bar?

Select the Toolbar and/or Status Bar commands from the View menu in the folder window. This is a particularly convenient method for viewing a folder's contents, as it puts a hierarchical list of your drives and folders into the toolbar that lets you change to another folder easily. The toolbar also contains a number of useful commands in button form. The status bar explains the purpose of any command that you highlight, and Tooltips appear when you move your pointer over a particular button or control. Figure 4-9 shows you a folder with these two commands turned on.

WORKING WITH ICONS

 I want to make it easier to spot a particular file type by assigning it a custom icon. How do I change the icon for a file in a folder?

To change the association of a file of a particular file type with an application, you need to do the following:

1. Select the Options command from the View menu.

2. Click the File Types tab.

3. Click the icon for the file type you wish to change.

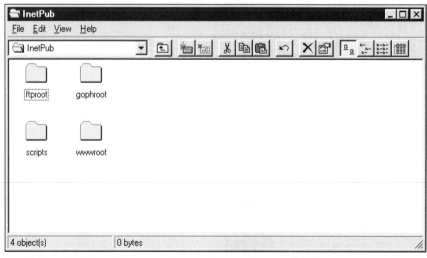

Figure 4-9.   A folder with the toolbar and status bar enabled

4. Click the Edit button.

5. Click the Change Icon button.

6. Specify the icon file (.ICO) that you wish to be displayed for this file type.

7. Click the OK button, and then two Close buttons to return to your folder view.

How do I change the icons of standard elements on my desktop?

The properties for modifying desktop icons, showing a window outline while dragging, using anti-alias fonts (making their borders fuzzy so that they read more easily), and stretching wallpaper to fit on the entire screen are set in the Plus! tab of the Display control panel. This tab is shown in Figure 4-10.

The Plus! package was an add-on first released for Windows 95. It offered such features as Desktop Themes, the Microsoft Internet Explorer, Internet access and dial-up support, and others. Windows NT Workstation and Server install the Plus! tab in the Display control

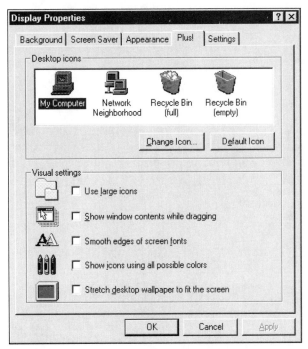

Figure 4-10. The Plus! tab of the Display control panel

panel, but do not install the Desktop Themes control panel from
Windows 95.

What is the purpose of the various Desktop icons?

Figure 4-11 shows you the standard Windows NT desktop. The icons
and their functions are as follows:

⇨ *My Computer.*   This is the icon for a folder that displays all of your
computer's drives (floppy disk, CD-ROM, and hard-drive volume
icons). You will also find folders for the Control Panel, Printers,
and Dial-Up Networking (if you install Dial-Up Networking as an
option) folders. Figure 4-12 shows the My Computer window.

⇨ *Network Neighborhood.*   This opens a window with a browsed list
of servers and workstations on your network. If you have the
privilege to open a particular volume on a remote computer, you
can see that volume in this browse list and double-click on it to
open it.

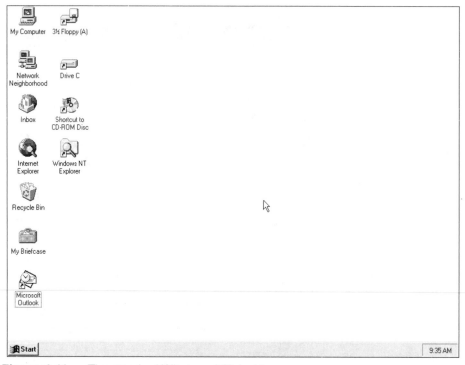

Figure 4-11.   The standard Windows NT desktop

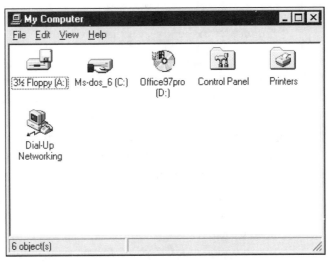

Figure 4-12.   The My Computer window

⇨ *Inbox.* This opens a window that contains all of your e-mail messages.

⇨ *Recycle Bin.*   This is a folder containing your recently deleted files. If you need to recover a deleted file, you can open this folder, select the file(s), and return it to its original location using the Restore command on the File menu. See Chapter 6, "Recovering Deleted Files," for more information on this topic.

⇨ *Internet.*   This launches the Microsoft Internet Explorer, a Web browser. If connected to the Internet or an intranet you will see your home page first and be able to navigate to additional resources.

⇨ *My Briefcase.*   This is a folder that contains files you use on a regular basis on a laptop. By synchronizing the contents of the Briefcase you can keep your work current on both your laptop and desktop computers.

USING THE CONTROL PANELS

How do I open the Control Panel folder?

There are two ways to open the Control Panel folder:

⇨ Select the Control Panel command from the Settings submenu of the Start menu.

⇨ Double-click the My Computer icon to view the Control Panel
folder in the My Computer window.

Every Control Panel folder may contain a somewhat different set of
Control Panel icons depending on what software has been installed on
your system. Figure 4-13 shows you a Control Panel folder for reference.

? There are some system components that weren't installed during the standard installation. How do I add and remove program and system components?

Open the Add/Remove Programs control panel. This is a wizard that
lets you install and remove programs from your system. It also allows
you to install system components for Windows NT that are installed
as an option. See Chapter 3 for more information about this feature.

? How do I change the appearance of my desktop and my monitor?

Open the Display control panel. It controls the appearance of your
desktop, and the characteristics of your display device.

Figure 4-13.   A typical Control Panel folder

Tip: Right-click on the desktop and select the Properties command to view the Display control panel.

How do I change features in a Command Prompt window?

Open the Console control panel. This lets you configure the Command Prompt window in which you can run MS-DOS programs. This feature was covered in detail in the previous chapter.

I want to use my computer in a language other than English or in another region of the world. How do I change the way numbers, dates, times, and currencies are displayed?

Open the Regional Settings control panel. This allows you to select a region or nationality, and to control how these other formats are used on your computer. Settings you select are used by applications in a variety of ways, such as sorts, display characteristics, and other features.

How do I change my system's date or time?

Open the Date/Time control panel. Use this control panel to set your system's date and time, to set your system's time zone, and to control whether your system observes daylight savings time (Windows NT makes the necessary adjustments automatically). Date and times you set are used as a system attribute to mark modification and creation dates, compare files for backups, and so forth. Figure 4-14 shows you the Date/Time control panel.

Tip: Your system's time appears in the status area of the Taskbar. Double-click on the time to open the Date/Time control panel.

Where do I get information about the peripheral devices that my computer is supporting?

Open the Devices control panel. This shows you an inventory of connected devices and their properties, and allows you to alter the configuration of your devices.

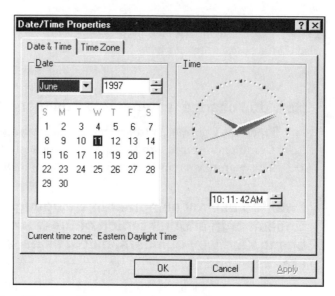

Figure 4-14.   The Date/Time Properties control panel

❓ How do I make it easier for people with disabilities to use my computer?

Open the Accessibility Options control panel. This lets you set options that make it easier for physically challenged people to use a computer. One option allows mouse behavior to be entered with a keyboard, another allows for single-finger operation from the keyboard, while still other options offer sound and visual feedback.

❓ How do I view, add, and remove fonts on my computer?

Open the Fonts control panel. This "control panel" is actually a shortcut to the Fonts folder on your system. It opens a folder that lets you add and remove fonts from your system. You can drag system and TrueType fonts directly into this folder, or use the Install New Fonts command on the File menu to open a dialog box to install new fonts. To remove fonts, delete the files from the Font folder.

If you are installing Postscript fonts on a Windows NT computer, you will need to use the installation program that comes with your

Postscript fonts package. Those fonts (screen and printer description files) are installed in different folders on your system than the Fonts folder. They also do not appear in the Fonts folder once installed because they are stored in other special PostScript font folders instead.

 Tip: *To see a sample of a particular font in the Fonts folder, double-click on that font file.*

❓ How do I change my Internet browser and session configuration?

Open the Internet control panel. This offers you several pages of settings that affect how your browser operates, how Internet connections are established, what security measures are in place, and so forth. See Chapter 15 for more information on this topic.

❓ How do I change my keyboard assignments?

Open the Keyboard control panel. The keyboard mapping to a character set or language is assigned here. You can also control features like the repeat rate and delay, as well as install a new device driver for your keyboard.

You cannot change the assignments of most keys on your keyboard using the Keyboard control panel. There are third-party programs that allow you to do this.

❓ How do I control where mail is delivered to?

Open the Mail control panel. This lets you direct mail from various services into a central Inbox. Additionally, you may see the Microsoft Mail Postoffice control panel. This lets you set up a PostOffice used by Microsoft Mail.

❓ Where do I configure and install a modem?

Open the Modems control panel. This opens a wizard that lets you install a new modem from the Add button. You can choose from hundreds of supported modems, or configure your own. Along with installing a modem driver, this control panel stores configuration settings for your modem, dialing instructions, and so forth. Chapter 14 describes "Managing Modems" in more detail.

How do I change my mouse button assignments?

Open the Mouse control panel. Right-click, left-click, and double-click behavior is assigned in the Mouse control panel. You can also control features like cursor speed and the pointers that are used, as well as install a new device driver for your mouse.

How do I install and configure multimedia equipment?

Open the Multimedia control panel. This lets you view and install multimedia devices, configure sound and video, work with MIDI files, and perform other tasks.

How do I install and configure network equipment and software?

Open the Network control panel. This lets you install network interface cards, install and configure network protocols, and assign addresses and service parameters. Chapter 14 describes the many features of this control panel in more detail.

How do I control PCMCIA cards installed on my laptop?

Open the PC Card (PCMCIA) control panel. This lets you view your installed PCMCIA cards and see their address assignments.

How do I configure a communication connection or port to a peripheral device?

Open the Ports control panel. This lets you alter the assignment of your serial and parallel ports connecting your computer to printers, modems, and other devices.

How do I manage and install printers?

Open the Printers control panel. This control panel is actually a shortcut to the Printers folder. You can also open this folder by selecting the Printers command from the Settings submenu on the Start menu.

To use items in the Printer folder:

⇨   Double-click the Add New Printer icon to open the Add Printer wizard and install a new printer.

⇨ Double-click on an installed printer to view the spooled print jobs in the print queue, and alter them.

⇨ Right-click on a printer to view and alter a printer's properties.

Chapter 9 describes printing issues in more detail.

How do I alter the behavior of multimedia files?

If they are QuickTime files, double-click on the QuickTime 32 control panel. This lets you set up and assign devices used to playback QuickTime multimedia files. It is installed as an add-on to Windows NT. See Chapter 10 for more information on this subject.

How do I see what devices are attached to my SCSI adapter?

Open the SCSI Adapters control panel. SCSI adapters let you attach up to eight SCSI devices in a chain, or up to 15 devices on a PCI controller. This control panel lets you view the device properties of any installed devices.

How do I see what services are running on my computer?

Open the Services control panel. Processes running on your computer appear here. You can start, stop, or pause a service here. You can also control whether this service starts up automatically when your computer boots. This control panel is described in more detail at the end of this chapter.

How do I assign sounds to various system events?

Open the Sounds control panel. Specific events are assigned to sound files there.

How do I get information about my computer system?

Open the System control panel. This displays general information about your system, its configuration, and attached devices, including hardware and user profiles, environment information, and startup/shutdown behavior. Right-click on the My Computer icon and select the Properties command to view this same information as a dialog box.

Another method you can use is to open the Microsoft diagnostic program WINMSD. To open the WINMSD program:

1. Select the Run command on the Start menu to open the Run dialog box.

2. Enter **WINMSD** into the Run dialog box, and press ENTER.

How do I install a tape device?

Open the Tape Devices control panel and install your device from there.

How do I configure my computer's telephone and dialing characteristics?

Open the Telephony control panel. Any MAPI device that can utilize the telephone interface of Windows NT is configured there.

How do I install and configure a UPS (uninterruptible power supply)?

Open the UPS control panel. A UPS device is a fancy battery that turns on when the electrical power fails. It provides additional time for your workstation to function while power is restored. Windows NT Workstation and Server has a feature that is configured through this control panel that allows the computer to be shut down gracefully after a period of time when the UPS device is functioning. You configure this connection with the UPS control panel.

How do I see who is using my workstation or server?

Open the Server control panel by double-clicking on the Server icon in the Control Panels folder. You will see what users are running processes. You can disconnect a user from a service in this control panel.

MAKING PROGRAMS LAUNCH AT STARTUP

There is a program that I always want to have running on my system. How do I make a program start up automatically?

To have a program start up automatically:

1. Right-click the Start button and select the Open or Explore command from the shortcut menu.

2. In the Startup folder that appears, double-click on the Programs folder, and then double-click on the Startup folder.

3. Select the Windows NT Explorer command from the Programs submenu of the Start menu.

4. Locate the program icon or a shortcut for that program in the Windows NT Explorer.

5. Or (instead of Steps 3 and 4) locate the program icon or a shortcut on your desktop.

6. Drag that icon to the Startup menu.

If you wish to leave your shortcut in the original location and create a new shortcut, right-click on the shortcut and drag it to the Startup folder. Then select the Copy Here command from the shortcut menu.

? I want to control a program that runs automatically on my system. How do I configure such a program?

You can control various features of how a program runs at startup. The procedure is the same as controlling how the program runs when you launch it from the icon on your desktop. You make selections from the program's Properties sheet.

To specify how a program runs at startup:

1. Open the Startup folder.

2. Right-click the shortcut icon and select the Properties command.

3. Click the Shortcut tab of the Properties sheet, as shown in Figure 4-15.

4. In the Target text box you will see the command line that launches that application. You can add any parameters or switches you desire to this line.

5. In the Run list box, select Minimized (Normal window Maximized).

6. In the Start in text box, enter the working directory that you want the program to have.

7. Click the OK button.

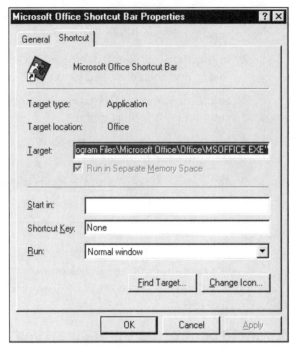

Figure 4-15.   The Shortcut tab of the Properties sheet

❓ How do I configure a service to start up automatically?

You can configure a service to start up automatically when you boot your Windows NT Server or Workstation. Some of the configuration utilities that these services install in the Administrative Tools folder may offer you the option of setting the automatic startup feature, but not always. The most general method for having a service start up automatically is to set that behavior in the Services control panel. The procedure below documents the use of the Services control panel to set startup behavior.

1. Select the Control Panel command from the Settings submenu of the Start menu.

2. Double-click the Services Control Panel icon.

3. Highlight a service in the Services list box.

4. Click the Startup button in the Services control panel.

5. In the Services dialog box (see Figure 4-16), click on the startup behavior you desire: Automatic, Manual, or Disabled.

Figure 4-16.   The Services dialog box is where you set startup behavior

6. Set the log-on behavior in the Log On As section of the Service dialog box.

7. Click the OK button in the Service dialog box, and then the Close button in the Services control panel.

You may need to reboot your workstation or server to enforce your settings, although many services do not require you to reboot your computer.

Using the File System

Answer Topics!

The File System @ a Glance

⇨ You can format a hard drive using either a FAT or NTFS **file system**. Use a FAT file system when you want any kind of client to access the volume. Use the NTFS file system when you want to enable advanced security and fault tolerance features.

⇨ You can subdivide physical drives into logical **partitions**. You can create a single partition as a primary partition. You can also create extended partitions and subdivide those partitions into individual logical drives, each of which has its own file system and drive letter. Each partition has its own file system. You can create partitions using the Disk Administrator tool or the Format command.

⇨ Windows NT offers **file and directory security**. Files and folders or directories can be secured to allow only particular users and groups to access them. You can also control what those users and groups can do when they access that resource. You can specify folder or directories and volumes that can be **shared** across a network. A share can be limited to a particular user or group, and you can control what privileges these users have when they access the shared resource.

⇨ When you install a program in Windows NT, that program normally registers what file types it will be responsible for. You can **change a file association** at any time and add new ones as an option.

⇨ **Files** are items that are tracked by the file system. When you create a file, it is stored to disk, along with a name and a set of attributes. If the file is of a type that is registered with the Windows NT Registry, Windows NT knows what icon to display for that file and what program to use when you open the file. Unknown file types are stored with a generic document type and require that you intervene and specify how they are used. You can easily create files and folders, and move, copy, and rename those objects using the shortcut menu on the desktop or in the Windows NT Explorer.

⇨ A **folder** is an iconic representation for a directory in the file system. Folders that appear on your desktop are actually directories that appear in the Desktop directory of your user profile. All other folders appear in the appropriate place that they occupy in the file system. Windows NT maintains some special folders. The Desktop folder is one such folder, as are the Start Menu and Startup folders. All of those folders are part of your Profile.

⇨ As Microsoft moves to a fully object-oriented operating system, more and more files, folders, volumes, disks, and other things that you manipulate in the interface take on the trappings of objects. One of the features of objects is that they have attributes. In Windows NT you manipulate an object's attributes by changing **object properties** in the Property sheet. Certain properties of an object are tracked by the system automatically: object type, location, size, dates and time created and modified, and so forth.

ABOUT THE FILE SYSTEM

 I want to make more efficient use of my disk space. Is there a way that I can control disk cluster size?

Use the Format command. Unlike the Disk Administrator, it allows you to have a finer control over the size of clusters on a drive.

To specify a cluster size, use the /A switch:

```
FORMAT /A:size
```

to control cluster size. The following cluster sizes are allowed:

⇨ FAT supports 8192, 16KB, 32KB, 64KB, 128KB, and 256KB.

⇨ NTFS supports 512, 1024, 2048, 4096, 8192, 16KB, 32KB, and 64KB.

For a cluster size above 4096 in NTFS, you cannot compress the disk.

? **Can I convert between file systems already installed on my hard drive?**

You can convert from FAT and HPFS to NTFS using a conversion program. The only way to convert an NTFS volume to FAT is to reformat the volume in the Disk Administrator program.

? **I have a FAT volume on my hard drive and I want to upgrade it to NTFS to take advantage of the newer format's security features. How do I convert from FAT (or HPFS) to NTFS?**

Use the CONVERT program to convert a file system after Windows NT is installed. Open the Command Prompt window and use the following command:

```
CONVERT drive: /FS:NTFS [/V]
```

The different switches in this command have the following explanations:

⇨ *Drive.* The letter of the volume you are converting to NTFS. The drive you are converting cannot be the drive from which you booted Windows NT. If you try to convert your boot drive, Windows NT must reboot the system before it can enable this option.

⇨ */FS:NTFS.* This switch specifies that you wish to convert the volume to the NTFS file system. The current version of Windows NT does not let you convert the NTFS file system to FAT.

⇨ */V.* The so-called "Verbose" switch posts numerous messages and prompts during the conversion.

When a volume is formatted during installation with the NTFS file system, Windows NT formats the drive as a FAT volume and converts the drive to NTFS after the system reboots.

When you install Windows NT 4 on a computer that contains the HPFS file system, the installer will ask if you wish to convert the volume to either the FAT or NTFS file system. You must perform this conversion, or reformat the drive prior to the installation as either FAT or NTFS.

? I want to be able to have other operating systems read my hard drive. Can I convert from NTFS to FAT?

There is no way for you to convert a volume that was formatted in the NTFS file system to the FAT file system. The only method you can use at the moment is to reformat the volume that contains the NTFS file system and specify that it is a FAT volume. If you do that, all of your data is destroyed on the NTFS disk, and all of the security attributes and other NTFS options that you enabled are also destroyed.

? What file systems does Windows NT support?

When you install Windows NT, you have the choice of installing different file systems:

⇨ *FAT.* The File Allocation Table file system is the one supported by MS-DOS and Windows 3.*x*.

⇨ *NTFS.* The New Technology File System is designed to exploit features in Windows NT.

⇨ *HPFS.* The High Performance File System was developed for OS/2, and was supported by Windows NT version 3.5 and earlier. Windows NT can access HPFS file systems, but no longer creates them.

Although FAT duplicates the file system DOS users are already familiar with, actually Windows NT expands on the FAT file system to allow the use of long filenames and other extended attributes. This virtual FAT file system first appeared in Windows 95.

? What happens to the data when I format a floppy disk in Windows NT?

When you format a floppy disk, you mark it so that areas on the disk can be identified by the file system. Formatting may or may not wipe your entire disk clean, depending upon what option you choose. If you format a floppy disk using the Quick Format method, most of the information remains on your disk with the exception of the boundary areas that are marked. The full format method overwrites your entire floppy disk.

Note: *You may be able to recover some or all of the data on your floppy disk using a third-party program like Norton Utilities for NT on a floppy disk that has been quick-formatted.*

? How do I format a floppy disk?

To format a floppy disk:

1. Insert the floppy disk into your disk drive.

2. Right-click an icon for the floppy disk drive in the My Computer or Windows NT Explorer window, or on a shortcut to that drive; then select the Format command from the shortcut menu (see Figure 5-1).

 Note: *The contents of the floppy disk cannot be displayed in the right pane of the Windows NT Explorer or you will not be allowed to format that disk.*

3. Select the correct capacity for your floppy disk in the Capacity list box, if necessary.

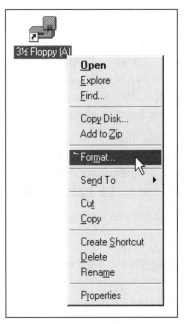

Figure 5-1.   A floppy disk's shortcut menu

Warning: *Do not format a floppy disk with a different capacity than the one at which it is rated. Doing so will either cause the format to fail or produce an unreliable disk.*

4. Enter a label in the Volume Label text box if you wish that name to appear next to the disk icon.

5. If you are reformatting a disk, click on the Quick Format checkbox. This option delete the entries in the file system for all of your files but leaves the file otherwise intact. To both delete the entries in the file system and overwrite all sectors with blank data you must use a full format and format the entire disk.

6. Click the <u>S</u>tart button, and then click the OK button in the warning box that appears.

7. When Windows NT finishes formatting your floppy disk, click OK in the message box.

You can only format a floppy disk with the FAT file system.

Warning: *Do not use the Format command on a hard drive or a volume on your hard drive unless you are certain that you wish to reformat the hard drive. Pay attention to the disk drive that you are formatting as this action can destroy all of your data.*

Note: *If you are displaying the contents of a floppy disk in the Windows NT Explorer in the right panel of the program, you will not be able to format the floppy disk. Click on another folder, right-click on the floppy disk, and select the Format command to circumvent this problem.*

❓ I want to overwrite all of the data on my disk, and to make sure that any suspect areas on the hard drive aren't used. How do I format a hard drive?

There are three methods you can use to format a hard drive:

⇨ Right-click the hard drive icon in the My Computer window, and select the For<u>m</u>at command as was described in the previous section.

⇨ Open a Command Prompt window and use the FORMAT command.

⇨ Open the Disk Administrator program in the Administrative Tools folder on the Programs submenu of the Start menu.

You can use the first method to create both FAT and NTFS file systems from an entire hard drive or from a volume that already exists. This method does not allow you to change the volume size, label, or other features. It follows the same procedure described above.

The Format command is both extensive and powerful. It can be used for both hard drives and floppy disks. Visit the online Help system and search for the Format command to view information about this command's syntax.

The Disk Administrator offers probably the easiest method to use with the most options to format a hard drive. In that utility you have the option of creating either FAT or NTFS volumes, rearranging volumes, combining and splitting volumes, setting up fault-tolerant features like RAID, and other options. To access the Disk Administrator, you must have administrative privileges.

❓ What file system should I use?

Use the FAT file system when:

⇨ You want to allow access to a volume on Windows NT Workstation or Server to MS-DOS or Windows 3.x clients.

⇨ You want a dual boot system.

⇨ You want the fastest possible disk performance.

Use the NTFS file system when:

⇨ You want the most efficient storage of your data.

⇨ You need to work with large volumes (FAT has a limit of 2.1GB; NTFS supports volumes up to 16 billion gigabytes!).

⇨ You want to use Windows NT's disk compression utility.

⇨ You want to enable the advanced security methods that are part of Windows NT.

⇨ You want access to the many fault tolerance features that are part of NTFS.

There are so many advantages to using NTFS and so few to using FAT that most Windows NT installations should install and use the NTFS file system. In those instances where FAT drives are required, an administrator or user may wish to consider installing both file systems in two different partitions.

MANAGING PARTITIONS

 Note: *See Chapter 7, "Understanding RAID," to learn about issues relating to establishing and managing volume sets.*

What is a partition?

A partition is a volume that is mapped to a letter or has a name associated with it on a computer. Partitions can span almost the entire hard drive space, or any part of that space. Most often, partitions occupy contiguous space on a hard drive, but that isn't a requirement.

Windows NT allows you to create both primary partitions and extended partitions. You can create multiple logical drives in an extended partition, but only a single logical drive in a primary partition. Your physical hard drive can support one primary partition, which maps to a single volume letter. You can create one or more logical drives in an extended partition, each one mapping to their own volume letter.

❓ I have several operating systems on my hard drive. How do I assign the boot drive?

The partitions that contain the startup and operating system files are often called the *system* and *boot partitions*, respectively.

To assign a boot volume for the system:

⇨ Select the desired volume in the Disk Administrator, and then select the Mark <u>A</u>ctive command from the <u>P</u>artition menu.

The words "Active Partition" appear in the status bar of the Disk Administrator when you select that disk.

Partitions for RISC-computers (which only support the FAT file system) are not marked active in the Disk Administrator. Use the boot manager or configuration program that comes with your RISC computer to determine the active partition on that type of computer.

Boot and system partitions can be mirroring, but no other RAID technique may be used for those partitions. A system partition contains hardware drivers and any I/O routines needed to boot Windows NT. A system partition must not only be a primary partition, but it also has to be marked as the active system partition.

The NT boot partition is the volume formatted for a NTFS or FAT. Versions of Windows NT earlier than 3.5.1 can also format a boot partition as an HPFS file system. A boot partition can also be the system partition, if that system partition was marked as bootable.

How do I create a partition?

To create a new partition:

1. Open the Disk Administrator by selecting it from the Administrative Tools folder in the Programs folder.

2. Click on an area of free space on a disk in the Disk Administrator.

3. Select the Create command from the Partition menu to create a primary partition, or select the Create Extended command to create an extended partition.

4. A Create Partition dialog box appears, as shown in Figure 5-2.

5. Enter the size of the partition; then click the OK button.

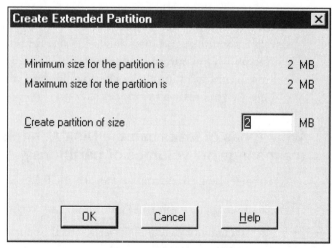

Figure 5-2.   The Create Extended Partition dialog box

I no longer need a particular volume. How do I delete a partition or a logical drive?

You delete partitions, volumes, or logical drives in the Disk Administrator. You cannot delete your boot partition, or any partition that has system files in use on an Intel x86 computer, but RISC computers do not offer this same protection. You cannot delete a volume that is part of a mirror or a striped set without removing that feature first.

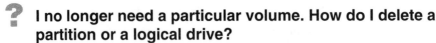

Warning: Information in deleted volumes cannot be recovered.

To delete a partition, volume, or logical drive:

1. Open the Disk Administrator and click on the partition, volume, or logical drive you wish to delete.

2. Select the <u>D</u>elete command from the <u>P</u>artition menu; then click the Yes button in the dialog box.

Your partition, volume, or logical drive is deleted and becomes free space.

Note: To delete an extended partition, you must delete all volumes or logical drives that are part of that extended partition.

If you are deleting a volume that is part of a RAID set, you will need to remove that feature first. Break any mirror set to create an orphan volume, and then delete the second mirror volume. You can reestablish the mirror at another time. It's a good idea to save and store a configuration disk prior to deleting a mirror set. That disk can help you re-create a mirror set later on.

 What types of tasks can the Disk Administrator do to help me manage my volumes or partitions?

You use the Disk Administrator for the following:

⇨ To format or reformat a volume, and to change its file system.

⇨ To create or delete disk partitions that appear as mapped volumes on your network.

⇨ To create extended partitions that store additional file attributes.

⇨ To create a partition that is a volume set and which spans two or more physical drives.

⇨ To create stripe sets with or without parity that can aid in data recovery.

⇨ To establish or break a mirrored set of drives managed via NT software drivers, or perform disk duplexing—both of which are RAID features.

⇨ To check for disk errors and set volume and disk labels.

Stripe sets, mirror sets, and disk duplexing are different levels of RAID (Redundant Array of Independent Disks). Establishing a RAID feature protects your data, and gives you great flexibility in the way you organize your hard drives.

A large part of my hard drive space is unused. What can I do with free space?

Free space is unused and unformatted space. You can have free space on a drive or in an extended partition. Free space on a drive can be partitioned into a volume; in an extended partition it can be used to create logical drives.

The Disk Administrator can convert free space to:

⇨ A new primary partition

⇨ Additional partitions (up to four per physical disk)

⇨ An extended partition, each containing one or more logical drives

⇨ RAID drives: volume sets and stripe sets

I want to create additional volumes on the same hard drive that already contains some partitions. How do I create logical drives?

A logical drive is a volume in a partition formatted with its own file system. Use the same procedure to create logical drives in an extended partition that was described for creating an extended partition. Select the free space in an extended partition, and then issue the Create command.

To create a new logical drive:

1. Open the Disk Administrator by selecting it from the Administrative Tools folder in the Programs folder.

2. Click on an area of free space on an extended partition.

3. Select the Create command from the Partition menu to create a primary partition.

4. In the Create Partition dialog box (see Figure 5-2) enter the size of the partition

5. Click the OK button.

❓ How do I partition a new disk?

To create a partition on a new disk:

1. Select the Disk Administrator command from the Administrative Tools folder of the Programs submenu on the Start menu.

2. In the Disk Administrator window shown in Figure 5-3, click on the new disk.

3. Select the Create command from the Partition menu.

4. Set the size of the partition that you desire; then click the OK button.

This creates the primary partition. By default, the Disk Administrator assumes that you wish to use the entire disk for a partition unless you lower the suggested partition size.

Continue formatting your partition:

1. Select the Commit Changes Now command from the Partition menu.

2. Select Format from the Tools menu.

3. Choose the type of file system you desire: FAT or NTFS.

4. Disable the Quick Format checkbox only if you are certain that the hard drive has no bad sectors and you want to avoid the

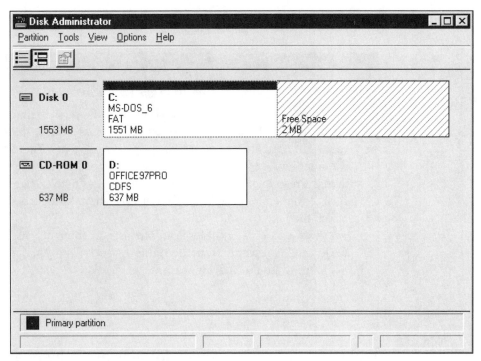

Figure 5-3.   The Disk Administrator

time-consuming surface scan. Otherwise, leave the feature enabled.

5. Click the OK button, and then confirm the action.

After Windows NT formats the drive, it assigns a letter to the volume. You can use that volume without having to reboot your system.

? I intend to use the next drive letter for a special purpose. How do I reassign a drive letter for a volume that has been automatically assigned?

Select the volume in the Disk Administrator. Up to 24 drive letters (25 when there is no floppy disk) can be assigned to volumes or to CD-ROM drives using the Drive Letter command on the Tools menu.

SETTING FILE AND DIRECTORY SECURITY

Who has access to a file?

As the creator of a file or folder, you have full access to that resource. In order to allow other users to access a file or folder, that right needs to be granted by the resource owner. There are different levels of privileges that users can be allowed when they access a resource. You specify access privileges to folders, and the files contained in those folders inherit the shared properties of the folder they are contained in.

Access to a file or folder is an intrinsic attribute of that file and folder, and is separate from the rights and privileges that you assign through the Sharing feature.

What types of access levels for files and folders are possible?

The following access levels are available to users and groups accessing folders and files:

⇨ *Take Ownership.* This user or group has the right to take over ownership of the resource.

⇨ *Change Permissions.* This user or group can alter the access of other users to this resource.

⇨ *Delete.* This level allows a resource to be deleted.

⇨ *Execute.* File attributes, permissions, and owner can be displayed. Changes can be made to subdirectories. Program file can be run. Files can have their attributes, permissions, and owner displayed. (This permission does not include a Read permission.)

⇨ *Write.* This level lets a user or group have Read access, as well as allowing the creation of subdirectories and files within a directory. It can also alter attributes of directories. Files can be read, and the file's data and attributes can be changed.

⇨ *Read.* This level allows a user to display filenames in a directory and see their attributes, permissions, and the owner of the directory. A file's data, attributes, permissions, and owner can also be viewed.

One thing that you should know is that access privileges are additive. If you give a user one set of privileges to a resource as part of their belonging to one group, and another set of privileges to another group that they belong to, the user has the most restrictive level of access to the resource. An example of this is if you establish SHARE permissions of CHANGE yet NTFS permissions are READ, then that user only has READ permissions.

I want to control who can access a file or folder on my computer. How do I add (or remove) a user or group to the permission list for a file or folder?

To add a user or group to the list of permitted users of that resource:

1. Click the Add button in the Directory Permissions dialog box.

2. Select the domain in the List Names From list box, if necessary.

3. Select the name of the group in the Add Users and Groups dialog box, as shown in Figure 5-4.

4. Or click the Show Users button to view users and click the name of the user account you wish to add, if necessary.

5. Click the Add button.

6. Select the access level in the Type of Access list box.

7. Click the OK button to return to the Access Through Shared Permissions dialog box.

To remove permission for access from a user or group:

⇨ Select the user or group in the Access Through Shared Permissions dialog box Name list box; then click the Remove button.

How do I change the access privilege to a file or folder for a user and group?

To change access privileges to a file or folder:

⇨   Select the name of the user or group in the <u>N</u>ame list box of the
     Directory dialog box, and then select the level of access you want
     them to have in the <u>T</u>ype of Access list box.

When you click the OK button to close the Directory Permissions
dialog box, the new level of access is granted.

How do I set file or folder permissions?

In order to allow another user to view and manipulate a file in a
folder, you have to specify that property on the Security tab of the
folder's Properties sheet, as shown in Figure 5-5.

Note: *The Security tab of the Properties sheet is not available on a FAT
volume, and does not appear. You cannot set file or folder permissions on FAT.*

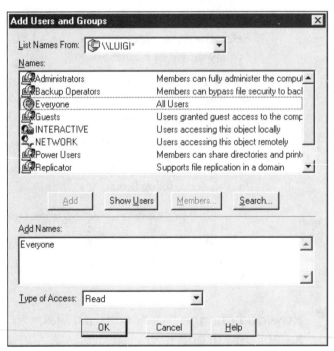

Figure 5-4.   The Add Users and Groups dialog box

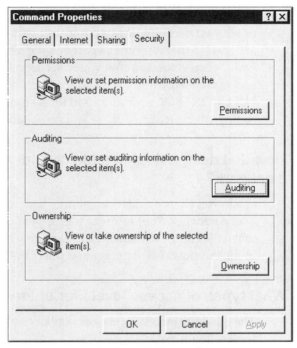

Figure 5-5. The Security tab of a folder's Properties sheet

? Who can take ownership of my files or folders?

An Administrator can take ownership of another person's files, folders, or volumes. If that occurs, the original owner will no longer be able to access those resources, which makes this action obvious. You will no longer have ownership the next time you try to access the file or folder.

? Are share permissions the same as file and directory permissions?

No. Windows NT lets you define two sets of privileges. The difference between them is best seen when considering local vs. networked access. You can access resources on a local computer for which you have the privileges even if those resources aren't shared. If you log in remotely, without the resource being part of a share, you will not be able to access that resource even if you have permission to do so.

When you access a share over a network, you can still be denied or allowed access to files and folders based on the access privileges assigned to that resource as part of a file or folder's security attributes. Only NTFS volumes allow you to set security attributes, so that if you access a shared volume on a FAT volume, the share access level of FULL CONTROL is what is used for all users. This is the default setting when creating a share and can be changed.

? How do I designate that a file or folder can be shared over a network?

When you share a folder or volume, you make that item viewable over a network. That resource will appear in a browsed list of folders when the computer is accessed. To share a folder, right-click the folder in the Windows NT Explorer and select the Sharing command.

? What types of access levels for shares are possible?

The following access levels are available to users and groups sharing folders and files:

⇨ *Full Control.* This user or group can change the file or folder. They have the right to change access permissions, and can take over ownership of the resource.

⇨ *Change.* This level allows a resource to be modified and files and folders to be deleted. Access permissions cannot be changed, nor can ownership be assumed by this level.

⇨ *Read.* This level allows a user to view a resource, but not to modify it. Files can be viewed, but not changed. Folders can be opened and browsed, but their contents cannot be altered, added, or subtracted to. Applications can be run, but not modified.

⇨ *No Access.* This level does not allow a user to access the resource in any way. It overrides privileges granted to other types of users, and can make the resource unavailable even to an administrator. The only way for an administrator to access a No Access resource is to take ownership of it.

One thing that you should know is that access privileges are additive (with the exception of the No Access privilege). If you give a user one set of privileges to a resource as part of their belonging to one group, and another set of privileges to another group that they belong to, the user has the higher level of access to the resource.

? How does sharing on a FAT drive differ from an NTFS drive?

Only an NTFS volume will allow you to assign file and folder security attributes. The Security tab appears in a file or folder's Properties sheet, and you can assign access privileges to that file or folder. You create shares on either a FAT or NTFS drive, but on a FAT drive your share sets the access level of its contents.

When you set file- and folder-level security on an NTFS volume and specify a share containing either of those elements, you have finer control over who can access that resource. The individual file and folder's privileges take precedence over the access privileges that you give users and groups to the network share.

? I don't have an NTFS volume installed, but I still want to share my files or folders. How do I share resources on a FAT drive?

The procedure for sharing a resource on a FAT drive is no different than sharing a resource on an NTFS volume.

To share a folder on a FAT drive:

1. Right-click the folder on your desktop or in the Windows NT Explorer.

2. Select the Sharing command from the shortcut menu.

3. The Sharing tab of the Properties sheet appears (see Figure 5-6).

4. Click the Shared As radio button.

5. Enter a Share Name, set the User Limit, and set the Permissions as described in the section "How do I set file or folder permissions?"

6. Click the OK button.

? I want to see who has been using my files and folders. How do I keep track of who has accessed files and directories?

Turn on directory and file auditing. This feature is available on NTFS volumes.

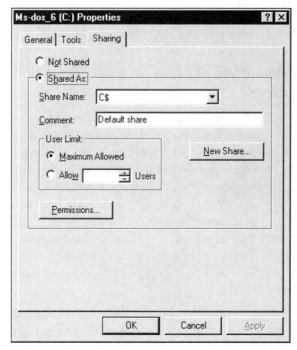

Figure 5-6.   The Sharing tab of the Properties sheet for a FAT drive

To perform file or directory auditing:

1. Right-click the file or folder and select the Properties command.

2. Click the Security tab; then click the Auditing button.

3. In the Directory Auditing dialog box shown in Figure 5-7, click the Add button to view the users and groups in the Add Users and Groups dialog box (see Figure 5-4) that you want to audit.

4. Select the Events To Audit checkboxes that are appropriate.

5. Click the OK button.

When you select a file, the File Auditing dialog box appears, which looks identical to the Directory Auditing dialog box.

Auditing by default is done on the top level folder you selected. If you want to audit subfolders, enable the Replace Auditing on Subdirectories checkbox at the top of the dialog box.

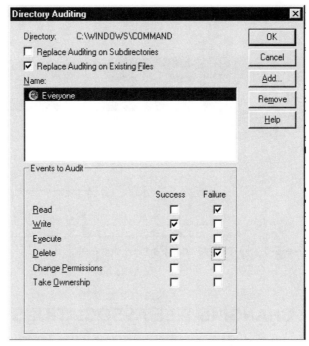

Figure 5-7.   The Directory Auditing dialog box

? How do I review who has what access privileges?

To review permissions for a file or folder:

1. Find the file or folder on your desktop or in the Windows NT Explorer.

2. Right-click on the folder and select the Properties command from the shortcut menu.

3. Click the Security tab, and then click the Permissions button.

4. In the Directory Permissions dialog box (when a folder is selected) shown in Figure 5-8, click on each user group in the Name list box to see what access privileges they have in the Type of Access list box.

An identical dialog box called File Permissions appears when you select a file and set its permissions.

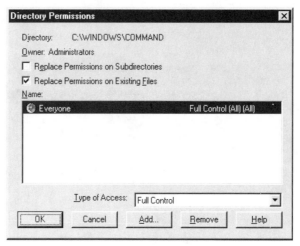

Figure 5-8.   The Directory Permissions dialog box

CHANGING FILE ASSOCIATIONS

Where do file extensions show up?

Although you don't see file extensions in the Windows NT file system, they are still used. The file extensions are displayed as a File Type attribute in both a desktop folder and Windows NT Explorer Detail view. There is a mapping of three-letter file extensions to more friendly names such as "Microsoft Word Document" based on the assignment of that file type in the Windows NT Registry. The file of any registered file type can be opened automatically when you double-click on that file. For any file that does not have an associated (registered) program you have to specify the application to be used to open that file when you attempt to open it.

? How do I associate a program with a file type?

The process of associating a file type with a program is often done automatically when you install a program, and is called *registering a program.* The association is made in the Windows NT Registry between that particular program and an associated file type. In many instances a program might be responsible for one or more file types, and you may see a dialog box appear during installation asking your permission to create that association.

If you attempt to open a file that has no program associated with it (or registered for it, if you will), you will see the Open With dialog box appear, as shown in Figure 5-9. You can select the application you wish to use to open that file from the Choose the Program You Want to Use list box.

You are free to make a new association between a file type and an installed program, at any time.

? I want to control what program opens a particular type of file. How do I change an association?

To edit a file type association:

1. Select the Windows NT Explorer command from the Programs submenu of the Start menu.

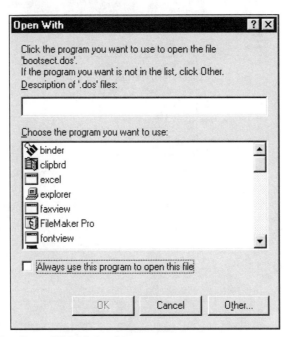

Figure 5-9.   The Open With dialog box

2. Select the Options command from the View menu.

3. In the File Types tab of the Options dialog box (see Figure 5-10), click on the file type in the Registered File Types list box to select it.

4. Click the Edit button.

5. Select the action that you want to edit in the Actions list box of the Edit File Type dialog box shown in Figure 5-11; then click the Edit button.

6. In the Editing Action dialog box shown in Figure 5-12, enter the new program you wish to associate with this file type and action.

8. Click the OK button and then the two Close buttons to return to Windows NT Explorer.

You can alter not only the open behavior, but also how files of this type are printed, and other supported commands.

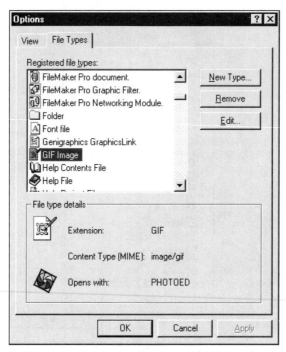

Figure 5-10.   The File Types tab of the Options dialog box

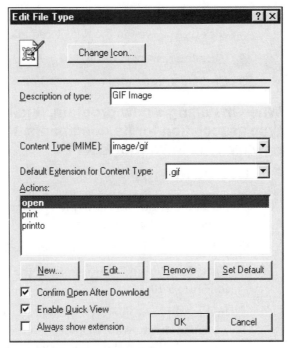

Figure 5-11.   The Edit File Type dialog box

? I no longer need a particular file association. How do I delete it?

To delete a file association, do the following:

1. Select the Windows NT Explorer command from the Programs submenu of the Start menu.

2. Select the Options command from the View menu.

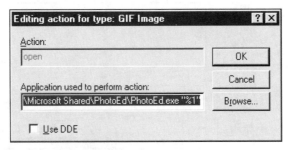

Figure 5-12.   The Editing Action dialog box

3. In the File Types tab of the Options dialog box (see Figure 5-10), click the file type in the Registered File Types list box to select it.

4. Click the Remove button.

5. Click the Close button.

When installing a new program, it failed to register the file type association for its documents. How do I register a new file type in Windows NT?

To register a file type:

1. Select the Windows NT Explorer command from the Programs submenu of the Start menu.

2. Select the Options command from the View menu.

3. Click the File Types tab; then click the New Type button as shown in Figure 5-10.

4. In the Add New File Type dialog box (see Figure 5-13), enter the information you want displayed in the File Type column of Detail view in the Description of type text box.

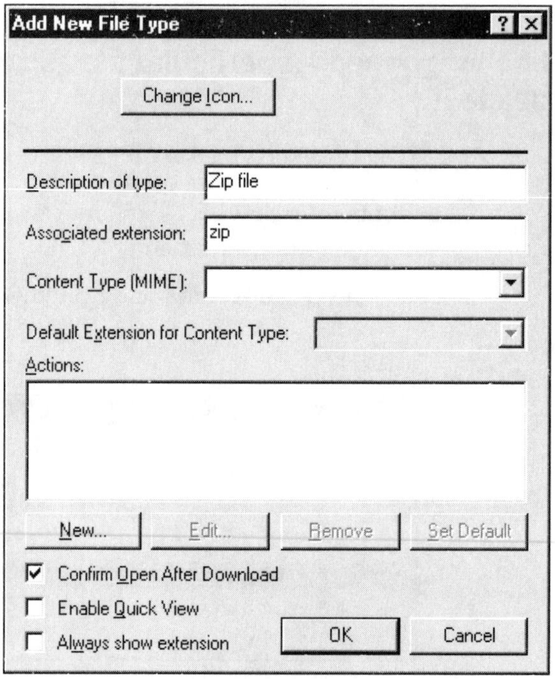

Figure 5-13.   The Add New File Type dialog box

5. Enter the three-letter file extension that maps the file type to the icon that will be displayed in the Associated file extension text box.

6. Click the New button to display the New Action dialog box shown in Figure 5-14.

7. Type **open** in the Action text box to have this file type open when you double-click on the file.

8. Click the Browse button and select the application that is used for this file type. Your selection appears as a path to the .EXE file in the Application Used to Perform Action text box of the New Action dialog box.

9. Click the OK button to return to the Add New File Type dialog box; then check that the icon displayed in the top-left corner is the one you wish this file type to have.

10. If not, click the Change Icon button and select a different icon for the file type.

11. Click the Close button to write the association to the Windows NT Registry.

I'm looking for a file that I think is either hidden or a system file. How do I see all of my files in the Windows NT Explorer?

Some files are given a hidden attribute and normally hidden from view. Other files such as system files and device driver files may also be hidden. The reason for this is twofold: to prevent these files from accidentally being modified or deleted, and to simplify your folder and file view.

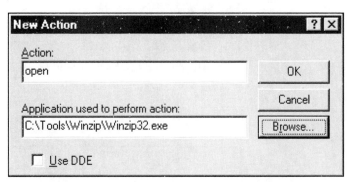

Figure 5-14.   The New Action dialog box

To view all files:

⇨ Enable the Show All Files radio button on the View tab of the Options dialog box (see Figure 5-15).

All hidden files then appear in your folders or in the Windows NT Explorer.

Warning: *If you select this option, even system privilege files will be displayed. Tampering with or removing these files will have a deleterious effect on your system!*

? I want to see the file extensions for files in the Windows NT Explorer, and not the friendly explanation of the file type. How do I view file extensions?

To see file extensions in folders and in the Windows NT Explorer:

1. Select the Options command from the View menu.

2. On the View tab (see Figure 5-15), click the Hide File Extensions for Known File Types checkbox to remove the check.

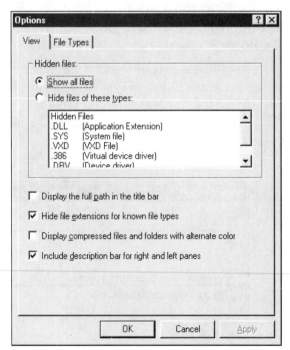

Figure 5-15.   The View tab of the Options dialog box

3. Click the OK button.

If Windows NT doesn't know what program created the file, the file extension will always appear.

WORKING WITH FILES

? I know I can create files within an application. How do I create a file quickly from the desktop or the Windows NT Explorer?

You can create a file from within an application, and the file type of that application is correctly saved to disk. You can also create files directly in the file system.

To create a file:

1. Right-click on the desktop or in the Windows NT Explorer.

2. Select the New command.

3. Select the file type from the shortcut menu.

4. Enter a new name for the file that is created.

Only applications registered with Windows NT have their file types appear on the New submenu.

? My hard drive seems to be getting slower. Do I need to defragment a disk in Windows NT?

Microsoft advertised that Windows NT 4 does not require defragmentation when the operating system was introduced. And, in fact, this operating system has far fewer problems relating to file fragmentation and loss of performance than other operating systems. However, fragmentation does occur on Windows NT. There are now a number of utilities like DisKeeper that will defragment files on Windows NT.

One other reason that a hard drive might get slower is if a part of a striped set fails. This feature is described in full in Chapter 7.

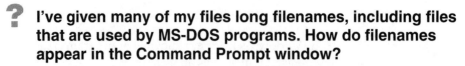 I've given many of my files long filenames, including files that are used by MS-DOS programs. How do filenames appear in the Command Prompt window?

When you open the Command Prompt window, you will notice that the DOS commands that are part of Windows NT recognize and use long filenames. Figure 5-16 shows you a window with several files. Figure 5-17 shows you the same directory listed with the Dir command in the Command Prompt window.

I know Windows NT allows me much more flexibility in naming files. What filenames are permitted?

The system of extended attributes that was introduced in Windows 95 is part of Windows NT Workstation and Server 4. Most prominent among its features are long filenames. Filenames can be up to 258 characters long and can include embedded spaces (no initial space characters), a comma (,), semicolon (;), equal sign (=), and square brackets ([ ]).

The following symbols cannot be used as a part of a valid filename:

```
/ \ * < > : ? " |
```

You may recognize these symbols as being part of paths, wildcard symbols, redirection symbols, pipes, and so forth.

When you enter a name, you can use both uppercase and lowercase letters. Windows NT will display your case and remember it.

Figure 5-16.   A folder in Windows NT

```
Command Prompt                                              _ □ X
Microsoft(R) Windows NT(TM)
(C) Copyright 1985-1996 Microsoft Corp.

C:\users\default>cd c:\projects

C:\projects>dir
 Volume in drive C is SICILY
 Volume Serial Number is 354A-17D8

 Directory of C:\projects

01/09/96  11:32a        <DIR>          .
01/09/96  11:32a        <DIR>          ..
01/09/96  11:32a        <DIR>          books
01/09/96  11:32a        <DIR>          database
04/18/96  09:45p               21,504 4-19 Wellesley Memo.doc
05/06/96  11:39a               18,944 5-6 Wellesley Memo.doc
              6 File(s)        40,448 bytes
                       57,606,144 bytes free

C:\projects>_
```

Figure 5-17.   The same folder shown as a directory with its contents listed in the Command Prompt window

However, case is not considered when you search for a file by its filename.

 Note: *Case is important when you define passwords.*

❓ How does Windows NT work with filenames for MS-DOS?

MS-DOS is only capable of storing filenames of up to eight numbers and letters, with a three-character file extension. This is the familiar "eight-dot-three" naming convention. Windows NT starting with version 4 builds on MS-DOS' naming conventions, allowing you to view long filename information in the Command Prompt window. Older eight-dot-three filenames appear on the desktop or in the Windows NT Explorer as the first part of the name (up to eight characters) without the file extension.

❓ When I open files that I named in Windows NT in MS-DOS or Windows 3.x, I see that they are truncated. What happens to long filenames in DOS or Windows 3.x?

When you save a file with a long filename, that filename is internally held. The following procedure shows that long filenames are not lost:

1. Copy a file with a long filename to a floppy disk, or transfer the file across a network to a DOS or Windows 3.*x* client.

2. Open and edit the file.

3. Copy that file back to Windows NT.

4. View the file on your desktop or in the Windows NT Explorer.

You will see your long filename again.

? I want compatibility between the filenames I create and the ones that are assigned by MS-DOS. How are long filenames truncated for use in DOS and Windows 3.*x*?

Long names are truncated to eight characters and the three-letter extension. If there is more than one file with the same eight letters, Windows NT truncates the last two letters and adds the characters "~#" to the end, incrementing the number character. If additional numbers are required, three letters are truncated and "~##" is added.

WORKING WITH FOLDERS

? How can I quickly create a folder on the desktop or in the Windows NT Explorer?

To create a file:

1. Right-click on the desktop or in the Windows NT Explorer.

2. Select the New command.

3. Select Folder from the shortcut menu.

4. Enter a new name for the folder that is created.

? I've gotten used to using Program Groups, and I like them. What happened to Program Groups in Windows NT 3.*x*?

Program Groups were converted to folders that appear in the Program folder of the Start Menu folder. When you click the Programs command of the Start menu, you see all of your old Program Groups. Newly installed programs often add folders to the Programs folder maintained in the Start Menu folder, thus maintaining the Program Groups concept.

Warning: *Be careful about deleting folders in the Programs folder of the Start Menu folder. Doing so deletes the actual files, not the shortcuts to the files.*

❓ How do I select files and folders on the desktop or in the Windows NT Explorer?

In order to act on files and folders in some way, you have to select them first. A selected item in a folder window or in a folder on your desktop or in the Windows NT Explorer appears highlighted in the selected color that is part of the scheme you are using in the Appearance tab of the Display control panel.

The following techniques are used to *select items* in a folder:

⇨ Click on a single file or folder to select it.

⇨ Click-and-drag your pointer to enclose contiguous items in a folder.

Tip: *If you right-click and drag a selection box, when you release the mouse button a shortcut menu appears.*

⇨ Hold down the SHIFT key and click on the first item in a contiguous range of items; then click on the last item to select the range.

⇨ Hold the CTRL key and click on multiple items to select several items that are not contiguous.

⇨ To select all of the items in a folder: select the Select <u>A</u>ll command from the <u>E</u>dit menu, or press CTRL-A.

To remove items from a selection:

⇨ Click on another item or on a blank area in the folder.

⇨ Hold the SHIFT key and click on a selected item in a range to diminish the range.

⇨ Hold the CTRL key and click on selected items in a range to remove them from the selected range one at a time.

WORKING WITH OBJECT PROPERTIES

How do I view an object's properties?

To view an object's properties:

➪ Right-click the object on your desktop, volume, folder, or in the Windows NT Explorer, and then select the Properties command.

➪ Or click on an object to select it, and then select the Properties command from the File menu.

Figure 5-18 shows a folder's Properties sheet in Windows NT.

I want to make sure that a file or folder cannot be modified. How do I specify this?

In the Attributes section on the General tab of the file or folder's Properties sheet, turn the Read-only attribute on.

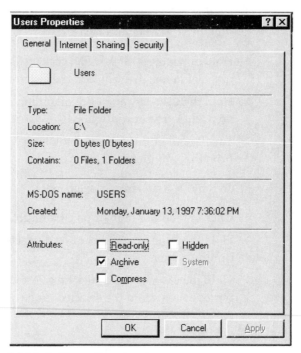

Figure 5-18.   A folder's Properties sheet

? How do I know if a file or folder has been backed up recently?

Many (but not all) programs set the Archive bit on and put a check in the Archive checkbox on the Attributes section on the General tab of the file or folder's Properties sheet.

 Warning: *You should not rely on the Archive bit to determine if your file was backed up unless you know that your specific backup program was run recently and reset all of the archive bits before marking backed up files.*

? How are creation and modification dates and times assigned?

Windows NT uses the date and time currently in your system to time-stamp objects when they are created, modified, and accessed. If your current date or time is wrong, change it in the Date/Time control panel.

? I do not want a file or folder to appear on my desktop, in the Windows NT Explorer, or in a browse window. How do I hide a file or folder?

In the Attributes section on the General tab of the file or folder's Properties sheet, turn the Hidden attribute on.

? The icon for a file on the desktop doesn't tell me very much, and I see what I need to know in the Explorer window. How do I get information about an object?

Information about files, folders, volumes, and other objects is displayed automatically in the top sections of the Properties sheet. They are assigned by the system and can't be altered. You can see the following information in the Properties sheet: type; location; size; MS-DOS name (converted from the long name); and date and time created, modified, and accessed.

I want to delete a large file from my disk. How do know if a file is needed by Windows NT to operate?

Check the Attributes section on the General tab to see if the System attribute is on. This attribute is always grayed out in a folder view so that you can't inadvertently change it.

6 Answers!

Working with Documents

Answer Topics!

Working with Documents @ a Glance

⇨ The **Windows NT Explorer** is a new and improved version of the File Manager. This program offers you a hierarchical view of your folders, volumes, the desktop, Network Neighborhood, Printers, and Control Panels, and the contents of each. The Windows NT Explorer is a very convenient place to go to find, copy, move, delete, and perform other types of file management. You can open folders in the Explorer view, and select options in the NT Explorer that change the way the file system is displayed and managed. File associations are controlled as an option through the NT Explorer.

⇨ A **shortcut** is a file that points to another file, folder, volume, disk, printer, and so forth. When you open a shortcut, the original item is opened. When you drag an item into a shortcut for a folder or volume, that item is copied or moved into that folder. When that shortcut is for a printer, a document dragged to it will print. Shortcuts are used to place startup items in the Startup folder, or to place programs or folders on the Start menu. The Windows NT operating system creates and manages a whole range of shortcuts for special purposes.

⇨ The Windows NT Start menu comes with a well-thought-out and powerful **Find** utility. You can search for files and folders by name and by a variety of attributes. You can search for computers and for other things, depending on the applications you have installed on your computer. Searches can be saved and retrieved, and the items found in a search can be directly manipulated through drag-and-drop. A find operation can be run in the background.

⇨ Deleted files are sent to the **Recycle Bin**. This special folder appears on your desktop, with each volume having its own Recycle Bin. Files deleted are stored on a first-in, first-out basis. When the Recycle Bin is full, the oldest files added to it are deleted. By default, Recycle Bins are large, often 10 percent of your volume. You can control the size of the Recycle Bin, and empty its contents when you choose.

⇨ You can **troubleshoot files** and folders to remove them when they get corrupted. Often, simply deleting those files from your file system is sufficient. In more extreme cases you may need to run a disk utility or reformat your volume and restore its contents from a backup.

USING THE WINDOWS NT EXPLORER

What is the Windows NT Explorer?

One Microsoft product manager described the Windows Explorer as the File Manager (from Windows 3.*x*) on steroids. You can use the Windows NT Explorer to view and manipulate files and folders in a hierarchical view of both My Computer and Network Neighborhood. The following illustration shows you a typical view of the Windows NT Explorer. Some special folders like the Control Panels and Printers also show up in the Windows NT Explorer to provide access to these features.

What is the Windows NT Explorer? *continued*

```
Exploring - Ms-dos_6 (C:)                                    _ □ ✕
File  Edit  View  Tools  Help

All Folders                          Contents of 'Ms-dos_6 (C:)'
📇 Desktop                           Name              Size  Type            ▲
└─ 💻 My Computer                    📁 Aol30a               File Folder
   ├─ 💾 3½ Floppy (A:)              📁 BO CD-ROM            File Folder
   ├─ 🖴 Ms-dos_6 (C:)              📁 Building VFP         File Folder
   ├─ 💿 Office97pro (D:)            📁 Dos                 File Folder
   ├─ 🖳 Control Panel              📁 Exchange            File Folder
   └─ 🖨 Printers                   📁 Figs10              File Folder
   ├─ 🖧 Network Neighborhood       📁 Figs11              File Folder
   ├─ 🗑 Recycle Bin                📁 Figs12              File Folder
   └─ 💼 My Briefcase               📁 InetPub             File Folder
                                     📁 MailMan             File Folder
                                     📁 MS Internet Explor...  File Folder
                                     📁 Nta03               File Folder
                                     📁 Nta04               File Folder
                                     📁 OQRFigs             File Folder
                                     📁 P.A.M. stuff        File Folder
                                     📁 P.J                 File Folder  ▼
                                     ◄                          ►

78 object(s)          47.6MB (Disk free space: 641MB)
```

When you install Windows NT, shortcuts to the Windows NT Explorer are placed on the Start menu in the Programs folder. You may find it convenient to add the shortcut for this program to other locations. In a number of other instances, the NT Explorer is invoked as a method of browsing and finding files. For example, when you click the Advanced button in the Start menu's Properties sheet, the Windows NT Explorer opens and allows you to add shortcuts to the Start Menu folder (found in a user's Profile folder).

The Windows NT Explorer shows you a view of your system's contents in two panels. The left panel contains a folder hierarchy. Dotted lines show you the volume and folder tree, with a plus symbol next to an icon indicating that the folder or volume has additional contents that can be viewed. The right panel, which shows the contents of the folder, can be viewed and arranged just like any other folder window on your desktop.

? I can't figure out how to copy or move a file between two open folders in Explorer. How can I do this?

Open up two instances of the Windows NT Explorer and click-and-drag a file from one Explorer window to the window of the second instance of Windows NT Explorer.

? I use a compression utility to compress my files. How do I know which files and folders are compressed?

To view compressed files and folders in a different color in the Windows NT Explorer:

⇨ Click on the Display Compressed Files and Folders with Alternate Color checkbox on the View tab of the Options dialog box to enable it.

? I need to find a particular type of file. What happened to file extensions in Windows NT Explorer?

Windows NT hides file extensions for files that are associated with a registered program in order to display more meaningful information like "Microsoft Word document" in place of .DOC.

If you want to see the file extensions for your files in the Windows NT Explorer, do the following:

1. Select the Options command from the View menu.

2. Click on the Hide File Extensions for Known File Types checkbox to remove the check mark.

3. Click the OK button.

? I don't like the Windows NT Explorer. Can't I have the File Manager back?

Yes. You can find the old File Manager in the SYSTEM32 folder. To open the File Manager:

1. Open the Windows NT Explorer and navigate to the <root>\WINNT\SYSTEM32 folder.

2. Double-click on the WINFILE.EXE file to open the File Manager.

If you intend to use the File Manager again, create a shortcut for this program and add it to the Start menu by right-clicking and dragging the file to the Start button.

I like the hierarchical view I find in the Windows NT Explorer. How do I open a folder in the Explorer view?

To open a folder in Explorer view:

⇨ Right-click on the folder and select the Explore command from the shortcut menu.

I need the full path to a file to manipulate it in a DOS session. How do I know the full path to the selected file or folder?

To view the path of a file and folder in the Windows NT Explorer:

⇨ Click on the Display the Full Path in the Title Bar checkbox on the View tab of the Options dialog box to enable it.

How do I add a shortcut to Explorer to my desktop?

To add a shortcut for Windows NT Explorer to your desktop:

1. Select the Files or Folders command on the Find submenu of the Start menu.

2. Enter **EXPLORER.EXE** into the Named text box.

3. Click the Find Now button.

4. Drag the Explorer icon from the list of found files onto your desktop to create the shortcut.

    The program is found in the WINNT folder at <root>\WINNT.

There are a lot of files in a folder, and I need an easy way to view them. How can I sort items in Windows NT Explorer?

To sort items in the Explorer window:

1. With the contents panel displayed in Details view, click on any of the column labels to sort by that attribute.

2. Click again on a column header to sort in the opposite sort order.

WORKING WITH SHORTCUTS

What is a shortcut?

A *shortcut* is a file that points to another file, folder, or volume. A shortcut icon contains a small arrow in the lower-left corner. When you double-click on a shortcut, it opens the original file, folder, or volume. The following illustration shows you several different shortcut icons. You can create as many shortcuts for a resource as you wish and put them anywhere you like in the file system or on your desktop. Shortcut files take the .INK file extension.

Since shortcuts are very small (200 bytes to 1KB), you can have literally thousands of shortcuts on your system. Windows NT creates and uses many shortcuts so that you see folders or programs on the Start menu, printer resources in the Printers folder, and so forth. Shortcuts provide another entry for using the resource.

Note: *In previous versions of Windows NT, the word "shortcut" was used to mean a keyboard shortcut for a menu command. In Windows NT 4, shortcuts are pointers and keyboard shortcuts are used when a keyboard key combination is referred to. Keyboard shortcuts are also referred to as accelerator* keys, *or* hot keys.

I know that I can modify how a program runs when it launches. How do I control the behavior of a program that starts up from a shortcut?

To specify the behavior of a program launched from a shortcut:

1. Right-click on the shortcut and select the Properties command from the shortcut menu.

2. Click the Shortcut tab (shown in the previous illustration).

3. Tab to the Start in text box and enter the location of the working directory for that program.

4. Tab to the Run list box and select either Normal window, Minimized, or Maximized to set the window start when the program launches.

5. Click the OK button.

How do I create a shortcut?

There are several different ways of creating shortcuts. Here are the most common ones:

1. Right-click on an object and drag that object (dragging is optional) to a location; then select the Create Shortcut command from the shortcut menu, as shown here.

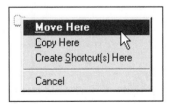

2. Highlight the object and select the Create Shortcut command from the File menu.

When you manipulate an object directly, there are no restrictions on the type of object that you can create a shortcut for. You can even create a shortcut from another shortcut icon. In that instance, the second shortcut still refers to the original file of the first shortcut.

To create shortcuts using the New command:

1. Right-click on a folder, on your desktop, or in the Windows NT Explorer and select the Shortcut command from the New submenu of the shortcut menu, as shown in Figure 6-1.

2. In the Create Shortcut screen (Figure 6-2) of the wizard, enter the command line for the file or program; or use the Browse button to locate that object. Then click the Next button.

3. In the Select a Title for the Program screen (Figure 6-3) of the wizard, enter the name you wish the shortcut to have, and then click the Finish button.

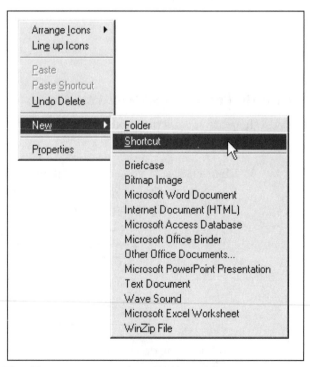

Figure 6-1.   The Shortcut command on the New submenu

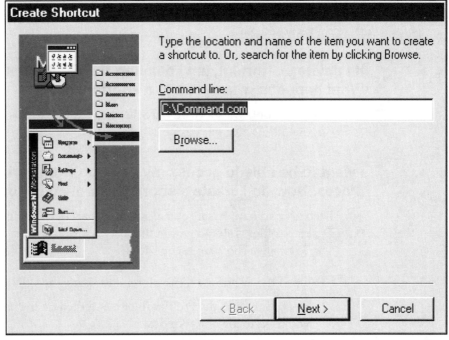

Figure 6-2.   The Create Shortcut screen

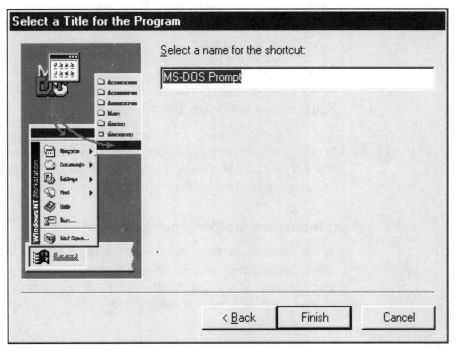

Figure 6-3.   The Select a Title for the Program screen

Windows NT creates the shortcut in the location that you right-clicked on.

If I delete a shortcut, am I deleting the file it points to? What happens when I delete a shortcut?

When you delete a shortcut, only the shortcut file itself is deleted. The original file, folder, or volume is not deleted.

I want to be able to access my desktop from various places. How do I create a shortcut for my desktop?

Each user account has its own desktop as part of its profile. The Desktop folder is stored within that user's Profile folder.

To create a shortcut to your desktop:

1. Open the Windows NT Explorer and locate the WINNT folder.

2. Double-click on the Profiles folder, and then on the username that you used to log onto Windows NT.

3. Right-click on the desktop and drag that folder to it.

4. Release the mouse button and select the Create Shortcut(s) Here command from the shortcut menu.

If you drag the Desktop folder onto the Start menu you add the Desktop folder to the top of your Start menu. Any system folder such as My Computer and the Recycle Bin will not appear in the Desktop folder when it is accessed from the Start menu.

 Note: *In some instances, a system administrator assigns you a desktop that you can't change as part of your profile. In that case you will not be able to access your Desktop folder to create the shortcut.*

What filenames are possible for a shortcut?

When you create a shortcut for an object, it is given the name "Shortcut to <objectname>." There is no good reason why you can't give the shortcut a different and more meaningful name, if you choose. Any valid filename can be used.

To rename a shortcut:

⇨ Click on the shortcut name to edit it directly

⇨ Or right-click on the shortcut and select the Rena̲me command
from the shortcut menu.

Any name that doesn't start with a space character or contain the
following characters is valid:

/ \ < > | : " ? *

❓ The icon for my shortcut looks just like the icon for the program or a program's document. How do I make this icon more distinctive?

The icon for a shortcut is controlled by the program that the shortcut
is associated with. A Word document shortcut will display the icon for
a Word document, for example. However, you can associate another
icon with a shortcut.

To change icons:

1. Right-click the shortcut icon and select the Properties command
from the shortcut menu.

2. Click the Shortcut tab and then click the Change Icon button.

3. Select an icon in the Change Icon dialog box, as shown in Figure
6-4; then click the OK button.

If the shortcut is a document or file, then the icon associated with
the shell library for the interface SHELL32.DLL is displayed. If you
have selected a shortcut for a program or application, only a single
icon for that program is displayed. You can display additional icons to
select from for a program (or other file) by clicking on the Browse
button and selecting the WINNT\SYSTEM32\MOREICONS.DLL file.

Tip: *Many icons (.ICO files) are available as shareware libraries.*

Note: *Some .DLL files are hidden from view and won't be seen during a
normal Browse of files. Make sure that you select Show All Files on the View
tab of the Options dialog box of the Windows NT Explorer. Select the
Options command from the V̲iew menu to view that dialog box.*

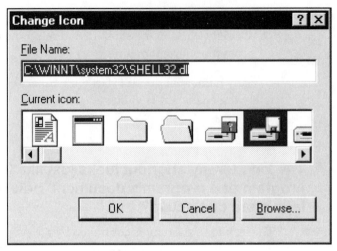

Figure 6-4.   The Change Icon dialog box

❓ I want a way to quickly jump to a specific place or resource on the Internet. How can I make a shortcut for an Internet address?

To create a shortcut for a resource found on the Web:

1. Move your pointer over a resource in the Microsoft Internet Explorer or another browser; it will change to a hand icon.

2. Right-click on that location and select the Copy Shortcut command.

You can combine this with a click-and-drag to your desktop or to a mail message to place the shortcut in that location.

❓ I use a shortcut frequently. Can I create a keyboard shortcut to open my shortcut?

To create a keyboard shortcut for a shortcut:

⇨ Tab to the Shortcut key text box and press the keys you want to use for your shortcut.

A valid keyboard shortcut is the CTRL and/or ALT key plus another keyboard character. You cannot use the ESC, ENTER, TAB, SPACEBAR, BACKSPACE, or PRINT SCREEN key to create a keyboard shortcut. Any keyboard shortcut that you create in a program takes precedence over the keyboard shortcut that you define for a shortcut. When there is a conflict, the keyboard shortcut for the shortcut will not work.

? I've moved the original file and now my shortcut won't work. What happened, and how do I reestablish the connection?

To find the original file for a shortcut:

1. Right-click the shortcut icon and select the Properties command from the shortcut menu.

2. Click the Shortcut tab, and then click the Find Target button.

If the original shortcut is still located in the same place, Windows NT opens the folder containing the file directly. If the target is on the desktop, a message box appears asking you to close all open windows. Otherwise, Windows NT begins a search for an identical filename and returns the location of the first one it encounters. If you've deleted the original target file and no file with the same filename is found, the search will fail.

That file may or may not be the target file for the original shortcut, and you can continue the search if needed. You may find that you get better results when you manually indicate the target for the shortcut.

? How can I create a shortcut to an MS-DOS program? Is there anything different about this type of shortcut?

You create shortcuts to MS-DOS programs in the standard way:

⇨ Right-click the icon for the program (the .EXE file) and select the Create Shortcut command.

Shortcuts to MS-DOS programs contain a few more settings and pages than you find on Windows programs. These settings let you define batch files, command line execution, Command Prompt window fonts and screen characteristics, and memory configuration. Figure 6-5 shows you the Program tab of an MS-DOS program's Properties sheet. All of these options were described in Chapter 3 in the discussion on the Command Prompt window.

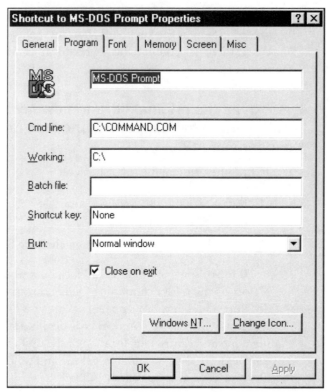

Figure 6-5.   The Program tab in the Properties sheet of an MS-DOS program

? How can I use shortcuts to make it easy to send items various places?

The Send To submenu is a particularly convenient place to add shortcuts to printers, directories, computers, and other resources. If you add these items to the Send To folders in the Profiles folder, they will appear in any application that uses this menu command.

To add a shortcut to the Send To submenu:

1. Open the Windows NT Explorer and navigate to the Profiles folder for the username that you wish to modify.

2. Double-click on the Send To folder (\Profiles\<username>\Send To) to open it.

3. Add any shortcuts you wish to the Send To folder.

4. Close the Send To folder.

Of particular value are the following shortcuts:

⇨ Folders

⇨ Drives

⇨ Printers

⇨ The Recycle Bin

How can I use shortcuts to automatically start up a program?

To have a shortcut launch when Windows NT boots:

1. Right-click the Start button and select the Open or Explore command from the shortcut menu.

2. Double-click on the Programs folder, and then on the Startup folder.

3. Drag any shortcuts for programs that you want to open at startup into that folder.

4. Or right-click on a shortcut on your desktop or in the Windows NT Explorer and drag it to the Startup folder; then click the Copy Here command.

What objects can I make shortcuts for?

You can make a shortcut for the following objects:

⇨ *Data files.* Any kind of file created by an application can be made into a shortcut.

⇨ *System files.* All system files can be made into a shortcut, provided that you are able to view them and access them.

⇨ *Programs.* MS-DOS and 16- and 32-bit Windows applications.

⇨ *Disk drives.* Hard drives, CD-ROM drives, volumes and partitions, and read-only and removable storage. If it mounts on your system and the file system displays an icon for it, you can create a shortcut.

⇨ *Computers.* Any computer that shows up in the Network Neighborhood or that you can connect to using a Dial-Up Networking connection can be made into a shortcut. These types of shortcuts are quite useful, as they can often work when the computer isn't properly browsed on the network. They also offer much faster connection to the computer than opening it up from the Windows NT Explorer.

⇨ *Remote connections.* A Dial-Up Networking connection or a HyperTerminal connection can be made into a shortcut. Double-clicking on this shortcut initiates the sequence that attempts to establish the connection.

⇨ *Internet Resource Locations.* When you create a Favorite "bookmark" in the Microsoft Internet Explorer, you are creating shortcuts that contain the URL (Uniform Resource Locator) or UNC (Universal Naming Convention) location to that resource. If you double-click on a shortcut of this type Windows NT will attempt to locate the resource, and if necessary establish an Internet connection to do so.

FINDING DOCUMENTS AND APPLICATIONS

Things you should know about the Find command

There are many options and variations to using the Find command. Some are particularly valuable for accessing system resources. Some things you should know about using Find are:

⇨ The Find dialog box is fully drag-and-drop enabled.

⇨ You can open multiple instances of the Find command and perform additional searches.

⇨ Finds can be run in the background as you work in another application.

⇨ The more information you supply for a search, the narrower the search becomes and the faster it is performed.

⇨ FIND is network-aware as well, allowing it to find other computers in your Network Neighborhood.

The only exception to this last point is that when you search for text within a file using the Containing text option on the

Advanced tab, your search is slower than when you search the file system for file information.

The following illustration shows you the Name & Location tab of the Find dialog box.

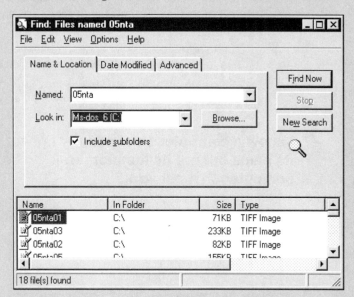

Windows NT's Find command on the Start menu allows you to search for:

⇨ Files and folders on local and networked drives

⇨ Other computers on a network

⇨ Using Microsoft Outlook (if you install that component of Office Professional 97)

⇨ On the Microsoft Network (for some versions of that software)

I don't remember the filename, but I do remember other things about it. How do I search for a file or folder by an attribute or property?

Additional search criteria are listed on the Date Modified tab of the Find dialog box, and on the Advanced tab. These two tabs are shown in Figures 6-6 and 6-7, respectively. The criteria you enter on these two tabs are added to the criteria you entered on the Name & Location tab to *narrow your search*.

On the Date Modified tab you can specify a search for a file or folder with a date created or modified before a certain date or between two dates. If you do not specify a date, the default All Files radio button is selected.

If you know the file type, or some text contained within the file, or the size of the file, then you can specify these search parameters in the Advanced tab. Any file type that is currently registered with your system can be chosen from the Of Type list box.

? I know a computer exists on my network, and I remember its name but not its location. How do I search for a computer on a network?

To search for a computer on a network:

1. Select the Computer command on the Find submenu of the Start menu.

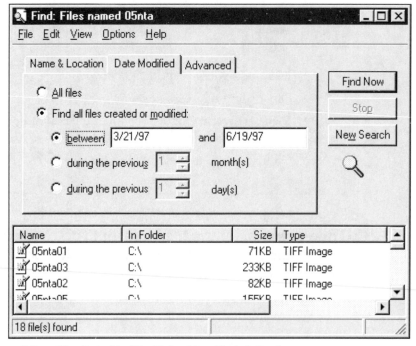

Figure 6-6.   The Date Modified tab of the Find dialog box

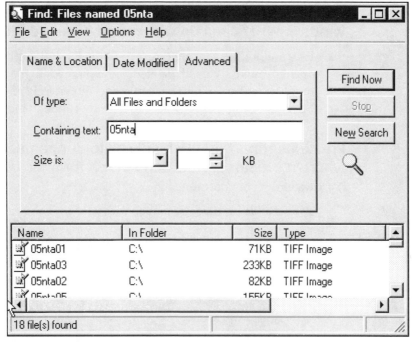

Figure 6-7.   The Advanced tab of the Find dialog box

2. Enter the name of the computer you wish to search for in the Named text box.

3. Click the Find Now button.

Matching computers are returned in the list box at the bottom of the Find dialog box. This dialog box is a simplified version of the one that you saw earlier, and contains no additional search parameters. In a search, any matching computers in your own domain, and in any trusting domains are returned in the result set.

 Tip: In some instances where the browse list of your domain is not up-to-date, or where you cannot see a computer that you know is on your network, you can use the Find Computer command to establish the path to that computer. If you right-click on the computer in the Find window and drag it to your desktop, you can access that computer's resources using the shortcut you create.

 Tip: Click-and-drag that computer from the Find window to create a shortcut to the computer on your desktop.

? **There are matches to my search returned in the Find window. What can I do with found files and folders?**

Files and folders that are returned in the Find dialog box can be opened, moved, copied, deleted, and renamed. Right-click on the file or folder to display the shortcut menu shown in Figure 6-8. Click-and-drag a file or folder to a new location to move or copy them.

? **I remember part or all of a file or folder name, but not where it's located. How do I search for a file or folder by name?**

To find a file or folder by name:

1. Select the Files and Folders command on the Find submenu of the Start menu.

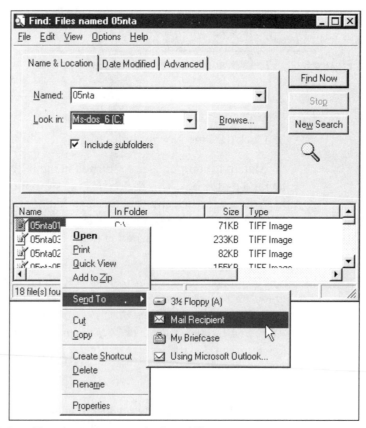

Figure 6-8.   The shortcut menu of a found file

2. Click the Name & Location tab, if necessary.

3. Enter the name of the file or folder you wish to search for in the Named text box.

4. Select the location of your search in the Look in text box.

5. Click the Find Now button.

Matching files or folders are returned in the list box at the bottom of the Find dialog box, an example of which is shown in Figure 6-9.

Here are some things you should know about the Find command that should help you with your searches:

⇨ Searches are case insensitive.

⇨ You can use wildcards for searches: the "?" character for any single character; and the "*" character for any set of characters.

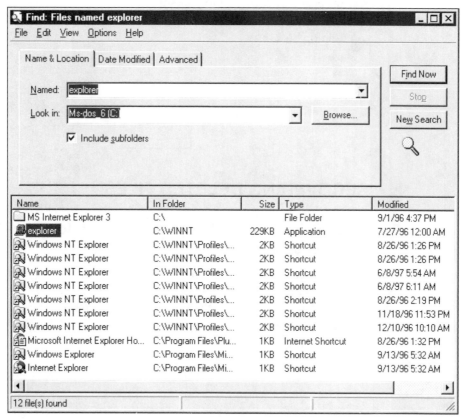

Figure 6-9.   A set of matching files found in a search in the Find dialog box

⇨   The Find command remembers previous searches, and you can
select them from the Named list box.

⇨   Don't forget to click on the Include subfolders checkbox to enable
it if you wish to search an entire directory tree.

❓ As part of my routine, I perform the same search that I have just specified. How do I save a search so that I can reuse it?

To save a search criterion:

⇨   Select the Save Search command from the File menu.

To save the matches to a particular search:

⇨   Select the Save Results command from the Options menu.

When you select either of these options, an icon for the search
appears on your desktop, as shown here. If you double-click on
that icon, your search criterion or result set is returned in the Find
dialog box.

Files named
explorer

RECOVERING DELETED FILES

❓ I see the icon for the Recycle Bin. What does the Recycle Bin represent?

The Recycle Bin is a folder (directory) that contains recently deleted
files. Each volume (file system) has its own Recycle Bin.

Files are added to the Recycle Bin in a first-in, first-out system.
When the Recycle Bin is full, the oldest files are deleted to make room
for new files.

? **I've made a mistake and deleted a file without using the Recycle Bin. What happens to files I delete from the Command Prompt or in applications?**

Older programs that allow you to delete files from within an application, or to use the DEL command from within a Command Prompt window, are simply deleted. They do not go into the Recycle Bin. In this regard, their behavior is similar to deleting a file(s) from a floppy disk.

? **I know what I'm doing when I delete files, and I don't need a reminder. I also know how to recover files from the Recycle Bin. So how do I get rid of those pesky confirmation dialog boxes?**

To delete files without seeing warnings:

⇨ Remove the check mark from the Display delete confirmation dialog checkbox in the Recycle Bin Properties sheet.

? **I no longer need a particular file(s). How do I delete files?**

Deleted files are stored in the Recycle Bin. There are several ways to delete a file.

To delete files on the desktop or in the Windows NT Explorer:

⇨ Select the file(s) and drag it to the Recycle Bin icon on the desktop.

⇨ Select the file(s) and press the DEL key.

⇨ Right-click on a file and select the Delete command from the shortcut menu.

⇨ Highlight the file(s) and select the Delete command from the File menu.

Windows NT posts the confirmation dialog box shown here asking you if you really wish to send the file to the Recycle Bin. Click the Yes button to move the files to that folder.

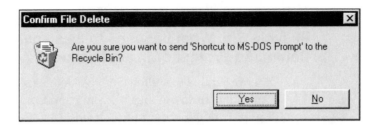

? Oops. I've accidentally deleted the Recycle Bin with the DEL key. What happens when I delete the Recycle Bin?

If you try to delete the Recycle Bin, the operating system will re-create another one when you restart your system. You will not see the deleted files that the original Recycle Bin contained. References to the locations of those files are lost.

Not only can the Recycle Bin not be deleted, it can't be renamed or removed from the desktop.

If you accidentally delete the Recycle Bin and need to recover a file that it contained, you will need to use a third-party undelete program like Norton Utilities for NT to recover the deleted file. It is likely still on your disk unless you have written additional information that overwrites it.

? Floppy disks don't have Recycle Bins. What happens to files I delete on my floppy disks?

When you delete files on your floppy disks, they are simply deleted. If you want to save a copy of a file(s) deleted from a floppy disk, here's how:

1. Open the Windows NT Explorer.

2. Highlight the file(s) you wish to move to the Recycle Bin on your floppy disk.

3. Right-click on the file and select the Cut command.

4. Right-click on the desktop and select the Paste command.

5. Highlight the file(s) you wish to delete on the desktop

6. Press the DEL key and click the Yes button in the Confirm File Delete dialog box to move the file(s) to the Recycle Bin.

? Where is the Recycle Bin folder actually found?

The Recycle Bin folder is a hidden system folder stored in a volume's root directory (top folder).

? I'm running out of room on my hard drive. How do I reclaim space from the Recycle Bin?

You can delete everything in the Recycle Bin by emptying it. Doing so makes the space occupied by these files available to the file system for use once again.

To empty the Recycle Bin:

⇨ Right-click on the Recycle Bin icon on your desktop and select the Empty Recycle Bin command. The same command is found on the Recycle Bin's File menu.

? I've mistakenly deleted a file(s) or folder of files that I need. How do I recover a deleted file?

To recover a file in Windows NT 4:

1. Double-click on the Recycle Bin icon on the desktop.

2. Select the file(s) you wish to recover.

3. Select the Restore command in the File menu to return the file(s) to its original location(s).

4. Or right-click on the file and select the Restore command from the shortcut menu.

5. Or click-and-drag the file(s) to the location you wish.

 Tip: *You may find it easier to locate one or more files when the Recycle Bin folder is displayed in either Details or List view.*

Tip: Sorting by the Date Deleted column in the Recycle Bin in Detail view is a very nice way to find something recently deleted. Click on the Date Deleted Column header to sort your files in this way. You can click on that header again to sort in the opposite order.

Figure 6-10 shows you the Recycle Bin in Detail view with a file and its shortcut menu.

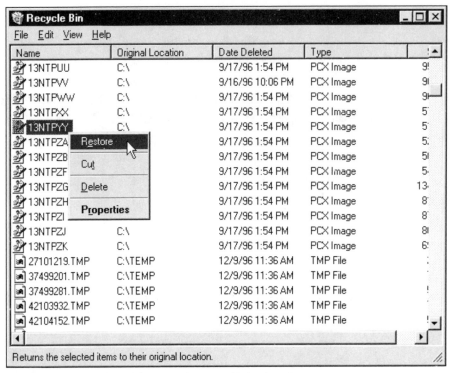

Figure 6-10.   The Recycle Bin showing a file's shortcut menu

? ## The Recycle Bin really consumes a lot of my disk space. How do I control the amount of space the Recycle Bin uses?

By default, the Recycle Bin is 10 percent of your volume's space. That can be a lot of megabytes on a large volume, and it gives you a reasonable amount of time to change your mind before the file is deleted by the file system (in most instances). If you are tight on disk space, you might want to lower the amount of space that the Recycle Bin occupies; or if you want to save deleted files longer on your file system you might want to increase the size of the Recycle Bin. Here's how.

To change the size of the Recycle Bin:

1. Right-click the Recycle Bin icon and select the Properties command from the shortcut menu.

2. In the Global tab of the Recycle Bin Properties sheet shown in Figure 6-11 click-and-drag the slider left to make the Recycle Bin smaller or right to make it larger.

3. If you want all of your Recycle Bins to be the same size on your volumes, click the Use One Setting for All Drives radio button (the default).

4. Or click the Configure Drives Independently radio button if you wish to control the size of each of your volumes' Recycle Bin.

5. Click the Apply button or the OK button to set these options.

If you set the option to individually control your volumes' Recycle Bin, you will need to use the tab in the Properties sheet for each Recycle Bin to set its properties.

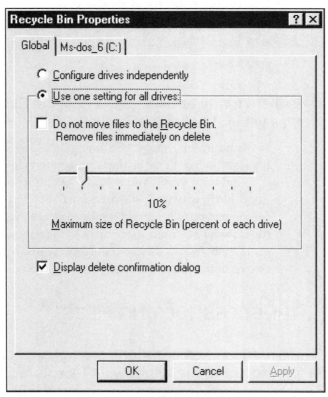

Figure 6-11.   The Global tab of the Recycle Bin Properties sheet

? Windows NT 3.5*x* doesn't have a Recycle Bin. How do I recover files on Windows NT 3.5*x*?

There were no provisions made for recovering a file in version 3.5*x* of the operating system. To undelete a file in 3.5*x* requires a special third-party utility.

? I'm sure that I won't ever need this file. How do I delete a file without sending it to the Recycle Bin?

To delete a file without storing it in the Recycle Bin:

⇨ Hold down the SHIFT key when you select the Delete command or press the DEL button.

Windows NT will post a confirming dialog box. Once you click the Yes button, the file is gone forever.

 Warning: *If you delete a file and bypass the Recycle Bin, that file is gone forever.*

? Is there a way to disable the Recycle Bin? How do I delete files without using the Recycle Bin?

You can turn off the Recycle Bin by checking the "Do not move files to the Recycle Bin. Remove files immediately on delete" checkbox.

But why would you want to? Doing so would require that you use a third-party undelete program (like Norton Utilities for NT), and even then your files might not be recoverable. Files deleted from the file system have their space marked for reuse and can be partially or completely overwritten. No third-party utility will be able to recover the file in that case, although some may retrieve file fragments.

TROUBLESHOOTING FILES

? Hard drives and partitions are not appearing on my desktop or in the Windows NT Explorer. What should I do?

There may be a hardware problem due to either an incompatibility or a disk problem. If Windows can mount the disk but not access the partition, the problem may be in the partition table or in the boot sector. These problems can often be fixed through the use of third-party disk utilities. Any detected hardware will appear listed in the NT Registry in the HKEY_LOCAL_MACHINE\HARDWARE key.

? How do I fix a disk with files and folders that have corrupted names or data?

If you see a file or folder that is corrupted, you can try deleting it from your disk. Typically you notice this problem when you see scrambled names. For files that are corrupted internally, you may see strange behavior or that your application may freeze when you try to read a section of it.

If you have a backup volume for your files, try reformatting the volume and restoring the files from your backup. The formatting process often removes problems relating to disk errors.

If deleting the file(s) or folder(s) doesn't solve the problem, you may want to run a third-party disk utility like Norton Utilities for NT.

? There seems to be a problem when I use a particular file. How can I recover a file that is internally corrupted?

Often you can open a file that is corrupted and copy parts of it to another file. Do this in pieces, saving the pasted resulting file each time. Eventually you will find the corrupted piece of data and be unable to copy and paste it. But you will have recovered most, if not all of your file's data.

? Can I use MS-DOS utilities to fix filename problems with FAT volumes?

As a general rule, no. Many third-party disk utilities often destroy long filenames, and can destroy files themselves.

Utilities that can be used in FAT volumes are:

⇨ MS-DOS 6.x tools

⇨ SCANDISK

⇨ DEFRAG

⇨ CHKDSK

⇨ Windows 95 disk utilities

? **I don't want my files to use long filenames. What can I do?**

To suppress the use of long filenames on a FAT volume, do the following:

1. Double-click on the RegEdit program in the WINNT folder.

2. Open the HKEY_LOCAL_MACHINE\SYSTEM\ CurrentControlSet\Control\FileSystem\Win31FileSystem and change the value to 1.

3. Close REGEDIT, saving changes.

chapter

7 Answers!

Fault Tolerance Features

Answer Topics!

Fault Tolerance Features
@ a Glance

⇨ Windows NT Server supports three levels of **RAID**. This feature based on a Redundant Array of Inexpensive Disks has the operating system write extra data to two or more volumes on different physical disks. If a volume fails, the system fails over to the working volume. Mirrored disks can be created where a duplicate volume is created and dynamically managed. You can also create striped sets with parity where the information is written across three or more volumes with redundant information that checks for parity and that allows the striped set to be regenerated should a member fail.

⇨ You can replicate directories between Windows NT Server (import/export) and Windows NT Workstation (import only). In **replication,** an export server functions as the source of a duplicated directory, and an import computer serves as the target. Replication lets you update files automatically, copy vital system information, and provide for application and data distribution across a LAN or WAN to provide for better performance on the network through load balancing.

⇨ Using an Uninterruptible Power Supply (**UPS**), you can provide for continuation of service if power fails. Windows NT can be connected to a UPS device through a COM port and provide for messaging, timed service termination, and remote shutdown when the UPS device begins to discharge.

⇨ Windows NT provides for data recovery in a number of ways. You can **back up** your system by copying your volume(s) data to tape using NT Backup. This utility also allows you to restore missing or damaged files. If your boot partition fails, you can create a boot disk that you can use to start up your system and repair your volume. You can also create an Emergency Repair Disk (ERD) that contains several important system files on it, such as the Windows NT Registry. The ERD is also useful for repairing damaged volumes. Windows also stores the last known good configuration of your system based on a successful logon, and you can return to that state during a boot up should your system crash.

UNDERSTANDING RAID

What is RAID?

Windows NT Server supports in software a number of fault tolerance features provided by Redundant Arrays of Inexpensive Disks, or RAID. This system lets you write duplicated or redundant information across two or more logical volumes using two or more physical disks so that you can continue to have access to your data should there be a disk failure, power outage, or a corrupted operating system. RAID supplements an actively maintained backup system by providing a live backup that can be active and failover to a working volume.

There are different levels of RAID, given numbers 0 to 5. The numbers do not represent more powerful implementations, just different methods. Windows NT Server specifically supports RAID level 0, striping without redundancy; RAID level 1, mirrored sets; and RAID level 5, stripe sets with parity; both of which are implemented in software at the operating system level. Other levels of RAID are available for Windows NT as hardware/software solutions from third party vendors.

RAID 1 Mirrored sets creates a set of identical volumes on two different physical drives. The FDISK.SYS fault tolerance driver writes data simultaneously to both logical volumes. Should one member of the mirrored set fail, the FDISK.SYS driver fails over to the working disk. RAID 1 requires two disks, but can offer enhanced read performance and a slight decrease in write performance.

When both disks in a mirror are connected to the same disk controller, failure of the controller can make the mirrored set inaccessible. A variation of mirroring called *disk duplexing* attaches each member of a mirrored set to its own disk controller. Duplexing can improve bus traffic and read performance. Disk duplexing is a hardware solution, and is independent of mirroring. You install a mirrored set after you have installed duplexed disks.

RAID 5 stripe sets with parity writes your data across from three to 32 volumes with redundant information (check bytes) so that the data can be reconstructed if a physical disk fails. Since

---

What is RAID? *continued*

data is written across several disks, you have a substantially slower write to the disk, but a faster read than with mirrored disks. Also, striped sets can use volumes of unequal size and are flexible in terms of the location of the stripes. For a three disk RAID 5 set, 25 percent of the data written in a striped set with parity is redundant information used to reconstruct a failed volume. For an n-disk set, 1/N of the disk set stores parity information.

It is also possible to create stripe sets without parity, where redundant information is not written to disk, although this is not commonly done.

 Note: *RAID is not part of the current version of the Windows NT Workstation operating system. The discussion of RAID applies to Windows NT Server for version 4 of both operating systems.*

❓ Which version of RAID is faster?

Windows NT Server supports three levels of RAID:

⇨   RAID 0, disk striping without parity.

⇨   RAID 1, disk mirroring.

⇨   RAID 5, disk striping with parity.

Writing to a single disk without RAID is faster than any other arrangement of RAID. Writing to RAID 0 disks is faster than writing to RAID 5 because of the additional time required to write parity information. RAID 1 is slightly faster to write to than RAID 0 because there are fewer writes required.

Reading from a RAID 0 or a RAID 1 disk set is faster than reading from a single hard drive. Reading from a RAID 5 disk may be slower or comparable to reading from a single nonredundant hard drive. Although RAID 0 would seem to have the best performance characteristics, you give up data redundancy in RAID 0.

Note: *Performance aside, RAID 5 offers a much more secure environment for your data over RAID 0. Any performance difference is outweighed by this factor.*

Can mirrored sets and stripe sets with parity both exist on the same computer?

Yes. You can use the same set of disks to duplicate a volume in a mirrored set and still have part of those physical disks participate in a stripe set.

How do I break a mirrored set?

There are several reasons why you might want to break a mirrored set. Perhaps you no longer need the mirrored partitions because you've added a different fault tolerance feature, or you need the other disk for a different purpose.

To break a mirrored set:

1. Create a backup of the mirrored set (optional, but highly recommended).

2. Select the Disk Administrator command in the Administrative Tools folder on the Programs submenu of the Start menu.

Note: *You must be logged onto a Windows NT Server as an administrator to perform this operation.*

3. In the Disk Administrator, click on the mirrored set.

4. Select the Break Mirror command from the Fault Tolerance menu.

5. In the Break Mirror dialog box, click the Yes button. The mirrored (secondary) partition receives the next available volume or drive letter.

6. Select the Commit Changes Now command from the Partition menu.

7. Click the Yes button in the confirming dialog box.

8. A dialog box appears asking you to update your Emergency Repair Disk; click the OK button.

9. Select the Exit command from the Partition menu to close the Disk Administrator.

How do I create a mirrored set?

To create a mirrored set:

1. Select the Disk Administrator command in the Administrative Tools folder on the Programs submenu of the Start menu.

Note: You must be logged onto a Windows NT Server as an administrator to perform this operation.

2. In the Disk Administrator shown in Figure 7-1, click on the partition that is one part of the mirrored set.

3. Hold the CTRL key, and then click on the partition for the second physical disk in the mirrored set.

4. Select the Establish Mirror command from the Fault Tolerance menu

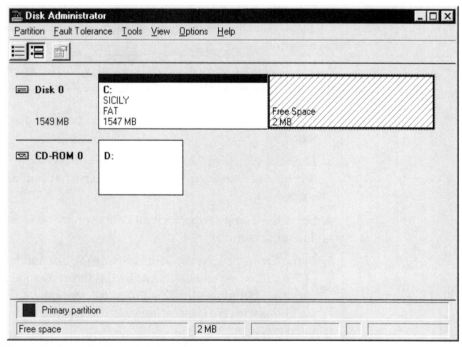

Figure 7-1.   The Disk Administrator

5. In the confirming dialog box, click the OK button. You will see the mirror partitions appear in the Disk Administrator as purple areas with the same volume label. (The partitions must be same size.)

6. Select the Exit command from the Partition menu to close the Disk Administrator.

7. Restart your computer.

You will be prompted to create an updated Emergency Repair Disk (ERD), which isn't a bad idea at this point. Click OK, update your ERD, and restart your system again.

Once you are back into the system, you need to initialize the mirrored set. Open the Disk Administrator program (as in Step 1 above), and you will see the mirrored set appear in red, which means that the mirror is being regenerated. Click on the mirror of the partition (the secondary partition) and its status should change from INITIALIZING to HEALTHY.

? How do I create a striped set with parity?

To create a striped set with parity:

1. Select the Disk Administrator command in the Administrative Tools folder on the Programs submenu of the Start menu.

Note: *You must be logged onto a Windows NT Server as an administrator to perform this operation.*

2. Click on an area of free space on the first physical disk used in the stripe set.

3. Hold the CTRL key; then click on an area of free space on the second and then the third disk that you wish to add to the striped set.

4. Select the Create Stripe Set with Parity command from the Fault Tolerance menu.

5. In the Create Striped Set with Parity dialog box, enter the size of the striped set you desire within the allowed range, and then click the OK button. The Disk Administrator creates the striped partitions with the same volume (or drive) letter and colors them green.

6. Select the E<u>x</u>it command from the <u>P</u>artition menu to close the Disk Administrator.

7. Restart your computer.

You will be prompted to create an updated Emergency Repair Disk (ERD), which is a good idea at this point. Click OK, update your ERD, and restart your system again.

Once you are back into the system, you need to format the striped set as either an NTFS or FAT volume. Select the striped set in the Disk Administrator, and then choose the Format command from the Tools menu to perform this operation. You can also format the striped set by using the FORMAT command in a Command Prompt window for that volume letter.

What do I do to repair a failed mirrored set?

When a mirrored set fails, the remaining member of the mirrored set is called the *orphan*. Any change in the data written to the orphan is not reflected in the disconnected mirrored volume. You need to reestablish the mirror to fix it.

To fix a mirrored set:

1. Select the Disk Administrator command in the Administrative Tools folder on the <u>P</u>rograms submenu of the Start menu.

 Note: *You must be logged onto a Windows NT Server as an administrator to perform this operation.*

2. In the Disk Administrator, click on the mirrored set.

3. Select the <u>B</u>reak Mirror command from the <u>F</u>ault Tolerance menu, and then confirm the action. The Disk Administrator assigns the next available drive letter to the secondary member of the mirrored set.

4. If the failed mirror was the primary volume, assign the drive letter to the volume you will use to reestablish the mirrored set.

Tip: *Use the Event Viewer if you need to determine which disk failed.*

5. Delete the failed partition.

6. Click on the orphan volume, hold the CTRL key, and click on another volume or free space on another physical disk to specify which volumes will be part of the mirror.

7. Select the Establish Mirror command from the Fault Tolerance menu.

8. Follow the procedure for creating a mirror described in this section from Step 5 onward.

❓ How do I regenerate a failed striped set with parity?

When a striped set with parity fails, your Windows NT Server will continue to function correctly. As data is required, the data must be reconstructed using the parity bits, and so you will notice a significant decline in performance. You need to regenerate the striped set with parity to regain both the lost performance and the fault tolerance that this RAID feature provides.

To regenerate a striped set with parity:

1. Replace the bad disk.

2. Open the Disk Administrator.

3. Click on the striped set to select it.

4. Select an area of free space equal to or greater than the member of the striped set that failed.

5. Select the Regenerate command from the Fault Tolerance menu.

6. Select the Exit command from the Partition menu.

7. Restart Windows NT Server.

Windows NT Server will read the data and the parity information on the existing stripes and then re-create the missing stripe.

REPLICATION

❓ How do I configure directory replication?

To configure directory replication on Windows NT Workstation (as an example):

1. Select the Control Panel command from the Settings submenu of the Start menu.

2. Double-click on the Server control panel.

3. In the Server control panel, shown here, click the Replication button.

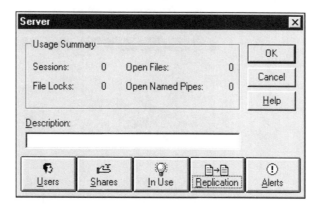

4. In the Directory Replication dialog box shown in Figure 7-2, click the Import Directories radio button, and then click the Add button to add directories to the Import list.

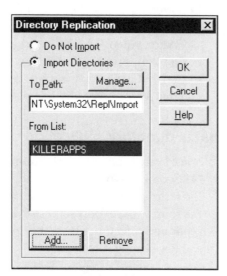

Figure 7-2.   The Directory Replication dialog box

5. Choose the domain where the data is to be imported from, and then the server from which to import the data. Click the Manage button to view the Manage Imported Directories dialog box shown here.

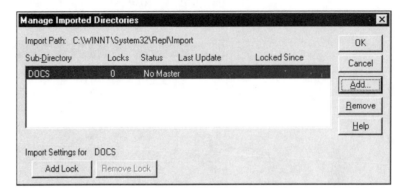

6. Click on <u>A</u>dd to choose an import directory. Add a name of the directory you are importing, and then click the OK button.

7. Click the OK button to complete the task.

You can use the Remove button to remove directories from your replication scheme, or the Do Not <u>I</u>mport radio button to disable replication entirely. The Add and Remove buttons in the Manage Imported Dialog box let you eliminate any restrictions placed on a directory through its use by a connected user.

When you open the corresponding Directory Replication dialog box on Windows NT Server, you see not only a directory export section, but a directory import section as well. Figure 7-3 shows you this dialog box on Windows NT Server.

❓ What is directory replication used for?

You can replicate directories from Windows NT Server to Windows NT Server or Workstation. Windows NT Workstation can only act as the recipient of exported directories (the import computer), and not as the source (the export server). Windows NT Workstation receives replicated directories from the domain server, by default.

Replicating directories:

⇨ Lets you maintain automatic updates of files

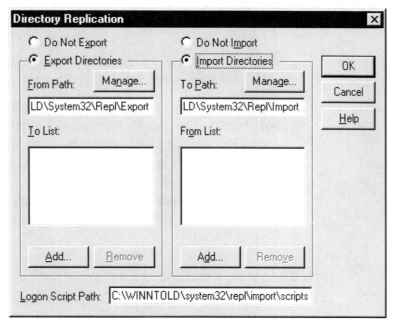

Figure 7-3.   The Windows NT Server Directory Replication dialog box

⇨ Gives you a uniform set of logon scripts and system policy files across network servers

⇨ Provides an automatic backup

⇨ Aids in network LAN and WAN performance by providing local copies of data for load balancing

How do I change the location of export and import directories?

To change the location, do the following:

1. Open the Server control panel.

2. Click the Replication button.

3. Specify a new location in the From Path and To Path text boxes.

Where do I change the replication parameters?

The Directory Replicator service is located in the Registry at the following path:

`HKEY_LOCAL_MACHINE\SYSTEM\CurrentControlSet\Services\Replicator\Parameters`

There are two Registry entries that you can add that are not configurable in the Server control panel. They are:

⇨ *Interval: REG_DWORD.* This parameter sets the interval that the export server uses to check a replicated directory for changes. The default is five minutes; the range is from one to 60 minutes.

⇨ *GuardTime: REG_DWORD.* This parameter controls the number of minutes that an export directory must have no changes written to it before it can be replicated. By default this is set to two minutes, but it can be in the range of from zero to half of the setting for the Interval you set.

How do I verify that files were replicated?

To verify replication of a directory on the export server:

1. Open the Server control panel.

2. Click the Replication button.

3. Click the Manage button on the Export Server.

4. Check the status in the Manage Directory Replication dialog box to see if the directory is OK.

5. Close the Manage Directory Replication dialog box, and then the Server control panel.

Then check the status of the directory in the import computer to see what the status of the import directory is in the Manage Directory Replication dialog box.

Where are the replicated directories kept?

All directories that need to be replicated on an export server are kept in a master export directory that by default is in the following master export directory:

`<systemroot>\System 32\Repl\Export`

This directory is shared as Repl$ when the Directory Replicator service starts up.

Note: *Directories to be exported need to be subdirectories in the Export directory or they are not replicated.*

All directories that are imported are kept by default at:

```
<systemroot>\System 32\Repl\Import
```

The directories that are imported from the export server are re-created as subdirectories in the Import directory.

CONFIGURING A UPS

How do I install a UPS device?

Both NT Server and NT Workstation come with a UPS control panel that lets you configure a COM port to install your UPS device on. When a UPS device is installed on an NT Server, you can enable messaging to other network nodes when the UPS device comes on. Both types of computers running Windows NT let you perform a timed or remote shutdown.

To install a UPS device:

1. Plug in your UPS device to a power line and connect the device to your computer's COM port.

2. Select the Control Panel command from the Settings submenu of the Start menu.

3. Double-click the UPS control panel icon.

4. In the UPS dialog box shown in Figure 7-4, check the Uninterruptible Power Supply Is Installed On checkbox and set the COM port in the list box.

5. Select the options appropriate to your UPS device:

    ⇨ Whether your UPS device is using a positive or negative interface voltage.

    ⇨ If you enable the Power failure signal checkbox, you will have to specify the anticipated battery life for your UPS, the recharge time, and the way you want NT to message the failure.

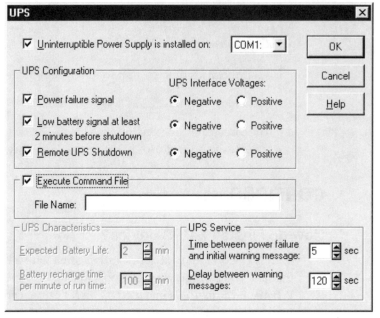

Figure 7-4.   The UPS control panel

⇨ If you enable the Low battery signal, you will receive a
warning when the battery power drops due to use or
discharge.

⇨ If you enable the Remote UPS Shutdown checkbox, you will
be able to log onto Windows NT and shut down the UPS
device.

6. Click the OK button to complete the installation.

How do I protect my computer in case the power goes off?

You can install a UPS (Uninterruptible Power Supply) device that
continues to supply power to your computer in case of power failure.
This is particularly valuable for Windows NT Server, as it allows
connected users to close their sessions in a graceful manner without
losing any unsaved work.

BACKING UP AND RESTORING YOUR SYSTEM

❓ How do I back up my data to protect it when lightning strikes?

Use the NT Backup utility to create a set of backup tapes to your tape drive; then run NT Backup.

1. Select the NT Backup application from the Administrative Tools folder of the <u>P</u>rograms submenu on the Start menu.

2. Put a tape in the tape drive.

3. Click on the checkbox(es) next to the volumes you wish to back up in the Drives window as shown in Figure 7-5.

4. To back up part of a volume, double-click on that drive to open the volume window as shown in Figure 7-6.

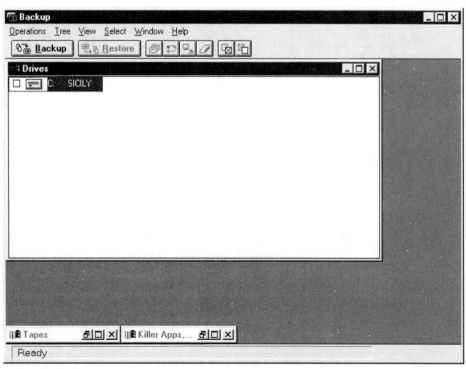

Figure 7-5.   The Backup window

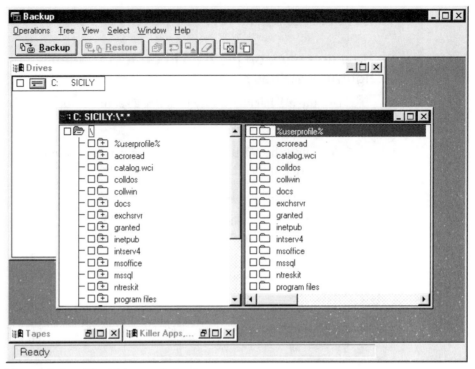

Figure 7-6.   The Volume window

5. Put a check mark next to each of the folders you want to back up; then click the Backup button.

6. In the Backup Information dialog box, enter a name in the Tape Name text box and a description in the Description text box. (A name or description with a date is a good idea.)

7. You create a different backup set for each volume you select in the Backup Drives window, so continue entering the information for Step 6 for each of the volumes you selected in the Backup Information dialog box.

8. Click on the Verify after Backup text box to make sure that you see the progress of your backup.

9. For a volume containing your system files, check the Backup Local Registry checkbox.

10. Select whether you want a Normal or full backup or a Differential or incremental backup in the Backup Type list box.

11. Click the OK button to begin the backup.

As the backup proceeds, a Backup Status dialog box appears that shows the progress of the backup.

? Can I back up my files by using a batch file to copy them?

If you want to back up a Windows NT Workstation volume to a server, consider writing a batch file. In order for this file to work correctly, you must copy files to a mapped volume on the server. The following is an example of this file's syntax:

```
COPY C:\DOCS\DATA\*.* F:\BACKUP\DOCS\DATA
...
COPY C:\APPS\FILES\*.* F:\BACKUP\APPS\FILES
EXIT
```

To run the batch file easily, save the file as a shortcut and run the command session by double-clicking that file icon.

? How do I create a boot disk for a mirrored set?

A computer that boots from a mirrored set of drives requires a different type of boot disk. Striped sets cannot contain both the boot partition and system, so only mirrored sets can provide fault tolerance for both the system and boot partition.

To create a boot disk for a mirrored set:

1. Format the disk in Windows NT Server.

2. Copy the files required to the boot disk.

3. Modify the BOOT.INI file to have your operating system point to the mirrored copy of the boot partition for Intel x86 systems.

4. Set your system so that it can boot from a floppy disk (if necessary), and test the disk.

The files required on the boot disk are different for the different types of computers that Windows NT Server runs on.

For Intel x86 computers, you must have the following files on disk:

➪ NTLDR

➪ NTDETECT.COM

➪ NTBOOTDD.SYS (when you use SCSI disks that are not using your computer's SCSI BIOS)

⇨ BOOT.INI

For RISC computers, you need the following files:

⇨ OSLOADER.EXE

⇨ HAL.DLL

⇨ *.PAL (the PAL code with the software routines that give the operating system control over the CPU)

For RISC systems, you will need to modify the BOOT.INI to change the following variables:

⇨ *OSLOADER.* Change that variable's value to multi(0)disk(0)fdisk(0)\OSLOADER.EXE.

⇨ *SYSTEMPARTITION.* Change that variable's value to multi(0)disk(0)fdisk(0).

⇨ *OSLOADPARTITION.* Change the path to the secondary mirrored partition.

⇨ *SYSTEMPARTITION.* Change the path to the Windows NT Server root directory.

Make sure that whenever your partition path information is altered, you update the BOOT.INI file on the fault tolerance boot disk.

？ If my hard drive fails, how do I create a Windows NT boot floppy?

When a partition table becomes corrupted or part of your mirrored set fails, you might need to have a Boot Floppy to start your system up. To create this disk, you must format the floppy disk on Windows NT and add the following files to that disk:

⇨ *NTLDR.* This is the Windows NT boot loader program.

⇨ *BOOT.INI.* This file contains the location of all of the boot partition information for each operating system that you have created on your computer.

⇨ *NTDETECT.COM.* This file detects the hardware that is installed on your computer.

⇨ *BOOTSECT.DOS.* This file allows you to dual-boot another operating system. You should only include BOOTSECT.DOS if you use a dual-boot system.

⇨ *NTBOOTDD.SYS.* This file contains a copy of the boot SCSI host adapter's driver file. You only need to include NTBOOTDD.SYS if you are using a SCSI drive or a SCSI driver as your boot drive.

Note: *Some computers require that you enable a BIOS setting before you can boot off of a floppy disk. Check your system's documentation or its BIOS setup program to see if you need to turn this feature on.*

There are no automated methods for creating a boot floppy disk, so you need to follow this procedure manually. Keep in mind that these files are hidden system files. Turn on the Show All Files option in the View menu of the Windows NT Explorer and make sure that these files have their Read Only, Hidden, and System Attributes set to on.

❓ How can I create an Emergency Repair Disk?

Windows NT comes with an emergency disk repair utility. This utility creates an Emergency Repair Disk (ERD) that contains a copy of your current system settings. Should vital system files on your drive become corrupted, you can use this disk to restore your disk. The only problem using this utility is that you need to make the Emergency Repair Disk and keep it current. When you install the Windows NT operating system, you are enjoined to create the ERD as part of your installation. However, you can create the ERD at any time. Here's how.

To create an Emergency Repair Disk:

1. Select the Help command from the Start menu.

2. Click the Index tab and enter the keywords **Repair Disk**; then double-click the topic "Using the Repair Disk utility to make an emergency repair disk" as shown here.

3. Click the Click Here button to open the Repair Disk Utility dialog box shown here.

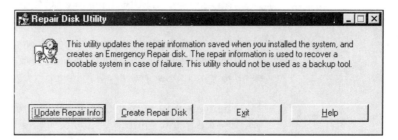

4. Click the Create Repair Disk button to create the ERD; the Repair Disk Utility will prompt you to insert a floppy disk.

5. Click the confirmation dialog box and the utility formats your disk and copies the information to it.

6. Click the Exit button to close the Emergency Repair Utility.

Note: *You can use the RDISK command from the Command Prompt window to create and update an ERD.*

If you want to update an existing ERD, click the Update Repair Info button in the Repair Disk Utility. When you update an ERD, your hard drive's configuration information is updated. That information remains unchanged when you simply create a new ERD. You should update your ERD whenever you change your system hardware, or when you make significant software changes.

? How do I know if my tape drive is properly installed?

To back up either a FAT or NTFS volume, first check to see if your tape drive is installed properly.

1. Select the Control Panel command from the Settings submenu on the Start menu.

2. Double-click the Tape Devices icon in the Control Panel folder.

3. Click the Devices tab; then select the tape drive in the list box, as shown here.

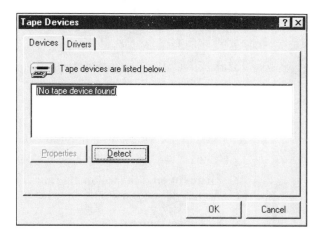

4. Click the Properties button to view the tape drives settings.

5. Or click the Detect button to have Windows NT search for the tape drive or other backup device.

6. Click the Drivers tab to see if the correct driver is listed for your backup device.

7. Use the Add button to install a new device driver; then select the correct driver from the Install Driver dialog box.

8. Or click the Have Disk button to specify the location of the device driver file; then click the OK button twice to install the driver and close the Control Panel.

How do I return to the last known good configuration?

When your system crashes and you cannot boot Windows NT, you can boot to the last known good configuration.

To do this, hold down the SHIFT key when you start up. The last known good configuration is stored after a successful logon.

How can I repair a damaged disk or volume?

If you get error messages when you start up your computer, you can use the Emergency Repair Disk to attempt to resolve those problems. The ERD is useful when system files have been corrupted, deleted, or damaged, or when the partition boot sector has been damaged.

To perform an emergency repair:

1. Boot Windows NT using a floppy disk with Setup Disk 1 on it.

 Note: *If necessary, make sure your BIOS supports booting from a floppy disk drive.*

2. Insert Setup Disk 2 when you are prompted.

3. You will see a screen asking you to select a new installation or a repair; press the R key to begin the emergency repair.

4. You are offered the following four choices (all of which are selected by default):

   ⇨ Inspect registry files

   ⇨ Inspect startup environment

   ⇨ Verify Windows NT system files

   ⇨ Inspect boot sector

5. Press the ENTER key to continue to repair your disk.

6. Setup posts a screen that tells you that it can detect your hard drives and floppy disks. Press the ENTER key to continue with auto-detection.

7. Setup can have problems with CD-ROM drives or tape backup units. To manually select SCSI devices, special disk controllers, CD-ROM drives, or other devices, press the S key and manually indicate the nature of attached devices.

8. When Setup posts the screen asking for the Emergency Repair Disk (ERD), press the ENTER key.

9. Windows NT displays a screen indicating each of the Registry files that it believes it requires to complete the repair process. It makes this selection based on comparing the files it finds.

10. Select any additional files you think are required. Use the UP or DOWN ARROW key to move to those files and press the SPACEBAR key to select them; or, press the letter A to repair all files.

11. Press the ENTER key to continue the repair, and then remove the floppy disk and press the ENTER key to reboot the system.

Warning: *When the Setup program copies your ERD files, it overwrites your current Registry information. Any changes you made to the Registry since the ERD was updated are lost.*

If you have difficulty booting your system after a repair, try booting from the Windows NT floppy disk and accessing the Disk Administrator utility in the Administrative Tools folder.

How do I restore my drive?

Using the tapes you create with NT Backup, you can restore a file, a folder, a set of files or folders, or an entire volume.

To restore from a tape backup:

1. Select the Backup command from the Administrative Tools folder on the Programs submenu of the Start menu.

2. Put the tape with your date into the tape drive.

3. Double-click on the Tapes window Title bar to maximize the window.

4. Select the Catalog command from the Operations menu.

5. A Catalog Status dialog box will appear, showing the information contained on the tape (name and description).

6. Select the volume(s) to be restored by adding a check mark next to the name.

7. Or double-click on a volume name to open the volume window.

8. Select the file(s) and folder(s) you want restored.

9. Click the Restore button.

10. In the Restore Information dialog box, select the following checkbox options:

   ⇨ The location the restored files are written to (overwriting the original location is the default)

   ⇨ If files are to have their original permissions (Restore File Permissions) or adopt the permissions of the folder to which they are being restored

⇨ Whether you wish to Verify After Restore

⇨ Whether you want to Restore Local Registry for a volume containing system files

11. Click the OK button to restore the files you selected.

NT Backup posts the Verify Status dialog box log files copied from your tape to your drive(s).

Can I back up my files using the XCOPY command?

The XCOPY command lets you copy all of the contents of subdirectories. You can use this command with FAT, and with NTFS volumes where you do not need to copy the file permissions.

XCOPY takes a number of switches that provide useful copying behavior:

⇨ /A. Copies files that have the archive attribute set and does not change the attribute

⇨ /M. Copies files with the archive attributes set and turns the archive attribute off

⇨ /D:m-d-y. Copies files changed after or on the date specified when you use the D switch with no date attribute

⇨ /S. Copies any subdirectories that contains files

⇨ /E. Copies any subdirectories, even ones that are empty

⇨ /C. Copies even when there are errors

⇨ /H. Copies hidden and system files

⇨ /R. Overwrites read-only files

⇨ /T. Re-creates the directory structure of the source

⇨ /U. copies files that already exist in the target

⇨ /K. Copies attributes

⇨ /N. Copies the truncated short filenames

⇨ /Z. Copies networked files in the restartable mode

Tip: *The Windows NT Workstation Resource Kit contains the SCOPY command. This command lets you retain the file permissions for an NTFS volume. However, SCOPY cannot copy only modified files. In other respects, the syntax of SCOPY is identical to XCOPY.*

What is the "Blue Screen of Death"?

When Windows NT starts up and freezes on the blue screen during loading, you are experiencing what is called a STOP error. There are many reasons why this can happen, among them:

⇨ A corrupt Registry file

⇨ Hardware configuration errors

⇨ A virus

⇨ A corrupt or missing partition boot sector

⇨ A hard drive error where the logical block addressing (LBA) is incompatible

To set options for this problem as an administrator:

1. Select the Control Panel command from the Settings submenu of the Start menu.

2. Double-click on the System control panel to view the System Properties dialog box.

3. Click the Startup/Shutdown tab.

4. Click on the options you wish to enable in the Recovery section (shown here).

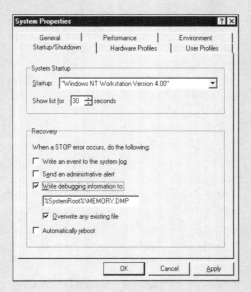

⇨ Write an event to the system log

⇨ Send an administrative alert

⇨ Write debugging information to: a file you specify

⇨ Automatically reboot

5. Then click the OK button.

All of the options require a paging file of 2MB. The memory dump debugging information is written to disk. This dump requires a paging file that is 1MB larger than the amount of installed RAM in your system.

chapter

8 Answers!

Working with the Security Model

Answer Topics!

Working with the Security Model
@ a Glance

⇨ Windows NT maintains a **security database** on the domain controller in which user and machine accounts and group definitions are kept; a portion of this security database is maintained on local machines. The Security Accounts Manager (SAM) uses this database to validate all resource access and logons in a domain.

⇨ Users are allowed certain privileges based on their logon. Individual user accounts are created to provide logon and resource access. A domain can also store a list of users in the security database. In order to simplify resource access management, a group account can be defined. Groups are a collection of users and other groups afforded the same access to resources. Access privileges are additive. Local groups are provided to give fine control over resource access; NT also contains prebuilt global groups that are available systemwide. This system of **users, groups, and domains** provides a flexible method for controlling and managing resource access based on the security you set in the file system.

⇨ Passwords are the key that enables you to log on to a user account. In order to protect **passwords**, Windows NT lets you set a period after which passwords expire. Users can change their passwords when that option is set, and a no-password password can be allowed to provide access to limited system resources.

⇨ A **user profile** is created whenever a user logs onto a system for the first time. You can also create user profiles with specific settings to maintain a desired look and feel of the desktop; access to programs, accessories, and printers; a Taskbar and Start menu configuration; Help system bookmarks; and options in the Windows NT Explorer. Profiles can be stored on the server and retrieved as a cached copy on a local machine when a user logs on. A stored local profile can be used when a problem occurs with a network connection or with a logon.

⇨ In order to enforce a set of rules on a computer, a network administrator can create a system policy that applies to a single user, a group of users, or all users in a domain. **System policies** can restrict network logon or access, customize the desktop, or limit access to settings in the Control Panel.

THE SECURITY DATABASE

How does the security database work?

When you log on to Windows NT, you get a Security Access Token (SAT) based on your user name and password from the machine you logged onto. When this logon is validated, you're passed on to the domain controller for validation and onto the domain resources as the next step. This SAT is a key that lets you access objects that Windows NT manages by maintaining a Security Descriptor (SD) file, which contains the access control list (ACL) for each resource.

There are two types of accounts that are created and managed in Windows NT: machine accounts (created with Server Manager) and user accounts (created with User Manager). Both of these accounts are maintained in the Security Account Manager (SAM) database stored on the Primary Domain Controller (PDC) and replicated to any Backup Domain Controllers (BDC) on the system. Accounts are assigned an internally issued and controlled System Identification number (SID).

You create and manage accounts in the User Manager for Domains. If you log on as an administrator, you have full access to create, modify, and delete accounts for machines and different levels of users. If you have a lower level of privileges, you have less access, and the changes you can make are more limited. An account is specified by the machine and user name, as in <computername>\BarrieS.

A group is an account that contains other accounts. Every computer contains a Users group to which all user accounts belong. There is also a Guest group that allows limited privileges to users who log on without a password (if you allow it).

? How big can a domain be based on the security database?

There is a current practical limit to the size of the security database of around 40MB. This size affects the number of users, groups, and machine accounts that you can define and the maximum size of users in a domain.

The three accounts you can define in a domain and their sizes are

➪ User accounts—1.0KB

➪ Group accounts—4.0KB

➪ Machine accounts—0.5KB

So as a practical limit, you can have as many as 40,000 users in a domain. Typically, domains are much smaller to allow for administrative division of resources.

I've made changes to a group or account, but they don't appear to have been enforced. When do changes take effect?

Changes you make in the security database don't take effect until a Security Access Token (SAT) is assigned. Windows NT assigns a SAT when a user logs on to the system. Therefore, you must log off first and then log on before the changes take effect.

USERS, GROUPS, AND DOMAINS

I want to monitor user account activity. How do I audit users?

You can set an audit policy in the User Manager for Domains by selecting the Audit command from the Properties menu. The Audit Policy dialog box that appears is shown in Figure 8-1.

The Audit Policy dialog box lets you audit events by marking them in the Security log. Use the Event Viewer to open this log and view audit events.

A new user has joined my company. How do I create a user account?

If no domain exists, you create a local user account on a computer. For a computer that is part of a domain, create a user in the User Manager for Domains.

To create a new user account:

1. Select the User Manager for Domains from the Administrative Tools folder on the Programs submenu of the Start menu.

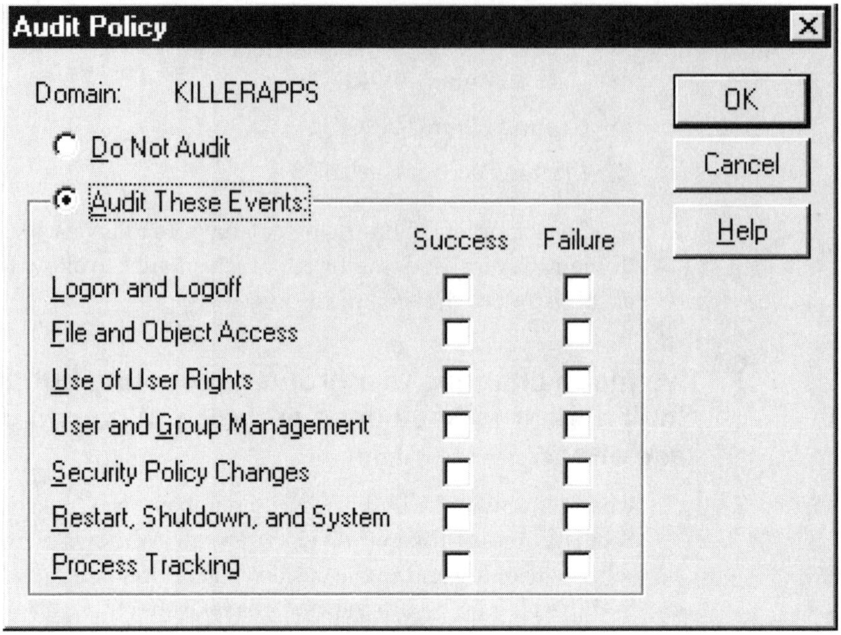

Figure 8-1.   The Audit Policy dialog box

2. Select the New Underline{U}ser command from the Underline{U}ser menu.

3. Enter the required information in the New User dialog box shown in Figure 8-2.

4. At a minimum, enter information into the Username, Password, and Confirm Password text boxes.

5. Click the Groups button and add the new user to existing groups.

6. Click the OK button to add the new user account to the security database.

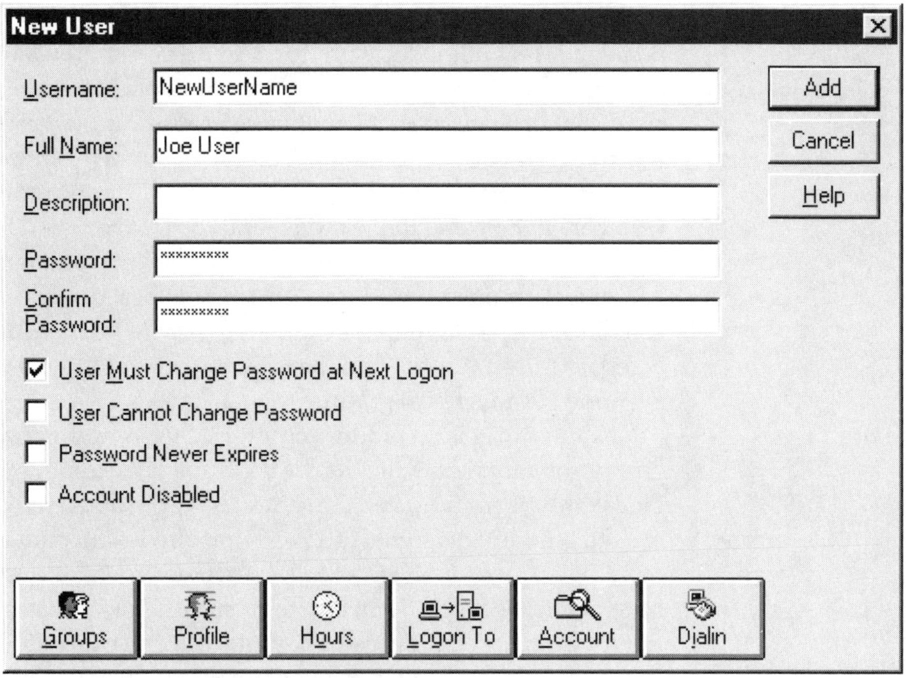

Figure 8-2.   The New User dialog box

What is the difference between a global group and a local group?

A named collection of user accounts with the same set of privileges and resource access is called a *group*. NT Server provides for some built-in local groups, but you can define your own and create global groups as well. By storing privileges in a group, every member of the group is given those privileges. Any user account that belongs to two or more groups has all of the privileges accorded those groups. Privileges are additive.

Most of the work done in the NT security system is performed setting up groups.

Some of NT's built-in local groups, like Administrator, are required; others, like Server Operators or Replicators, are a convenience. Careful analysis of these groups can suggest schemes that you might want to employ in your enterprise.

Local groups are local in the sense that they apply only to members that belong to the group, and the local group defines the set of privileges for those users. Local groups can contain users and global groups from a local domain, but local groups cannot contain other local groups. To add more privileges or resource access to a user, you can add the user either to additional local groups or to any global group.

Not only can local groups accept local users and global groups for a local domain, but local groups can accept users and global groups from trusted domains. However, an administrator can only modify the rights of a local domain during domain setup.

A *global group* is a named collection of users. Global groups have no privileges associated with them. You implement global groups to create a set of custom privileges, which are added by adding the global group to one or more local groups. You can base a global group on a local group, and modify its privileges; or you can create a global group from scratch. A global group is particularly useful because it can be used in other trusted domains.

A global group can contain user accounts from the same domain. This is useful because it provides a way of allowing users in one domain to have access to resources in other trusting domains. Global groups are typically designed to define an organization's membership, and therefore play a role in partitioning an enterprise into logical units. So a global group might apply to business units like administration, marketing, human resources, and so on. Doing this provides a finer control over domain architecture than defining an entire domain for each of these business units. An administrator typically starts off creating a domain by defining global groups for each user type, and then adding users to each global group.

❓ My company has a new project that requires group access. How do I create a new group?

You create a new group in the User Manager for Domains. The procedure isn't much different from creating a new user account.

To create a new group account:

1. Select the User Manager for Domains from the Administrative Tools folder on the Programs submenu of the Start menu.

2. Select the New Local Group command from the User menu to display the New Local Group dialog box, as shown in Figure 8-3.

3. Enter the group name and description in the New Local Group dialog box.

4. Click the Add button to open the Add Users and Groups dialog box to add users to your local group. (For a global group, you can also add local groups to the group definition.)

5. Click the OK button.

To create a new global group, select the New Global Group command on the User menu. The New Global Group dialog box is shown in Figure 8-4.

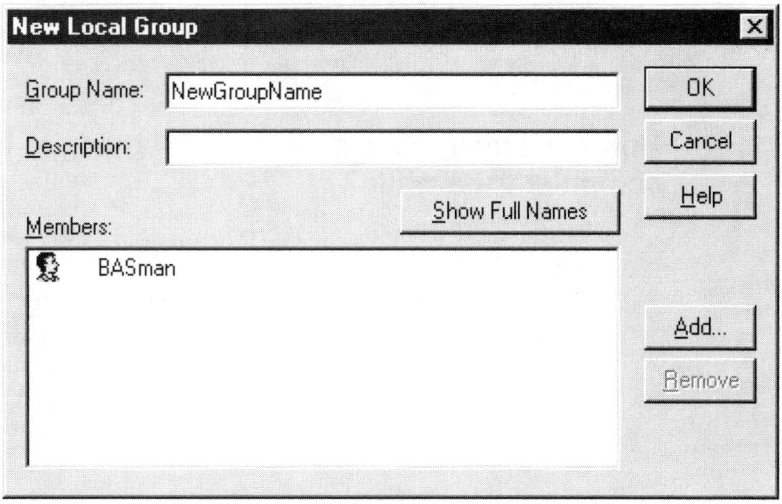

Figure 8-3.   The New Local Group dialog box

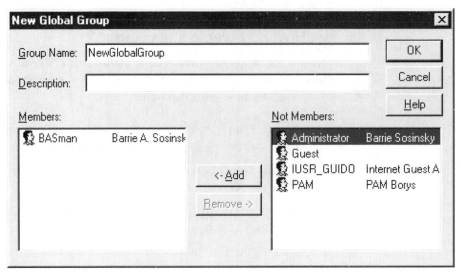

Figure 8-4. The New Global Group dialog box

What is the purpose of the Guest group, and why would I want one?

The Guest account is meant to provide limited privileges and access or for occasional use. A Guest logon can allow access to shares when the no-password option is set. The Guest password is particularly useful for an NT Server or Workstation running an FTP service where you want to provide access to a volume or folder for an anonymous logon.

How can I maintain a session if I'm going to leave my computer for a while?

If you log off when you leave, other users can log on to your computer while you are away. If you want to maintain your session, press the CTRL-ALT-DEL key to bring up the Security dialog box (Figure 8-5) and click the Lock Workstation button. This maintains your session and posts a Workstation Locked alert box (Figure 8-6), but requires that you press the CTRL-ALT-DEL keystroke to enter your password into the Unlock Workstation dialog box (Figure 8-7).

 Note: Use of the CTRL-ALT-DEL *keystroke helps defeat programs that post a simulated logon screen in order to collect user names and passwords.*

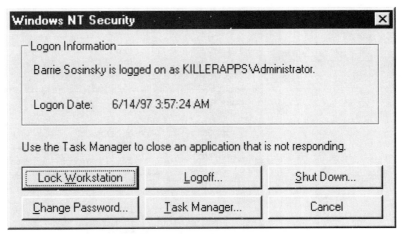

Figure 8-5.   The Windows NT Security dialog box

If you wish to lock your workstation during a session automatically, turn a 32-bit screen saver on and enable the Password Protected feature. The Windows screen saver is displayed in the Screen Saver tab of the Display control panel.

? How do I add or remove rights from a group or user account?

User rights are a group account policy that you specify from within the User Manager for Domains on Windows NT Server.

To add or remove a right from a group or user:

1. Select the User Manager for Domains from the Administrative Tools folder on the Programs submenu of the Start menu.

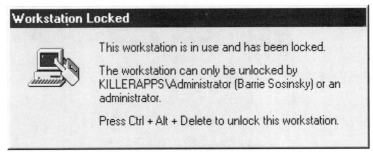

Figure 8-6.   The Workstation Locked alert box

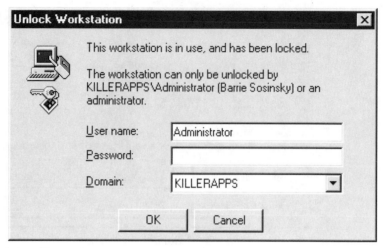

Figure 8-7.   The Unlock Workstation dialog box

2. Select the User Rights command from the Policies menu.

3. Select the privilege you wish to add or deny in the Right list box in the User Rights Policy dialog box shown in Figure 8-8.

4. Click on the group from which you wish to remove the right in the Grant To list box; then click the Remove button.

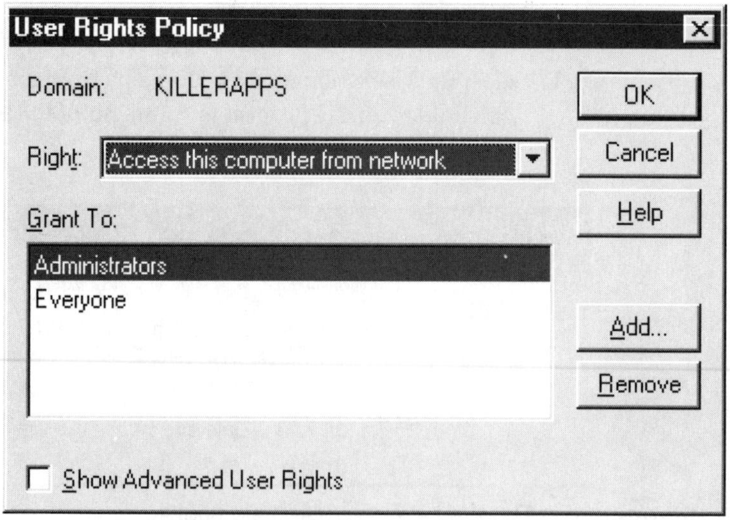

Figure 8-8.   The User Rights Policy dialog box

5. Or click the <u>A</u>dd button to view the Add Users and Groups dialog box as shown in Figure 8-9.

6. Select the user or group from the <u>N</u>ames list box, and then click the <u>A</u>dd button. The name appears in the A<u>d</u>d Names list box.

7. Click the OK button to add the account to the User Right Policy; then click the OK button to add the privilege to the security database.

In most instances you should assign privileges to groups and not to users. If you need to assign a right to a user, use the Show <u>U</u>sers button in the Add Users and Groups dialog box.

 ### How can I search for a user or group?

To search for a specific user or group:

1. Open Add Users and Groups dialog box (see Figure 8-9).

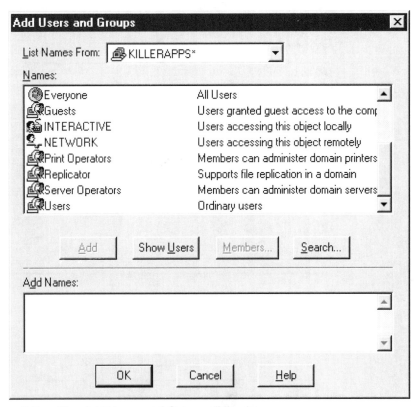

Figure 8-9.   The Add Users and Groups dialog box

2. Click the Search button to open the Find Account dialog box shown in Figure 8-10.

3. Enter the name of the user or group, and then click the Search button.

? I belong to one domain, but I want to use the resources in another domain. How do trust relationships work?

A user account is recognized in the security system by a username and a password. Users can log on to a domain at any computer in the domain, or at any computer in a trusted domain. A guest account does not require a password, but generally has very limited access. User accounts can be either global accounts that are validated by a

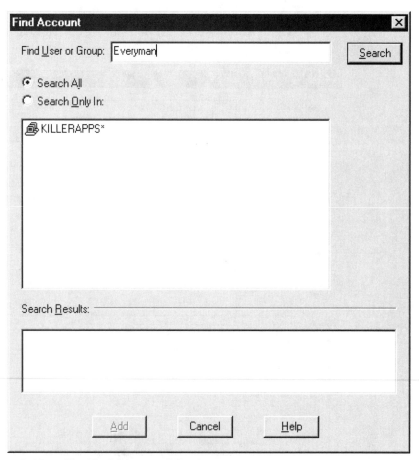

Figure 8-10.   The Find Account dialog box

domain's SAM, or local accounts that provide access to a specific service on the network.

When you log on to a domain, your logon is validated by the local security account (LSA) on the workstation first, and then the security database (SAM) of that domain. If your logon (user account and password) is not recognized by the domain SAM, the domain controller sends out a request to other trusted domains' controllers to validate the logon. The first one that recognizes the account and responds to the request sets the privileges and access rights for that user.

When you log on to your own domain, you can see resources for any domain involved in a trust relationship as a trusting domain. The access allowed to you is based on your level of access rights, and the nature of the access allowed by the specific resource you've accessed.

Not only can local groups accept local users and global groups for a local domain, but local groups can accept users and global groups from trusted domains. However, an administrator can only modify the rights of a local domain during domain setup.

Trust relationships in Windows NT 3.5x and 4 are a one-way relationship. There are trusted and trusting domains involved in any relationship. If you need a two-way trust relationship, you can define two different trust relationships between the same two domains.

 How can I tell which users belong to which groups?

To view the members of a particular group:

1. Highlight the group in the Add Users and Groups dialog box (see Figure 8-9).

2. Click the Members button to view the Group Membership dialog box.

3. Double-click on the group of interest.

PASSWORDS

 How do I change my password?

If your password has expired based on your Account Policy, Windows NT will prompt you to change your password when you attempt to log on to the system.

To change your password at any time, do the following:

1. Press the CTRL-ALT-DEL keystroke to view the Windows NT Security dialog box shown in Figure 8-5.

2. Click the Change Password button to view the Change Password dialog box shown in Figure 8-11.

3. Enter your password into the Old Password text box, your desired password into the New Password text box, and the new password once again into the Confirm Password text box.

4. Click the OK button to enter the new password into the security database.

I want to protect passwords by having them expire every so often. How do I change password options?

Passwords are controlled within the Account Policies dialog box of the User Manager for Domains.
To set password options:

1. Select the User Manager for Domains from the Administrative Tools folder on the Programs submenu of the Start menu.

2. Select the account name in the Username panel of the User Manager for Domains.

3. Select the Account command from the Policies menu.

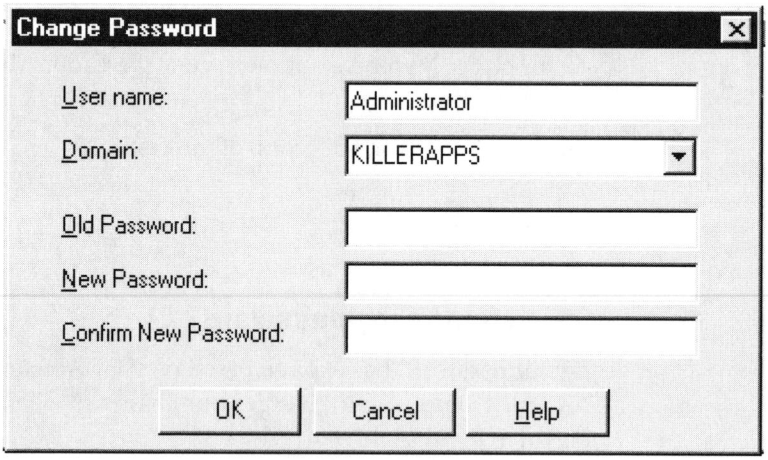

Figure 8-11.   The Change Password dialog box

4. In the Account Policy dialog box (see Figure 8-12), select the options you desire, and then click the OK button.

Among the options you can set are

⇨ Minimum and maximum password age before a password expires

⇨ Whether blank or no character passwords are permitted

⇨ The maximum length of a password

⇨ Whether a password list is maintained for an account, which allows the user to cycle between passwords

⇨ How many failed attempts to log on with a username result in an Account Lockout

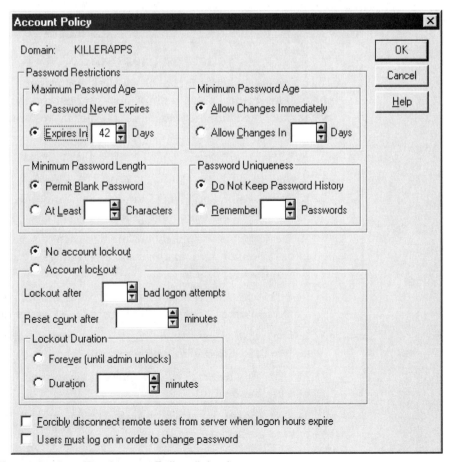

Figure 8-12.   The Account Policy dialog box

If you set an Account Lockout, set the Lockout Duration so that the account login can be re-attempted after a specified time.

 I've entered my password correctly, but the system won't log me on. What did I do wrong?

Unlike many other network operating systems, programs, Internet access, and other security systems, Windows NT passwords are case-sensitive. If you can't log on to the system, make sure that you have correctly entered not only the spelling of the password, but also the case. If you still can't log on, check to see that your CAPS LOCK key is not accidentally on.

USER PROFILES

What is a user profile?

The changes that a user makes on the desktop, printer connections, control panel settings, applications, and the Help system are saved into the user's local profile and restored when they log back onto the system.

The following settings are saved as part of a user profile:

⇨ *Accessories*. Many applets such as the Calculator, Clock, Notepad, Paint, and HyperTerminal can be modified. Those modifications are stored in a profile.

⇨ *Applications*. Many applications are designed to save information for particular users. These settings are stored as part of the user profile.

⇨ *Control Panels*. Many settings in the various control panels are stored to a profile. See the following bulleted list for details.

⇨ *Online Help bookmark*. If you create a bookmark for the Help system, it is stored with your user profile.

⇨ *Printers*. Any network printer connections and settings are part of your profile.

⇨ *Taskbar*. The configuration of the Start menu and all Taskbar options are saved.

⇨ *Windows NT Explorer.* Any user settings or options are part of a user profile.

Among the control panel settings that can be stored as part of a user profile are the following:

⇨ *Accessibility Options.* The keyboard, sound, display, and mouse can be modified to support users with special needs.

⇨ *Console.* The look and feel of the Command Prompt window can be modified.

⇨ *Display.* The user's desktop, interface items, and the nature of the display and resolution can be modified.

⇨ *Keyboard.* The keyboard repeat rate and delay can be specified.

⇨ *Mouse.* The double-click speed, tracking speed, and mouse button assignment can be determined.

⇨ *Regional Settings.* You can specify how numbers, dates, and times are displayed and managed.

⇨ *Sounds.* Sounds can be assigned to various system events.

When you log back in, these settings are restored for you based on your user account. User profiles are useful because they allow a single computer to be used by several users in a way that is customized for each one's use.

How do I create a new user profile?

When a user logs onto Windows NT for the first time, the system looks for a user profile for that user. If it finds the profile, it copies it as a roaming or server-based user profile on the local computer. If one does not exist, a copy of the default user profile is made and named for that user.

To create a new user profile:

1. Open the Windows NT Explorer on your domain controller (for a roving profile) or on a local Windows NT computer (for a local profile).

2. Find the folder for the user profile that you wish to use as a template at the location <root>\WINNT\Profiles\<Username>.

3. Copy the <Username> folder to the Profiles folder.

4. Click the folder name and rename the folder with the user account you desire.

When you log on as that user, the settings in your new folder are established.

When a user has an account on a local computer, that account stores a profile in addition to the profile that is stored on the server. Should there be a logon problem, the local computer can use the last saved local profile to allow workstation access.

? I want to control the environment of a computer based on a user's logon. How do I do that?

To create an environment based on the user account, select that user account in the User Manager for Domains, and then click the Profile button. In the User Environment Profile dialog box shown in Figure 8-13, you can specify a startup script that modifies the environment at logon. Scripts can be a BAT (batch), CMD (OS/2), or EXE (program or executable) file. Specify the path to the script, and the script name in the dialog box. The Local Path or Connect radio button specifies the location of the home directory.

When you create a new user, you can access the User Environment Profile dialog box using the Profile button in the New User dialog box.

? How do I allow people to log on to a computer and use their profile on a local computer?

If you want to have users log on locally using their user profile, enable this right for the Everyone group:

1. Select the User Rights command on the Policies menu in the User Manager for Domains.

2. Select the Log on Locally in the Rights drop-down list.

3. Select Everyone in the Names list box, and then click the Add button.

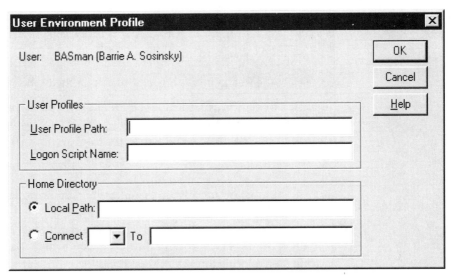

Figure 8-13.   The User Environment Profile dialog box

4. Click the OK button in the Add Names dialog box.

5. Verify that the Everyone group appears in the Grant To list box; then click the OK button and close the User Manager for Domains.

I've created program groups as part of my profile. Where do the other program groups come from?

Settings in the All Users folder are used in conjunction with individual user profiles. Any common program groups you see are stored with that profile. The All Users profile also stores settings used on the desktop and for the Start menu. Only an administrator can modify the All Users profile and create common program groups.

Where are user profile settings stored in the Windows NT Registry, and how do I change them?

User profile settings are stored in the Windows NT Registry in the HKEY_CURRENT_USER key. To change a setting in a user profile:

1. Log on to the system with the user name whose profile you wish to modify.

2. Open the Registry Editor (REGEDIT.EXE).

Note: *By default, the Registry Editor is installed in the <root>*
\WINNT directory.

3. Select the Read Only Mode command on the Options menu.

4. Click the HKEY_CURRENT_USER key to expand the settings;
then alter the setting you desire. Figure 8-14 shows you the
HKEY_CURRENT_USER key in the Registry.

5. Close the Registry Editor.

The setting you modify takes effect when you close the
Registry Editor.

The actual information that the Registry reads for a user profile is
contained in the NTUSER.DAT file of the user profile folder. This file
is cached on a local computer when the user profile is read.

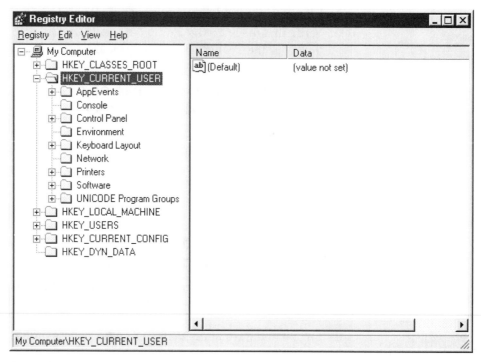

Figure 8-14.   The HKEY_CURRENT_USER key in the Registry Editor

I want to modify items in my user profile directly. Where are user profiles and items in that profile stored?

User profiles are stored in the Profiles folder in the system root. This is usually the C\WINNT folder. The default user profiles are stored in the Default User folder, and any individual user profiles are contained in a folder with that user name. Each user profile folder also contains an NTUSER.DAT file and a directory of shortcuts or link (.LNK) files to desktop items. Figure 8-15 shows you the structure of an individual user's profile folder.

 Note: *The NetHood, PrintHood, Recent, and Templates folders are hidden and do not appear unless you choose the Show All Files option on the View menu of the Windows NT Explorer.*

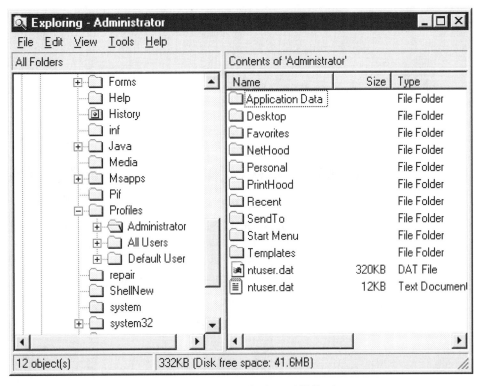

Figure 8-15.   A user profile folder in the Windows NT Explorer

The user profile folders contain the following shortcuts:

⇨ *Application Data.* Any application data or settings are stored in this folder.

⇨ *Desktop.* Shortcuts to files or folders are contained in the Desktop folder.

⇨ *Favorites.* Any shortcuts to programs, folders, or favorite locations on the Web are stored in this folder.

⇨ *NetHood.* This folder stores shortcuts to Network Neighborhood objects.

⇨ *Personal.* This folder contains program items.

⇨ *PrintHood.* Any network printer connections and settings are stored in this folder.

⇨ *Recent.* The list of files that appear on the Documents menu are stored as shortcuts in this folder.

⇨ *SendTo.* This contains shortcuts to document items.

⇨ *Start Menu.* Any items that appear on the Start menu are stored in this folder.

⇨ *Templates.* Any template items that are stored to disk by a user are contained in this folder.

SYSTEM POLICIES

What are system policies?

A *system policy* is a stored group of rules that control what a user can do and see on their computer when they log on to a Windows NT or Windows 95 workstation. A system policy can apply to a single user, a group of users, or all of the users in a domain.

In a system policy you can

⇨ Restrict network logon and access

⇨ Customize the desktop

⇨ Remove different options in the Control Panel

The two standard policies, Default Computer and Default User, control the options that apply to all computers in a domain or to all users.

You create a specific policy with custom options in the System Policy Editor. This utility lets you edit portions of the Windows NT Registry or edit system policy.

When I create a policy in Window NT, I see a set of options. Where do these policies come from?

Policies that you see in the System Policy Editor derive from template files in Windows NT. The two system policy template files that are used are WINNT.ADM and COMMON.ADM. Template files are a set of stored registry entries. You can modify a template file in the System Policy Editor, or create new template files.

I have restricted access to control panels, but the Control Panel icons still appear. Is there any way to make them disappear?

Although a system policy can restrict access to the control panel, it doesn't remove the icons from the user's view. To suppress the display of Control Panel icons, open the CONTROL.INI file and modify the [don't load] section.

I want to restrict usage by a user or on a computer on the network. How do I create a system policy for this?

The System Policy Editor (POLEDIT.EXE) is used by an administrator to create or change system policies.

To create a new policy:

1. Log on to the computer as an administrator.

2. Select the System Policy Editor from the Administrative Tools folder on the Programs Submenu of the Start menu.

3. Select the New Policy command from the File menu.

Two icons appear in the System Policy Editor window: Default Computer and Default User, as shown in Figure 8-16.

4. Select the Add User, Add Computer, or Add Group commands to add a policy.

5. Enter a name for the user, computer, or group in the Add User, Add Computer, or Add Group dialog box; then click the OK button.

6. Select the Exit command on the File menu to close the System Policy Editor.

The System Policy Editor will prompt you to save any changes that you make, if necessary.

When you place the System Policy Editor in policy mode to create and modify a system policy for the domain, you create or modify system policy files. These files take a .POL file extension. Changes you make for a specific user, group, or computer in the system policy are stored as an entry in the NTCONFIG.POL file.

You must save the policy file as the NTCONFIG.POL file in the NETLOGON share on the Primary Domain Controller (PDC) and have that file replicated to the Backup Domain Controller (BDC) before the policy is enforced when a user tries to log on.

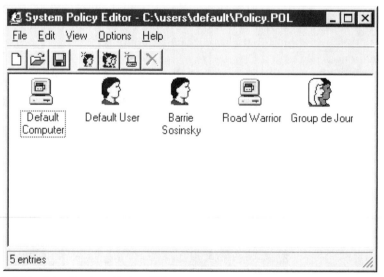

Figure 8-16.   The System Policy Editor

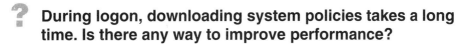

During logon, downloading system policies takes a long time. Is there any way to improve performance?

When you have a large number of users that log on to the network at the same time, you can experience delays if there are many different policies in the NETLOGON.POL file. If the clients accessing the policies are Windows 95 computers, enable load balancing. If the computers are Windows NT Workstations or Servers, enable manual updating and create system policy files on computers other than the domain controllers.

On a network, Windows 95 computers are able to download user policies at logon, but Windows NT users cannot. Why?

The system policy files that you create in the System Policy Editor for Windows 95 and Windows NT computers are not interoperable. You need to create a user policy for both types of computers in the CONFIG.POL and NTCONFIG.POL files to support a user logging onto the domain from either type of computer and to support both types of computers.

Why do group policies work on Windows NT computers, but not on Windows 95 clients?

In Windows NT, a group policy is installed by default using the System Policy Editor. For Windows 95 clients, a group policy must be installed locally in order to create and enforce those policies. Use the Add/Remove Programs control panel to add group policy support to a Windows 95 client.

I don't want the last logged-on user to appear in the Logon Information dialog box. How do I create a policy that suppresses this information?

By default, when a user presses CTRL-ALT-DEL, the Logon Information dialog box appears with the name of the person who last logged onto the system in the User Name text box. To suppress this display, change the Windows NT System\Logon\Do Not Display Last Logged on User Name option in the computer policy to off.

I want to use a local policy. Is it possible to have more than one system policy in a domain?

You can maintain more than one system policy in a domain. Since Windows NT searches the NTCONFIG.POL file on the domain controller when it validates a user logon, you need to change the Remote Update setting from automatic to manual in the computer policy section of the system policy in order to have the local policy enforced.

To set a manual Remote update:

1. Open the System Policy Editor on Windows NT Server.

2. Select the New Policy command from the File menu.

3. Double-click the Default Computer, and then click the plus sign next to the Network listing.

4. Open the System policies update setting, and then select the Remote update listing.

5. At the bottom of the screen, the Settings for Remote update dialog box appears.

6. Select the Manual (use specific path) listing in the Update mode list box.

7. Enter the path to the policy file (e.g. <path>\FILENAME.POL); then click the OK button.

8. Select the Save command from the File menu, and specify the computer for which you are changing the remote update setting in Network Neighborhood so that its name appears in the Save in box.

9. Type the filename for the system policy in the File name box; then click the Save button.

The file is saved by default in the root directory of the drive that contains the workstation's system files (systemroot). Whatever filename and path you use must be the same as the one you entered in the Path for Manual Update box.

？ Where are policy entries stored in the Windows NT Registry?

The various settings that you enforce for a system policy are stored in the Windows NT Registry in the HKEY_CURRENT_USER and HKEY_LOCAL_MACHINE keys. When you open the System Policy Editor in the registry mode, you expose various keys in this area of the Registry.

Changes that you make in the Windows NT Registry are updated and saved when you close the registry. You do not have to reboot your system or log off to have these changes take effect.

Tip: *Maintaining individual registry settings can be time-consuming and frustrating. Use a standard system policy for the domain and record individual settings as a separate policy entry for that user or computer in the NTCONFIG.POL file for the domain system policy using the System Policy Editor.*

To change the registry for a remote computer on the network, select the Connect command on the File menu of the System Policy Editor and specify the computer that you want to modify.

？ Why is the wallpaper that is part of a system policy not showing up on client computers?

The wallpaper bitmap file is not found in the path that is specified in the system policy file. There are some settings that require that the system policy refer to a component that is installed on the client locally. Create a copy of the wallpaper on the client computer and reference that copy.

Answer Topics!

Printing Issues @ a Glance

⇨ In Windows NT terminology, a "printer" refers to a component (queue, driver, etc.) that sends output to a print device, which is the actual hardware. Therefore, you can print to a fax, a file, or to an actual printer. You can **install a new printer** to be either a local printer or a network printer. You can also connect to an established printer that exists on your network. Printers can be both physical printing devices or logical printing devices in Windows NT.

⇨ You can **select and use printers** that are installed on your computer. A network printer must be shared by an Administrator or Power Users on the computer on which it is installed in order to allow other users to print to it. A printer share can be secured and audited in the same manner that a file or folder can be secured. One printer on your system is the default printer that is used to print to in an application session. You can specify a different printer as the target of your document.

⇨ You can control **printer properties** for a large number of settings in the Printer Properties dialog box. Additionally, you can find most printer settings stored as Registry entries in the HKEY_LOCAL_MACHINE\ SYSTEM\CurrentControlSet\Control\Print\Printers key.

⇨ **Fonts** are either stored in permanent memory in a printer or downloaded as soft fonts to the printer. If a font is missing, a printer will substitute another font. In some instances, a font may print incorrectly, or the document may not print at all due to a missing font. You can also embed fonts in a document to print them.

⇨ When you print a document, it is written as a temporary file on the print server and spooled to the printer's **print queue**. You have control over a printer's print queue if you manage or own the printer or the document.

⇨ The help system provides a utility to **troubleshoot** print problems. Since printing is a modular function in Windows NT, it is often possible to isolate print problems by working through the print process one step at a time. Several common problems are described in this chapter.

INSTALLING A NEW PRINTER

How does the printing process work?

The printing subsystem is modular and works in concert with several other systems in Windows NT to provide printing services. Printers can be either local printers attached to your computer or network printers attached to a print server. Unless a printer gets very heavy use and processes jobs rapidly, you may not find it necessary to actually dedicate a server to the purpose of being a print server.

When a printer is a local printer and a print job is specified by an application, data is sent to the Graphical Device Interface (GDI) for rendering into a print job in the printer language of the print device. This print job is passed to the spooler, which is a .DLL, and written as a temporary file to disk. The client side of the print spooler is WINSPOOL.DRV, and that driver makes a remote procedure call to the SPOOLSS.EXE server side of the spooler. When the printer is attached to the same computer, both files are located on the same computer. When the printer is attached to a Windows NT Workstation in a peer-to-peer relationship, those files are located on different computers.

SPOOLSS.EXE calls an API (Applications Programming Interface) that sends the print job to a router (SPOOLSS.DLL), which sends the print job to the computer with the local print device where the LOCALSPL.DLL library writes the file to disk as a spooled file. At this point, the printer is polled by LOCALSPL.DLL to determine if the spooled print job is capable of being processed by the printer, and altered if it is required.

The print job is then turned over to a separator page processor and despooled to the print monitor. The print device receives the print job and raster image processes it to a bitmap file or raster image, which is then sent to the print engine to output.

For network printers the scenario is similar, but there is a clearer separation of client request and server services. The routers—WINSPOOL.DRV, SPOOLSS.EXE, and SPOOLSS.DLL—are still the same, but a local print provider on the client LOCALSPL.DLL is matched to a remote print provider—WIN32SP.DLL (for Windows print servers) or NWPROVAU.DLL (for NetWare print servers)—on the server side. Similarly, print processors and print monitors use several different DLLs on the server side, each one required by a supported operating system.

How do I add a local printer to my computer?

The first step in adding a local printer is to attach the connecting parallel or serial port cable from your computer to your printer and turn the power on. Less frequently, a printer will require a specific add-in board or a SCSI cable connection. You should check with your printer's documentation to see what cables are required (some may not come in the box) and how they are connected.

Many printers come with an installation disk that contains a Setup or Install program for installing the required printer driver on your computer. These programs also install an icon for the printer in your Printers folder. You can certainly install your printer's software manually using the Add Printer Wizard, and there can be good reasons why this is desirable.

Note: *The printer drivers that come with the latest version of Windows NT are often the latest ones available. Frequently, the software is more up-to-date than what came in the box with your printer—which may have been manufactured several months prior to your purchase. If you are experiencing printer problems, you might want to check with the manufacturer to obtain the latest driver.*

To add a local printer to your Printers folder:

1. Select the <u>P</u>rinters command from the <u>S</u>ettings submenu of the Start menu.

2. Double-click on the Add Printer icon shown here.

3. In the first step of the Add Printer Wizard shown in Figure 9-1, verify that the <u>M</u>y Computer radio button is selected, and then click the <u>N</u>ext button.

4. Click on the checkbox next to the port the printer will connect to—usually the first parallel port, LPT1—in the Port selection list box shown in Figure 9-2.

5. Highlight the printer's company name in the <u>M</u>anufacturer list box, the model name in the <u>P</u>rinter list box as shown in Figure 9-3, and then click the <u>N</u>ext button.

6. If your printer is not listed, or you want to use the printer driver that came with your printer or that you downloaded from the Internet or a BBS, click the <u>H</u>ave Disk button and specify the appropriate printer driver file.

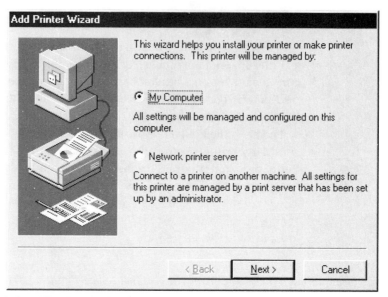

Figure 9-1.   The Printer Type dialog box

7. Enter the name of the printer as it will appear on your computer, and, for a second printer, whether this is the default printer, as shown in Figure 9-4; then click the Next button.

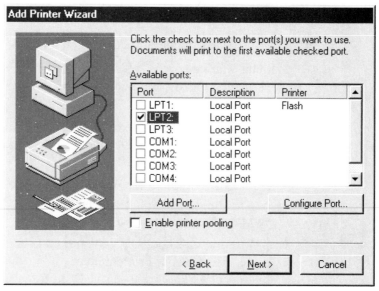

Figure 9-2.   The Port Selection step of the Add Printer Wizard

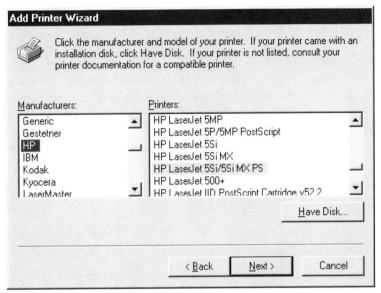

Figure 9-3.   Selecting a printer driver for a supported model

8. Click on the Shared radio button and enter a name in the Share Name text box to share your local printer with other computers on the network.

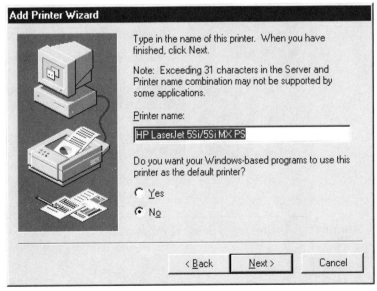

Figure 9-4.   The Name That Printer step of the Add Printer Wizard

9. Specify the operating systems that will print to your local shared printer and click the Next button, as shown in Figure 9-5.

Note: *Each operating system that you select installs a printer driver for that printer into your system. You will need the printer drivers supplied by each of the operating systems.*

10. Or click the Not Shared radio button to maintain this as a local printer that no other computer can access.

11. Click Yes to print a test page or No to bypass this step; then click the Finish button.

Tip: *It's a good idea to test-print a page at the end of your installation to check if your installation succeeded.*

Windows NT copies the appropriate printer driver files and places an icon for the printer you have created in your printer folder.

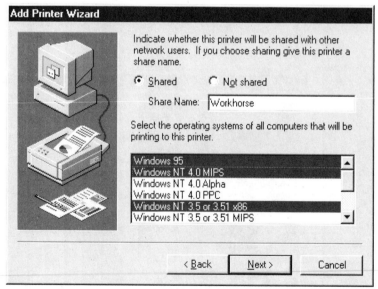

Figure 9-5.   Creating a Shared local printer

❓ How do I add a network printer to my computer?

A network printer must be installed prior to use:

⇨ The print device must be properly cabled and connected to the print server.

⇨ The printer must be installed as a local printer on the print server.

⇨ The printer must be shared and named, and appropriate permissions created.

When a printer is added to your network and shared so that you can use it, it doesn't automatically appear on your computer. You have to add the printer manually.

To add a network printer to your Printers folder:

1. Select the Printers command from the Settings submenu of the Start menu.

2. Double-click on the Add Printer icon shown earlier.

3. In the first step of the Add Printer Wizard shown in Figure 9-1, verify that the Network print server radio button is selected, and then click the Next button.

4. In the Connect to Printer dialog box shown in Figure 9-6, select the printer you wish to add from the domain and computer that will serve as the print server; then click the OK button.

Note: *The wizard will inform you if you need to install a printer driver for this computer locally, adding additional steps.*

5. Specify if you wish this printer to be the default printer, and then click the Finish button.

Tip: *You can also add a printer to your computer from the Network Neighborhood using the "point-and-print" method. Open the print server and locate the printer icon in Network Neighborhood; then put it into your print folder.*

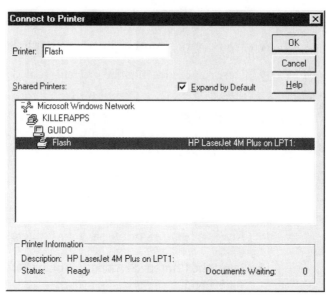

Figure 9-6.   The Connect to Printer dialog box

A printer no longer exists. How do I delete it?

To delete a printer:

1. Right-click on the printer's icon in the Printers folder and select the Delete command.

2. If you have appropriate permissions, Windows NT will post a confirming dialog box, and in some instances (for a local printer or a network printer with local printer driver files) ask you if you want to delete the files associated with the printer. Click on the Yes button.

Try as I might, I can't locate a printer driver for my printer. How do I emulate a print driver?

Your printer may emulate another popular printer model. It is not uncommon for printers to use print engines that accept output from popular printers like Epson dot-matrix printers or Hewlett-Packard LaserJets. This is particularly true of clone or off-brand printers. Check your printer's documentation, or ask the technical support line for this information when you talk with a representative of the company.

If all else fails, you might be able to get by for a while using the Generic text-only driver that ships with Windows NT. This will allow you to print only plain text, not graphics. Your printer should be set in the ASCII or ANSI text-only mode, which often involves a button or menu setting.

Note: *If your printer is a PostScript printer, the text-only mode is not available.*

Where can I find printer drivers?

These are the usual sources of printer drivers:

⇨ The Windows NT operating system distribution CD-ROM disks.

⇨ Microsoft's technical support line. You can contact Microsoft at (206) 882-8080. Their current printer driver library is on the NT Driver Library disk.

⇨ The Microsoft Web site. Use the search button to search for the keywords "NT driver," or search for the name of your particular model of printer.

⇨ CompuServe. Enter GO WINNT or GO WDL (Windows Driver Library) to access that area of the service.

⇨ The installation disks that come with your printer.

⇨ The printer manufacturer's BBS or Web site.

What sort of security options are available for a printer share?

If you click on the <u>P</u>ermissions button of the Security tab (see Figure 9-7) of the Printer Properties dialog box, you will see the Printer Permissions dialog box shown in Figure 9-8.

By default, a printer is assigned to allow access to Everyone and to allow queue management and configuration to an administrator, power user, or the owner of the print share. You assign rights or permissions to groups of users, not to individual user accounts.

The following access rights can be assigned:

⇨ *No Access.* A user with no access cannot print or modify the printer in any way.

⇨ *Print.* A user with print access can send jobs to the printer to print.

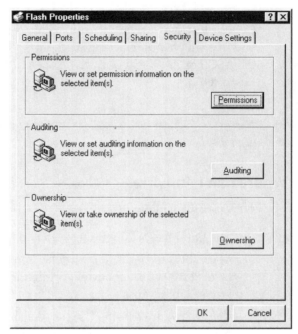

Figure 9-7.   The Security tab of the Printer Properties dialog box

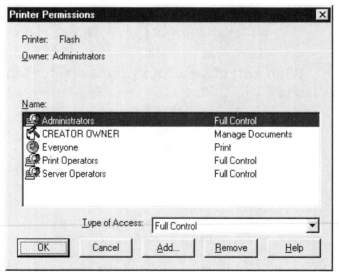

Figure 9-8.   The Printer Permissions dialog box

⇨ *Manage Documents.* This right allows a user to see and modify the print queue. This user can start, stop, pause, resume, and delete queued documents. These commands show up in the printer shortcut menu, and also in the print queue window. A user with Manage Document privileges can also change printer permissions and properties.

⇨ *Full Control.* A user with Full Control privileges can modify both the printer and any print jobs. This level of privilege also allows a user to delete a printer or remove it from network use.

 Warning: *Make sure that at least one group has Full Control privileges, or you will not be able to change future printer permissions without an administrator taking ownership of the printer share. To take ownership, an administrator needs to click on the Ownership button on the Security tab of the Printer Properties dialog box.*

As with other permissions, any user of two or more groups is assigned the highest-level access rights from any of the groups they belong to. However, if a user belongs to a group with No Access, that user has *no access* to the printer regardless of his or her other permissions.

I've installed a serial port printer and it doesn't seem to work properly. What could be wrong?

The first thing you should check is that you didn't assign your serial printer to the wrong port. Since any serial device is likely to be attached to the serial port it's assigned to, check to see if the label for the serial port you connected your printer to is the one you assigned in the Add Printer Wizard.

Serial port printers require that you configure their settings in the Configure Port dialog box (shown below) that opens when you click the button of that name in the Add Printer Wizard. Make sure that you have assigned the appropriate communication settings—baud rate, data bits, parity, start and stop bit, and flow control—that your printer requires. These settings should be listed in your printer's manual. Failure to configure these settings properly may result in your printer operating too slowly, improperly processing print jobs, or not working at all.

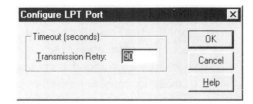

 I've installed a local printer, but I want other people to be able to use it. How do I share a printer?

To share a printer:

1. Select the Printers command from the Settings submenu of the Start menu.

2. Right-click on the printer icon and select the Properties or Sharing command from the shortcut menu, as shown here:

 Note: This option will only be available to you if you have the correct permissions. By default, only members of the Administrators and Power Users groups may share a printer.

Tip: As a shortcut, press the ALT-ENTER *key to open the Properties dialog box.*

3. If you selected the Properties command, click on the Sharing tab in the Properties dialog box, as shown in Figure 9-9.

4. Click on the Shared radio button and enter the share name into the Share Name text box.

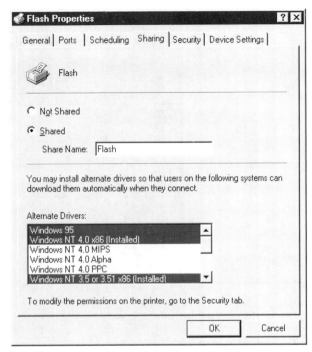

Figure 9-9.   The Sharing tab of the Printer Properties dialog box

5. Click on the General tab and enter a comment that describes the printer in the Comment text box, as shown in Figure 9-10.

6. In a large or distributed network, enter a description into the Location text box.

7. If you don't want Everyone sharing your printer, click on the Security tab (see Figure 9-7) and then click on the Permissions button to set the share access permissions. This feature was described for file and folder shares in Chapter 5, "Setting File and Directory Security."

Flash

8. Click on the OK button, and the printer icon turns into a printer with a hand beneath it, as shown here.

To disable a printer share, click on the Not Shared radio button on the Sharing tab of the Printer Properties dialog box.

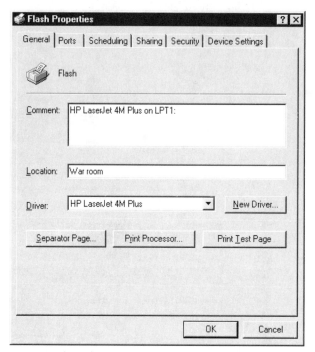

Figure 9-10. The General tab of the Printer Properties dialog box

? What is a valid printer share name?

If you have MS-DOS clients on the network, you should use the DOS file-naming convention to name your printer shares. The name can be up to 12 characters long and mustn't contain spaces or any special characters:

```
? * # | \ / = > < %
```

SELECTING AND USING PRINTERS

? I know that a printer exists on the network, but I can't see it on my computer. Why is that?

You may not be able to view a printer on your computer if you haven't been granted specific permission to access that printer. Printers are a share resource, and only an Administrator or Power User can grant you the right to use a printer.

I want to use a particular printer most of the time. How do I set a default printer?

To set a default printer:

1. Select the <u>P</u>rinters command from the <u>S</u>ettings submenu on the Start menu.

2. Right-click on the printer you wish to set as the default printer and select the Set As De<u>f</u>ault command from the shortcut menu.

If that printer is the default printer, a check mark appears next to the Set As De<u>f</u>ault command.

When a printer is the default printer, it is the one automatically chosen whenever an application starts a session. If you go to the Print Setup dialog box of any application and change the printer that is used, then the new printer you selected is used for the remainder of the session.

Note: Sometimes the Print Setup command is called the Printer Setup command, and normally it is found on the File menu. In many instances, an application may not have a Print Setup command. Try looking in the Print command's dialog box for a drop-down list of printers to select from.

How can I drag-and-drop print a document?

You can always print a document from within an application. However, you can drag-and-drop a document or multiple selected documents from your Desktop or within a folder of the Windows NT Explorer onto the icon for a printer or a shortcut to that printer and have the printer print your document. If the document has a registered file extension, the associated application loads, processes the document, spools it to the queue, and closes.

If the file extension of the document you attempt to drag-and-drop print isn't associated on your computer with a particular application, you will receive an error message.

Some simple programs like Notepad do not allow you to print to a printer that is not the default. If you attempt to drag-and-drop a Notepad document onto another printer, Windows NT will ask you if you want to make that printer the default printer.

Tip: *Most programs will allow their documents to print using the Print command on the document's shortcut menu. If you select the Print command, the document is printed to the default printer.*

How do I share a printer with some network users but hide it from the rest?

If you name your printer share with an ending dollar sign character (e.g., *printer sharename$*), the printer does not show up in the Connect To Printer dialog box (see Figure 9-6) that a user sees when creating a network printer using the Add Printer Wizard. The hidden share will also not appear when you browse network resources in Windows NT Explorer. A user who knows that this printer exists, and knows the name, can enter the path and the printer share name in the dialog box and connect to that printer.

How do I print-to-disk, and why would I want to?

When you print a file to disk, you create a file that contains not only the text but any graphics, formatting, control codes, margins, page breaks, and other formatting that a printer would require.

Note: *If you wish to print to disk only text, change the printer driver to the Generic/Text Only driver for that printer.*

Printing to disk might allow a database to output a file that can be used by another application, or allow a program to create a graphic that a PostScript page layout program can use. You can also use the print-to-disk feature to transport a print job to a service bureau, send it over the Internet, or print it at a later time even when you don't have the creator application in hand.

To print to disk:

1. Right-click on a printer icon in the Printers folder and select the Properties command.

2. Click on the Details tab.

3. In the Under Print to Following Port list box, select the File option.

4. Click the OK button.

You will notice that the printer's icon now contains a disk icon on it. When you print a file from a program, a Print to File dialog box appears that asks you to name and locate the print file. Print-to-disk files take the PRN file extension.

   Tip: *To print an EPS file, direct your print output to a printer that uses a PostScript driver, or create an imaginary printer that uses one. Make sure you give the file an EPS file extension.*

How do I share a printer with different groups of people on a network in different ways?

While you may assign different users or groups different levels of access to the same shared printer, you may gain additional flexibility by creating two different share names for the same printer on the print server. This also lets you:

⇨ Assign each group different printing priorities

⇨ Allow access to the printer at different hours for each group

⇨ Have one printer share name assigned for network use and another for local use

I have two types of print output that I use on a printer. Is there a quick way of switching between them?

When you define a printer and install a driver, you are creating a virtual printing device on your computer. You can create additional printer definitions for the same printer that print out in different ways. For example, if you use two printer trays, black and white or color, landscape or portrait mode, etc., you can specify these settings in different printer definitions. Just switch between the definitions to switch the settings.

I live on a network, and I don't have a printer attached to my computer. How do I find out what printers I can use?

Printers that are available for you to use are found in the Printers folder. To view available printers:

1. Select the Printers command from the Settings submenu on the Start menu.

2. Right-click on a printer and select the Properties command from the shortcut menu.

3. The General tab of the Printer Properties dialog box, shown earlier in Figure 9-10, shows you not only the assigned name, but printer type, location, and the installed driver.

SETTING PRINTER PROPERTIES

My printer has two or more ports. Can I use additional ports at the same time?

Some printers come with connections for multiple ports. To add more ports:

1. Right-click on the printer icon in the Printer folder and select the Properties command from the shortcut menu.

2. Click on the Ports tab, as shown in Figure 9-11.

3. Double-click on the additional port you wish to add.

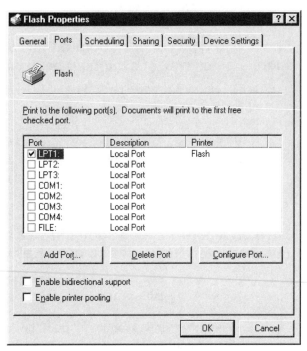

Figure 9-11.   The Ports tab of the Printer Properties dialog box

When you print to a printer with multiple ports, several print jobs can be queued at once.

If you don't see the port you require in the Ports list box, click the Add Port button and select the port from the Printer Ports dialog box shown here:

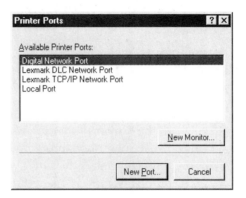

How do I delete a port, or recover a deleted port?

Deleting a port is easy; recovering a port is hard. Make sure that you really want to delete a port before you do so.

To delete a port:

1. Select the port in the Ports tab of the Printer Properties dialog box (see Figure 9-11).

2. Click the Delete Port button.

You will need to go into the Registry to recover a deleted port. In that case, do the following:

1. Open the Registry Editor program (REGEDIT.EXE), which is typically located in the <root>\WINNT folder.

2. Open the HKEY_LOCAL_MACHINE in the Local Machine hive and find the following subkey:

   `Software\Microsoft\Windows NT\CurrentVersion\Ports`

3. Select the Add Value command from the Edit menu.

4. Enter the printer port in the Value Name text box, retain the default value in the Data text box (REG_SZ), and then click the OK button.

5. Enter the value in the String text box that corresponds to the port you entered (see below for value).

6. Exit the Registry Editor.

When you log back onto Windows NT, the port should reappear. Table 9-1 shows which ports take which string values for the REG_SZ data type.

? Where do I change the printer settings for a printer that I manage or own?

If you right-click on a Printer and select the Properties command, you will open the Printer Properties dialog box. The many tabs of this dialog box are described throughout this chapter. Settings you make in this dialog box take effect after you restart your system.

Additionally, most of the settings that apply to your printers are stored in the Windows NT Registry in the following key:

```
HKEY_LOCAL_MACHINE\SYSTEM\CurrentControlSet\Control\
Print\Printers
```

 Note: *Be careful when you make changes to the Registry. If you make a mistake, you may have to reinstall the operating system to reestablish your correct settings.*

Table 9-1.   Assigning string values for ports

Port Name	String Value
LPT1	none
LPT2	none
LPT3	none
COM1	9600,n,8,1
COM2	9600,n,8,1
COM3	9600,n,8,1
COM4	9600,n,8,1
FILE	none

WORKING WITH FONTS

 ## How do I install downloadable fonts?

Downloadable fonts are soft fonts that can be sent to a printer's memory for use. Doing so saves processing time.

To install downloadable or soft fonts to a printer:

1. Right-click on the printer and select the Properties command from the shortcut menu.

2. Click on the Device Settings tab as shown in Figure 9-12.

3. Click on Soft Fonts.

4. Click the Soft Fonts button.

5. Enter the path to the fonts disk, and click the Open button.

6. Close the dialog boxes using the OK buttons.

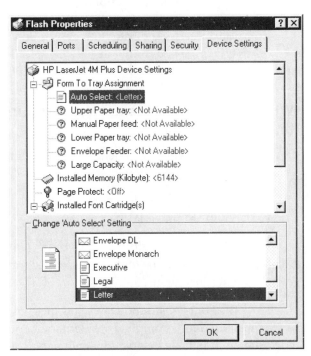

Figure 9-12.   The Device Settings tab of the Printer Properties dialog box

How can I embed fonts in a document in order to print that document on a computer that doesn't have these fonts?

You specify that fonts are embedded in a document within the application that you use to create the document. Typically these options are found in the Save Options for that document or for the application itself. Microsoft Word, for example, lets you specify embedded fonts on the Save tab of the Options dialog box that you open from the Tools menu.

Many applications let you choose from either embedding an entire font or character set or embedding only the characters that you have used in the document. Embedding fonts will make your documents much larger, so be sure you need this feature before you use it.

Why do my fonts look bad, or why won't my printer print my document's text at all?

If you used a raster font, it requires the correct size description in order to print properly. If you used an outline font, your printer may not support that font description, or the software necessary to render the font may not have been installed properly. PostScript fonts require separate screen and printer font descriptions and will not print properly if the latter is not installed. Typically, though, you get font substitution for a missing print font description.

When I print a document, I get font substitution. Why is that?

If the fonts in your document aren't soft fonts or aren't downloadable to the printer, font substitution can occur. To prevent this from happening:

⇨   Use TrueType or PostScript fonts.

⇨   Install font cartridges on the printer.

⇨   Or download the fonts to the printer's memory before printing your document.

The Font Substitution table specifies which printer font is to be substituted for a computer-resident font. You can edit the font substitution table by doing the following:

1. Right-click on a printer and select the Properties command from the shortcut menu.

2. Click on the Device Settings tab and double-click on the Font Substitution Table.

3. Click on a TrueType font in the table, and then click to select the substitution font.

4. Or click Download as Soft Font from the Change Setting list.

5. Click OK.

WORKING WITH THE PRINT QUEUE

 I want to know who has used my printer. How do I audit printer usage?

To turn on auditing of a printer share:

1. Enable File and Object Access auditing in the User Manager.

2. Enable printer auditing for a specific printer share: open the Security tab of the Printer Properties dialog box and click the auditing button, as shown in Figure 9-7.

3. In the Printer Auditing dialog box shown in Figure 9-13, click the Add button.

4. In the Add Users and Groups dialog box, select a group or user to be audited. (When in doubt, specify Everyone.)

5. Click the OK button to return to the Printer Auditing dialog box.

6. Select a user or group and click on the checkboxes in the Events to Audit section to track events your wish to log for that user and group.

7. Click the OK button.

Use the Event Viewer utility in the Administrative Tools folder to view logged events.

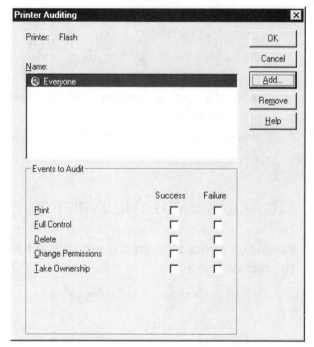

Figure 9-13.   The Printer Auditing dialog box

? How do I change the location of my spooled documents?

The default location of spooled files is %WINNT\System32\
Spool\Printer. A shadow file (SHD) is also written to this location.
To change the location of spooled documents:

1. Create a new spool directory.

2. Select the Printers command from the Settings menu of the Start
   menu.

3. Select the Server Properties command from the File menu.

4. Click on the Advanced tab, and then enter the location of the
   spool file directory

5. Click the OK button.

You can enable event logging to your spooler by adding a check
mark to the Enable spooler event logging checkbox on the Advanced tab.

You may want to create the spool folder on an NTFS volume and set security for this folder.

If you want to change the spooled location for one printer only, you can change the Registry setting found at:

```
HKEY_LOCAL_MACHINE\SYSTEM\CurrentControlSet\Control\
Print\Printers
```

Find the key for the printer you wish to modify, and then add a new SpoolDirectory value that points to the path you wish.

? I want to see what print jobs are pending. How do I open the print queue?

When you print to a printer, spooled jobs are placed in the print queue. These are temporary files written to disk. A printer icon appears in the Status area (also called the System Tray) of the Taskbar. The two easiest ways to open and view a print queue are to:

⇨ Double-click on the printer icon in the status bar to see all pending jobs

⇨ Double-click on the icon of a specific printer in the printer folder to see jobs sent to that particular printer

You must have the privilege of Manage Documents or greater to be able to open the print queue window and change the queue.

? How do I print directly to the printer and avoid having my print job spooled?

You can print directly to a printer from your application by turning off the print spooling feature. Before you print, open the Scheduling tab of the Printer Properties dialog box (see Figure 9-14) and select the Print directly to the printer radio button. When the printer next becomes available, your document prints.

Until your document finishes printing you will not be able to use the application that originates the print job. You can task switch to another application and continue working until your printing application becomes available.

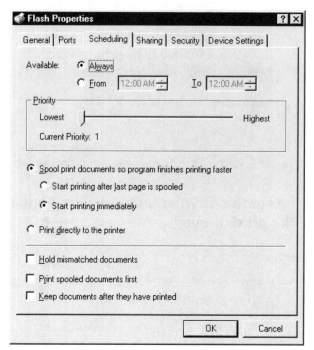

Figure 9-14.   The Scheduling tab of the Printer Properties dialog box

 A particular printer on the network gets very heavy use and is often busy. Is there a way to pool print jobs among a group of printers?

Printer pooling allows you to specify that two or more *identical* printer devices can be used for the same print queue. Creating a pool essentially creates one logical printer, printing the job to the first available printer and managing a single print queue.

To use printer pooling:

1. Select the Printers command from the Settings submenu of the Start menu.

2. Right-click on a printer icon and select the Properties command.

3. Click on the Ports tab (see Figure 9-11) and select the logical printer that you wish to print to.

4. Click on the Enable Print Pooling checkbox, and then close the Printer Properties dialog box.

To set up a logical printer, you can use the Add Printer Wizard to add a printer to a port and use the same share name. Although the printers need to be identical, the ports do not. You can mix and match local, serial, and parallel ports in the same logical printer.

What can I do with queued documents in the print queue window?

If you have access to the print queue window, you can

⇨ Delete print jobs by selecting them and pressing the DEL key

⇨ Move them around in the print order by clicking and dragging them up or down

⇨ Pause or resume printing and purge all print jobs with commands on the Printer menu

⇨ Pause or cancel a print job by selecting the Pause Printing or Cancel Printing command from that document's shortcut menu

⇨ Use the Document Default command to control the settings of a default document printed to that printer

⇨ Make the printer the default printer

Many of these commands are found on the shortcut menu of the printer involved.

 Note: *Use the* F5 *key to refresh the printer queue window.*

If you pause printing or shut down the computer, your spooled documents are still stored on disk. They will print when the printer becomes available again.

In the print queue, one of my documents is labeled Remote Downlevel Document. What does that mean?

Any client that doesn't support Microsoft Remote Procedure Call (RPC) will not be able to transmit a document name. This is most often true of a print job originating from a DOS application, but it can also come from a workstation that is running Windows for Workgroups, LAN Manager, UNIX, or NetWare.

? I have a large print job that I want to schedule for after-hours. How do I do that?

There is no way to specify when a particular job will print on a printer. However, you can control when a printer is available for printing.

To set availability times:

1. Click on the printer icon in the Printers folder and press ALT-ENTER to open the Printer Properties dialog box.

2. Click on the Scheduling tab of the Printer Properties dialog box, as shown in Figure 9-14.

3. Click on the From radio button in the Available section; then enter the starting and ending times that the printer is available.

Any print job that is printed off-hours is left in the print queue until the printer becomes available.

 Tip: *If you have two different named printer shares for the same printer, you can let one printer be always available and restrict the availability of the second.*

? Why can't I view the print queue for a network printer?

Only users with appropriate privileges can view a network printer's print queue. Typically, an administrator, power user, or the person who created the printer and shared it are allowed this privilege. These people can open the print queue and start, stop, or pause printing, or delete specific print jobs in the queue.

? My printer has stopped working and the documents in the print queue show a status of work offline. What does that mean?

When you see the words "User Intervention Required - Work Offline" in the Status column of a networked printer's print queue, printing has stopped due to a printer error. The error can be as simple as an empty paper tray or a printer that has its power turned off; or it can be more serious. When you open the print queue window, you should see an error message that suggests the nature of the problem. After you fix it, select the Work Offline command in the Printer menu to remove the check mark. Printing should begin again.

TROUBLESHOOTING PRINT PROBLEMS

 ### How do I get help troubleshooting printing problems?

Windows NT comes with an interactive Print Troubleshooter that is part of the online help system.

To access the Print Troubleshooter:

1. Select the Help command from the Start menu.

2. Click on the Index tab and enter the keyword **troubleshooting** into the "1 Type the first few letters…" text box. Figure 9-15 shows you this topic in the Help system.

3. Double-click on the problem type and follow the instructions in the Help system.

When I print to a PostScript printer, I get an out-of-memory error. How can I fix this?

On the Device Settings tab of a printer's Printer Properties dialog box, double-click on the Available PostScript memory and enter a larger value into the Change Settings box.

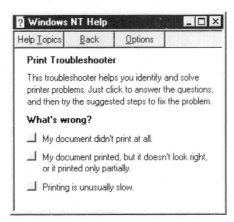

Figure 9-15.   The Print Troubleshooter topic in the Help system

? My printer is printing, but not correctly. How do I fix that?

A whole host of problems ranging from random characters to dropped pages and other general flakiness can be cured by turning a printer off and on again. This causes the printer to reset, clears its memory, and runs through all of the diagnostics. This simple act solves many unknown errors for a printer that is known to be generally functioning correctly.

If you're experiencing an application problem, you can diagnose it by printing a simple text file from an application like Notepad.

? My printer is powered on, but doesn't print. What's happening?

Most printers have a Printer Online button that allows you to leave the printer powered on but turn off printing to perform some action like changing a paper tray. Make sure that the Printer Online button is on.

? My serial printer has stopped printing and I see a message that the "Printer is Out of Paper." What is wrong?

Serial printers don't come with status indicators that show up on your computer, although some come with status lights on the printer itself. Typically, the following things can be wrong when this message appears:

⇨ The message is accurate and the paper tray is empty.

⇨ The printer has gone offline and needs to be put back online.

⇨ The printer is switched off.

⇨ A cable connecting the printer to the print server or local computer has gotten disconnected or malfunctioned.

10 Answers!

Multimedia Support

Answer Topics!

Multimedia Support
@ a Glance

⇨ Windows NT lets you **install** one or more sound boards into your computer. You will require a sound board to play MIDI or Wave files and to play music back on your system.

⇨ Windows NT will autoplay a **CD-ROM**, either playing music or launching a program. You can have multiple CD-ROM drives, map them to different volumes, and set a default device in Windows NT.

⇨ If you want to improve video performance, see more colors, and go to higher resolutions, **install a new video board**. You use the Display Properties dialog box to start the installation process and to change the display characteristics of your monitor.

⇨ Windows NT comes with several **multimedia applets** that let you record and play back sounds and video files. Some of these applets serve as the default players that appear when you double-click on AVI, WAV, MIDI, and other multimedia file types.

⇨ You can assign .WAV sounds to different system events, and save a collection of sound assignments to a scheme. Windows comes with different audio and video codecs for compressing and decompressing files for recording and playback. You can add more codecs as required. Use the Sound Recorder applet to record sounds, and the Media Player to play back both **sound and video** files.

INSTALLING AND CONFIGURING SOUND BOARDS

How can I quickly control audio levels and properties?

Most people know that if you click the Speaker icon in the Status bar on the right side of the Taskbar the pop-up sound-level dialog box shown here appears. You can use that dialog box not only to adjust the sound level, but also to mute your computer's sound output.

However, if you right-click the Speaker icon, and select the
Volume Controls command from the context menu (shown here), you
open the more complete Volume Control applet shown in Figure 10-1.
This applet lets you adjust volumes for CD Audio, Synthesizer, and
other output channels, as well as adjust their balances. The Adjust
Audio Properties command on the shortcut menu also offers you a
handy method for opening the Audio Properties dialog box shown
in Figure 10-2.

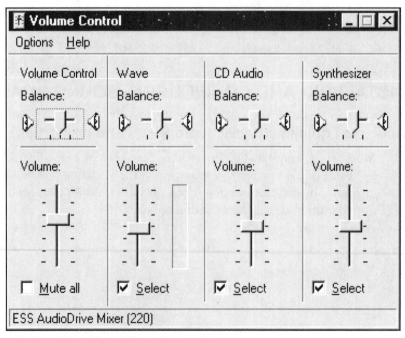

Figure 10-1.   The Volume Control applet

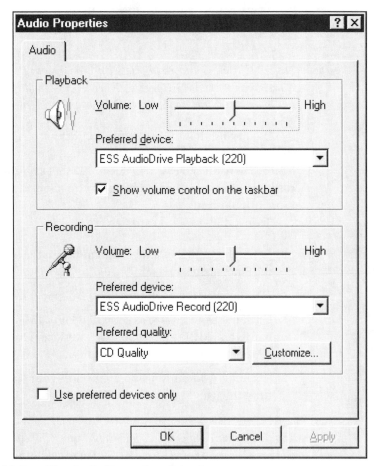

Figure 10-2.   The Audio Properties dialog box

❓ How do I install a sound board in my computer?

When you purchase a sound board compatible with Windows NT, the first step is to determine the appropriate settings required by that card. If those settings don't conflict with other cards in your system, you can install the card directly and continue with the software installation of the sound driver.

Typical settings for the popular Sound Blaster card are

⇨ IRQ 5

⇨ Base I/O Address: 220 and 330

⇨ DMA (Direct Memory Access) channels: 1 and 5

Many sound cards use these settings to emulate the Sound Blaster boards.

 Note: *Many network interface cards may want to use IRQ 5 as a setting. Make sure that your NIC uses a higher IRQ as an alternative. Many NICs, like Ethernet boards, will offer IRQ 11 as a secondary setting.*

If you find that these settings conflict with another card in your system, either change that card or change the setting for the sound board. There are several I/O addresses that you can use for a sound card, and this is rarely a problem. If you have an IRQ conflict, that is more troublesome.

To install the sound card driver:

1. Select the Control Panel command from the Settings submenu on the Start menu.

2. Double-click the Multimedia control panel icon.

3. Click the Devices tab, as shown in Figure 10-3. This tab lists the hardware, MCI (Media Control Interface) Drivers, and any supported audio/video decompression that are installed.

4. Click the <u>A</u>dd button, and then select your sound board's driver from the list.

 Tip: *If your copy of the Windows NT operating system is current and you have chosen a popular sound board, you will want to use the driver that comes with Windows NT. Otherwise, you will need to obtain the driver from your sound card vendor.*

5. Confirm the location of the operating system files, and then click the OK button. Windows NT copies the required sound driver file to your system.

6. Enter the two Base I/O addresses, the IRQ, and the two DMA channels into the dialog boxes that appear.

NT will ask to reboot your system and activate your sound board. In order to test your sound board, you will need to have either a speaker attached to the line out output jack, or a set of headphones. You should hear the Windows startup sound when the computer boots into Windows.

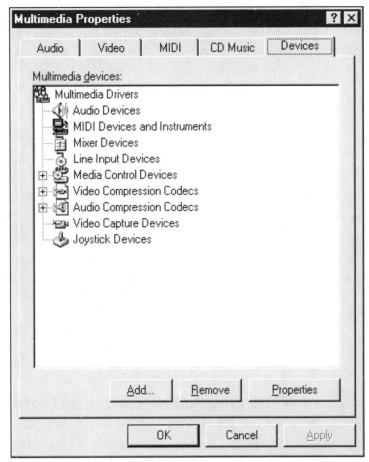

Figure 10-3.   The Devices tab of the Multimedia Properties dialog box

This startup sound tests the wave audio capability of your sound board, but doesn't test its MIDI capabilities. To finish testing your sound board, locate a MIDI sound file (.MID) on your computer and double-click on it. Examples are found in the WINNT folder, as well as many other places. Many games install these files. When you double-click on a .MID file, it runs within the Media Player applet.

? Windows 95 supports Plug-and-Play, but Windows NT 4 doesn't. What's the story?

Plug-and-Play or PnP is a module of the Windows operating system that auto-detects hardware and configures your system based on what it finds. The system works with your computer's BIOS to determine what I/O resources are required, and what can be addressed. In general, PnP has solved many configuration problems, and created a few new ones.

Three things must be true in order for PnP to work properly:

⇨ The operating system must support PnP

⇨ Your computer's BIOS must be PnP compatible

⇨ The devices being added to your system must conform to the PnP specification

Windows NT is expected to add full PnP support in version 5, due out in early to mid-1998. Most computers manufactured for Windows since 1995 have a BIOS that is PnP compatible—or can be upgraded to one that can. The same is true for most peripheral devices, expansion cards, and add-in boards that you probably purchased since 1995. Often these devices will advertise PnP compatibility on the box.

If you are installing a PnP device into Windows NT 4, you may want to disable the PnP functionality. Some devices will let you do this by changing a jumper switch or by running a software setup program. PnP may cause installation problems in non-PnP computers.

I don't hear the startup sound when I open Windows. What could be wrong?

The simplest explanation is that you forgot to turn your speakers on, or plug them into your sound board. Watch for the A/B plug on the rear of the speakers as some people plug one speaker into the B channel when it isn't even active. Assuming that your hardware is properly set up, you should then check that you turned the volume up both on the speakers themselves and in Windows. Click on the Speaker icon in the Status section of the Taskbar and check that you haven't enabled the Mute checkbox. Little things mean a lot.

If you have just installed a sound board or another piece of equipment and suspect a possible hardware conflict, you should check your hardware settings. Use the following procedure:

1. Double-click the Multimedia control panel icon.

2. Click the Devices tab, and then double-click the Audio Devices icon.

3. Check that the correct sound driver for your sound card is listed, and reinstall the sound card driver if it is incorrect.

4. Right-click on the sound card driver and select the Properties command from the shortcut menu.

5. Click the Settings button and check the values for the I/O addresses in the Settings dialog box. Change any incorrect settings there.

6. Close the Multimedia control panel and reboot your system.

If all of the settings in software were correct, you may need to check your sound board hardware. Check to see that the card is still seated properly in the expansion slot, and that any jumpers or DIP switches are set properly. If that still doesn't work, try the card on another computer, or swap in another known working sound card to determine if the sound card itself is defective.

RUNNING CD-ROMS

 What determines if a CD-ROM autoplays or not?

Windows looks for a file called AUTORUN.BAT, which contains the instructions on how to launch the program(s) on the CD that is to be executed. If the CD is an audio CD, Windows detects that and will run the CD Player applet (shown here) automatically.

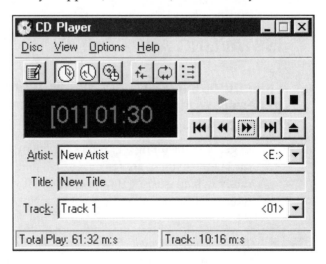

Which is a better purchase: a CD-ROM attached to my floppy disk controller or one that is attached to a SCSI chain?

As a general rule, a SCSI CD-ROM drive will be faster, easier to configure, and more trouble free than one that is attached to the floppy disk controller of your computer. A SCSI CD-ROM will also be somewhat more expensive than its floppy disk-based counterpart.

If you don't have a SCSI controller on your computer, you will need to purchase either an add-in board like an Adaptec controller to establish a SCSI chain, or a CD-ROM drive that comes with its own controller.

You can daisy-chain up to seven devices: hard drives, scanners, and CD-ROM drives on a SCSI chain. Windows NT shows a preference for SCSI hard drives, and will attempt to boot from one if it detects its existence.

 My CD-ROM drive and my headphones don't have a headphone volume control. Is there any way to control the sound level of CD output in my headphones?

Open the CD Music tab of the Multimedia Properties control panel shown in Figure 10-4, and move the Headphone slider left or right. If you have multiple CD-ROM drives installed on your computer, you will first need to select the drive letter for the CD-ROM drive that you wish to control.

INSTALLING AND CONFIGURING VIDEO BOARDS

 I just purchased a bigger, faster, more colorful, and generally wonderful video board. How do I install a graphics card?

In general, installing a graphics card is easier than installing a sound card because there are fewer settings that you need to adjust. Also, rarely will an existing device or one that you plan to add conflict with the default settings for the great majority of video boards.

 Tip: *Upgrading your video board is one of the best performance enhancements that you can buy for your computer.*

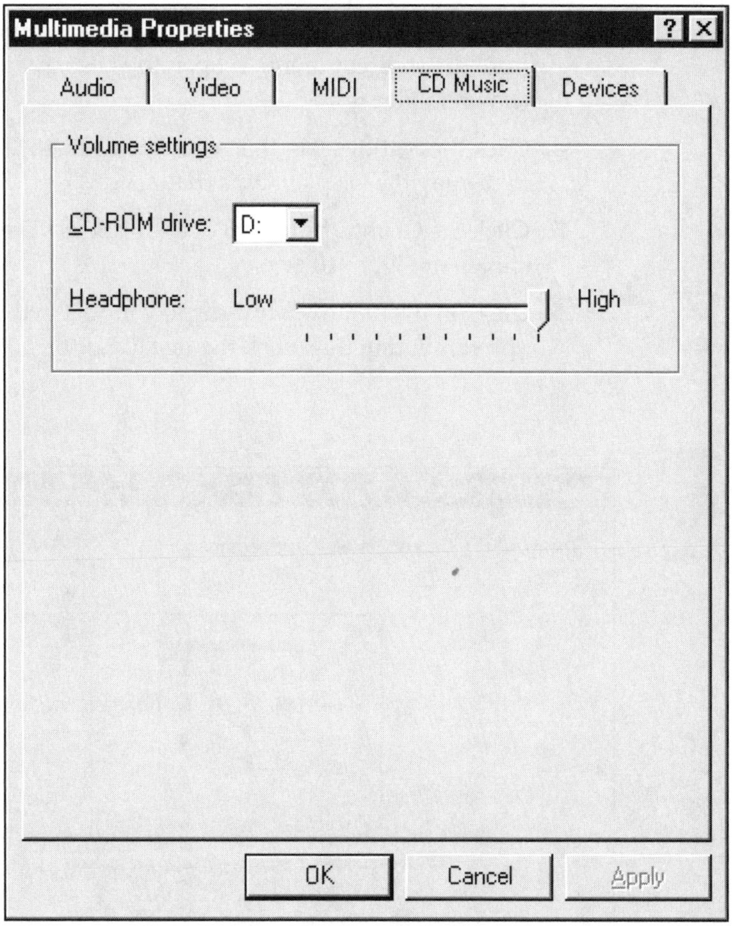

Figure 10-4.   The CD Music tab of the Multimedia Properties control panel

In general, your video drivers that worked with Windows NT 3.5*x* will continue to work with Windows NT 4. Still, it's a good idea to get updated NT drivers before you begin the installation of any video board that isn't listed in the Select Device dialog box.

To install a graphics board:

1. Install the video board into your computer and plug your display device into it.

2. Boot Windows NT and select the generic VGA boot mode. Almost any video board should be able to work in this mode.

3. Right-click on the Desktop and select the Properties command from the shortcut menu to open the Display Properties dialog box shown in Figure 10-5.

4. Click the Settings tab; then click the Change Display Type button to display the Display Type dialog box.

5. Click the Change button to open the Select Device dialog box shown in Figure 10-6.

6. Click on the name of your display model in the Models list box if you can find it; then click the Install button.

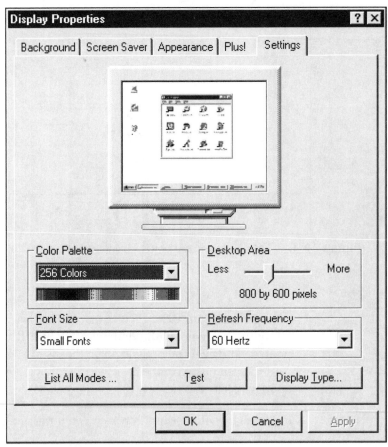

Figure 10-5.   The Display Properties dialog box

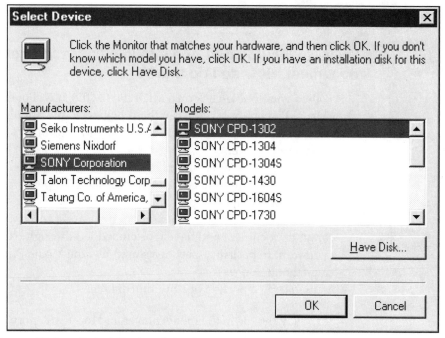

Figure 10-6.   Select Device dialog box

7. Or, if you can't find the model, click the Other button and supply the installation disk that came with your display or tell Windows NT where the device driver file is located. Make sure that you specify the Windows NT driver file, and not another operating system.

   If you use the drivers on the Windows NT Setup disk, NT will detect the model of the graphics board and install the appropriate driver automatically after you confirm the selection. Generally, Windows NT does a good job in this area.

8. Click the OK button and Windows copies the driver files to your hard drive and displays the message "Driver Installation was Successful."

9. Reboot your system.

WORKING WITH MULTIMEDIA APPLETS

 ### I want to include part of a multimedia file in another document. How do I do this?

When you double-click on a MIDI file (.MID), it will open in the Media Player applet. You can then click the Play button to play the sound. The Media Player will also play and control AVI files. It is one very useful critter.

You can also open and play WAV files using the Media Player, although the Sound Recorder is the applet that opens when you double-click that file type.

You probably know that you can drag-and-drop a sound file into another document and have it be embedded through OLE there. If you want to paste just part of a sound file, the Media Player provides a method to do so.

To copy a portion of a multimedia file:

1. Play the file in the media player and locate the portion that you wish to copy.

2. Drag the slider to a position in the file.

3. Click the Start Selection button to mark the beginning of the range you will select.

4. Click the End Selection button to mark the end of the range.

5. If you make a mistake, select the Selection command from the Edit menu and choose None. Or enter the start and end times in the Set Selection dialog box (shown here) directly.

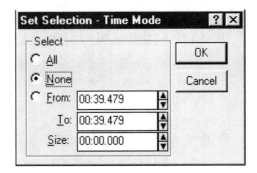

6. Select the Options command and click on the options that you
   wish the Media Clip OLE object to have in the Options dialog box,
   as shown here.

7. Select the Copy Object command from the Edit menu to copy
   that portion of the file to the Clipboard.

8. Go to the document that you wish to copy into and paste
   the object.

When you paste a media object into a document, you can
right-click on that object and select the Edit Media Clip command to
view the Media Player controls within that document.

? Is there a shortcut to setting the playback size of an AVI file in the Media Player applet?

You can double, triple, or quadruple the playback size of an AVI file when it plays in the Media Player if you hold down CTRL-2, CTRL-3, or CTRL-4 before you click the Play button.

? Where are all of the multimedia applets located?

Open the Multimedia folder in the Accessories folder on the Programs submenu of the Start menu to view the different applets that are installed with Windows NT. Figure 10-7 shows you the full suite of these tools. If your NT computer doesn't contain this folder or contains some but not all of these choices, open the Add/Remove

Figure 10-7.   The Multimedia folder on the Start menu

Programs control panel and click the NT Setup tab. Install the missing Multimedia components from there.

Keep in mind that some of these applets are players that are activated when you open a multimedia file of some kind. They are registered for WAV, AVI, and other standard file types when you install them. You can change that registration as you would any file type association.

WORKING WITH SOUND AND VIDEO FILES

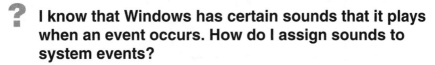

I know that Windows has certain sounds that it plays when an event occurs. How do I assign sounds to system events?

Windows NT allows you to assign sounds in the form of WAV files to a variety of system events. It's easy to do, and there is a variety of system events that aren't normally assigned by default. You can either download WAV files from online sources or record your own.

To assign sounds to system events:

1. Select the Control Panel command from the Settings submenu of the Start menu.

2. Double-click the Sounds control panel icon to open the Sounds Properties dialog box, as shown in Figure 10-8.

3. Click on an event and assign a WAV sound to that event. To test a sound, click the Play button to the right of the Preview box.

4. If you wish to save a set of sound assignments as a collection, enter a name in the Schemes text box and click the Save As button.

Tip: Windows NT comes with several sound schemes that are optionally installed. If you are interested in obtaining these additional sounds and trying them, custom install these schemes using the Windows NT Setup tab on the Add/Remove Programs control panel. Select these schemes from the Multimedia components.

What is a codec, and how does it relate to Windows multimedia files?

A *codec* is a compression/decompression module. These algorithms determine how a multimedia file is written to disk, and how that file

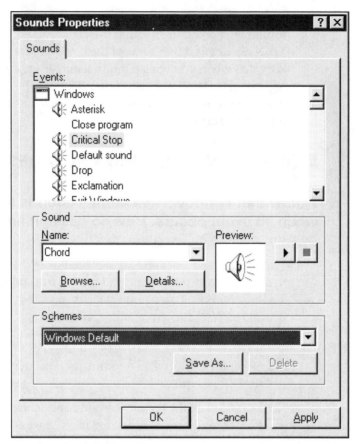

Figure 10-8.   The Sounds Properties dialog box

is read from disk and played back. Windows NT comes with both audio and video codecs, and when you install a program or multimedia title, additional codecs may be installed with those programs.

The four audio codecs that come with the Windows NT operating system are:

⇨ ADPCM (Adaptive Differential Pulse Code Modulation), from the International Multimedia Association

⇨ Microsoft ADPCM

⇨ Microsoft GSM

⇨ TrueSpeech

The latter two are for recording and playing back speech. They are lower in quality but highly compressed (10:1 to 20:1). The first two on the list are used for music recording and playback and achieve a compression of about 4:1.

The Windows NT operating system also comes with four video codecs:

⇨ Cinepack

⇨ Indeo

⇨ Microsoft RLE

⇨ Microsoft Video 1

Cinepak and Indeo are widely used in the industry for multimedia CD-ROMs, and are of good quality. RLE and Video 1 are older codecs that are there for backward compatibility.

One very important codec that isn't installed as part of the operating system but is very widely used is the MPEG (Motion Picture Expert Group) codec. MPEG requires hardware support, either an extra chip or an Intel Pentium microprocessor. MPEG contains a specification for both video and audio compression as part of the codec.

Other, less common codecs that you might see are the Motion-JPEG and the TrueMotion-S codecs.

If you want to see what codecs are currently installed on your computer, open the Devices tab of the Multimedia Properties dialog box, as shown in Figure 10-3. Both Video Compression Codecs and Audio Compression Codecs are listed on that tab.

Since many programs install codecs automatically for you, you may not ever need to know what codecs you have installed. However, if you need to manually install a codec, you would open the Devices tab and click the Add button. Have the codec files handy so that you can specify their location when the Select Devices dialog box appears—just as you would install any other device in Windows NT. A codec is a Windows NT "device" in the same sense that a DOS box is a device. It's implemented in software only.

 ## Is there any way to obtain detailed information on the various multimedia files that I find on my computer?

Right-click on any multimedia file and select the Properties command from the shortcut menu. The Properties dialog box for multimedia contains a wide variety of interesting and important details and features. Among the obvious things you will find there are file type descriptions, size, creation and modification dates, and all of the standard file system details. Figure 10-9 shows you the Details tab of the Properties dialog box of an AVI file.

Many of these dialog boxes will tell you which video or audio codecs are used to compress and play back the file, as well as offering a playback device. For example, when you open a MIDI file you will find that the Preview tab has a progress bar and an Apply button that lets you hear the sequence. Good stuff.

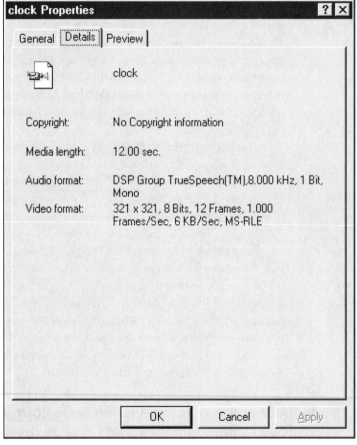

Figure 10-9.   The Details tab of the Properties dialog box of an AVI file

What is Apple's QuickTime, and what does it have to do with Windows?

QuickTime is a technology for video recording and playback that is a framework into which various codecs may be installed. The technology ships with some audio and video codecs, and can take others. A QuickTime Movie file is given the .MOV file extension and can contain audio, MIDI, and digital video data.

MOV files cannot be played on the Media Player, but require a special QuickTime player. You can obtain the QuickTime for Windows movie player from Apple and install it on your computer.

QuickTime is referenced in many places throughout the Internet. The latest and greatest files, including the latest Windows movie player, sample Movie (.MOV) files, and other resources are found on Apple's Web site at http://www.microsoft.com/hwtest/hcl/.

 How do I record a sound in Windows NT?

Use the Sound Recorder applet to record sounds as WAV files. Before you start the procedure listed below, make sure that you have your sound input device—a microphone, audio input, and so on—plugged into the appropriate jack of your sound board.

To record a sound:

1. Select the Sound Recorder from the Multimedia folder in the Accessories folder of the Programs submenu on the Start menu. The Sound Recorder is shown here.

2. Select the New command from the File menu.

3. Select the Audio Properties command from the Edit menu and select the quality of sound you desire.

4. Use the Volume Control applet to adjust the sound level for the input.

5. Click the Record button in the Sound Recorder.

6. Select the Save command from the File menu.

7. Choose the place where you want to store the file, name your WAV file, and then click the OK button.

If you change your mind about the sound quality and wish to save the WAV file in a lower quality version, click the Convert Now button in the Properties dialog box. Use the Properties command on the File menu to open the dialog box required to access the conversion utility. The following illustration shows you the Sound Selection dialog box used for the conversion.

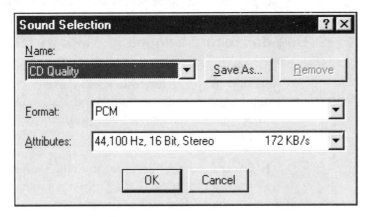

I want to record smaller sound files or hear better sound quality. Is there any way to do this without having to buy a new sound board?

If you open the Multimedia control panel and click the Audio tab shown in Figure 10-10, you will see a list box called Preferred Quality in the Recording section of that tab. You can set audio quality as any of the following:

⇨ *Telephone Quality.* This level records at 8KHz and 8-bit mono.

⇨ *Radio Quality.* This level records at 22.050KHz and in 8-bit mono.

⇨ *CD Quality.* This level records at 44.1KHz and at 16-bit stereo.

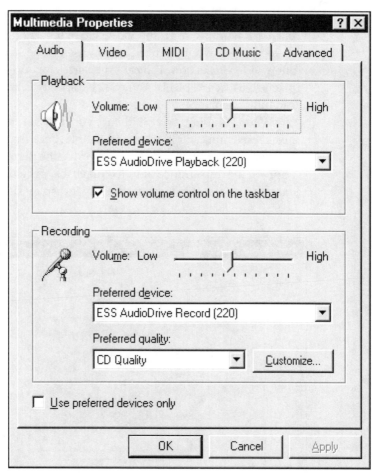

Figure 10-10.   The Audio tab of the Multimedia Properties dialog box

These settings control the quality and size of sound files that you record by adjusting the sampling rate and bit-depth. Although the setting won't actually improve the quality of your sound board, diminishing the quality of the recorded file will lower the quality of what you hear when you play back the sound.

? How do I control the size of the window that my video files run in?

Windows NT comes with a video playback device that automatically runs when you double-click on or open an AVI

(Audio-Video-Interleaved) file. If you wish to control the size of the
playback window, open the Video tab of the Multimedia Properties
dialog box shown in Figure 10-11 and select the size from the
Show video in section. Typical frame sizes for AVI files are 160 x 120
pixels to 640 x 480 pixels. You can also specify that the video file
run full screen.

When you blow an AVI file up, you may see the image become
pixelated (chunky or blocky) and the playback may become jerky.
Accelerated graphics boards can improve the display of video files to
improve the appearance of video playback, provided that sufficient
data was recorded to support the larger display size.

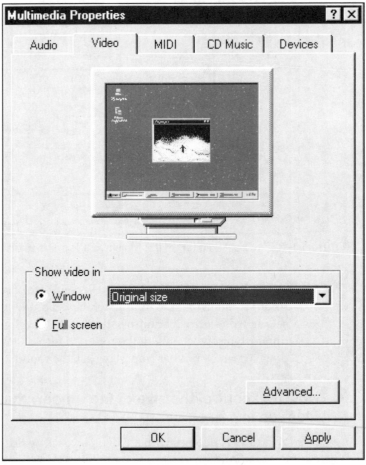

Figure 10-11.   The Video tab of the Multimedia Properties dialog box

? I don't see the volume control icon in the Taskbar. How do I add that icon?

To add the Volume Control to the Taskbar, open the Multimedia control panel to view the Multimedia Properties dialog box. Click on the Show Volume Control on the Taskbar checkbox. When you close the control panel, the icon will appear.

Answer Topics!

Monitoring and Performance Tuning @ a Glance

⇨ A number of **events** are generated by your computer that indicate error conditions, display information, indicate specific security or application activity, and so forth. Three event logs are kept by your system—Security, System, and Application—and each log can be viewed in the Event Viewer.

⇨ The Windows NT operating system is capable of creating and monitoring periodic activity called *counters*. Counters are processed by or acted upon by various objects in your system. By analyzing different objects' counters you can determine a whole host of performance factors. You can use the **Performance Monitor** to graph or chart various counters.

⇨ The key to **finding bottlenecks** is to observe various key counters and see how they interact. You can determine if your CPU or hard drives are too slow or if they are adequate for the processing that your system is doing. You can also use counters to determine if a device is about to fail.

⇨ You can **optimize disk storage and performance** by segregating fast and slow devices on different buses. You can also control the size and location of your pagefile, thus controlling virtual memory. While you can always upgrade a hard drive to a faster hard drive, you can often get dramatic increases in performance by adding more RAM to your system.

⇨ This chapter tells you how to calculate how much RAM you optimally need. The calculation for **working with memory** uses several counters and the size of the pagefile.

⇨ Processes running on Windows NT spawn threads of execution. Each thread is assigned a priority based on whether the application is a foreground or a background application, and other factors. You can **prioritize threads and processes** to improve a processes execution, and to alter the relative performance of a foreground to a background process.

MONITORING EVENTS

 How do I enable the security log?

When you install Windows NT, security logging is off by default. To enable security logging, you must turn it on. Open the User Manager and enable security logging, using the following steps:

1. Select the User Manager for Domains command in the Administrative Tools folder on the <u>P</u>rograms submenu of the Start menu.

2. Select the Audit command from the Policies menu to view the Audit Policy dialog box shown in Figure 11-1.

3. Click the Audit These Events radio button, and then click on the checkboxes for the security events you wish to audit.

4. Click the OK button to close the dialog box.

5. Select the Exit command from the User menu to close the User Manager for Domains utility.

? When I get error messages, how do I find out more information about what went wrong?

Most error messages, alert boxes, and condition indicators represent a specific event that has occurred on Windows NT. Those events are written to one of Windows NT's log files and are available for view with the Event Viewer.

To view details of an error message:

1. Select Event Viewer from the Administrative Tools folder on the Programs submenu of the Start menu.

2. Select the particular log of interest from the Log menu in the Event Viewer window, as shown in Figure 11-2.

3. Double-click on the event with an error icon, one with a red stop sign to the left of it.

The Event window, an example of which is shown in Figure 11-3, opens, displaying useful information about the event.

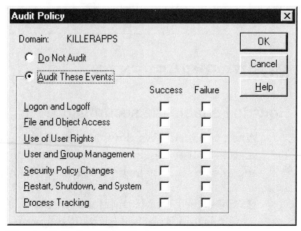

Figure 11-1.   The Audit Policy dialog box

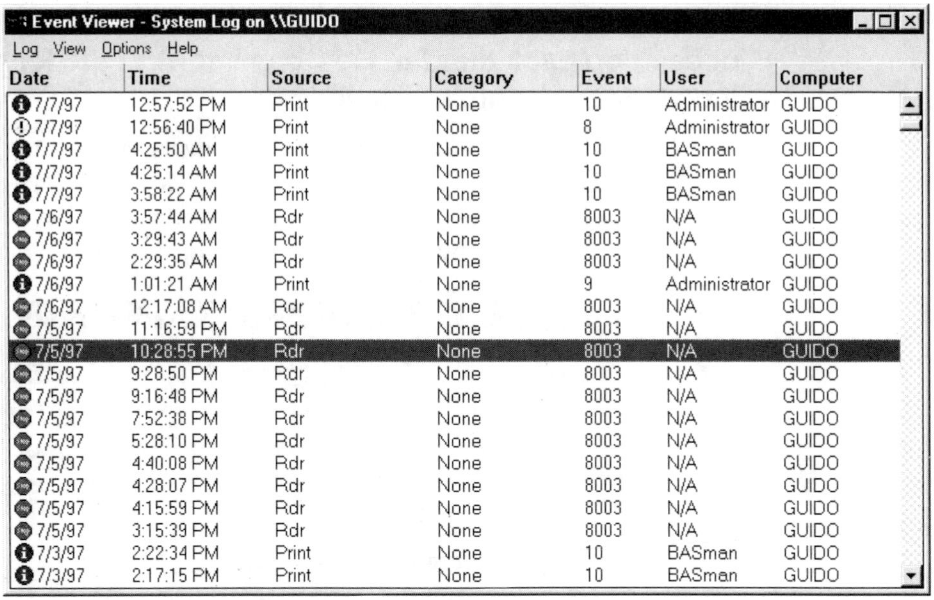

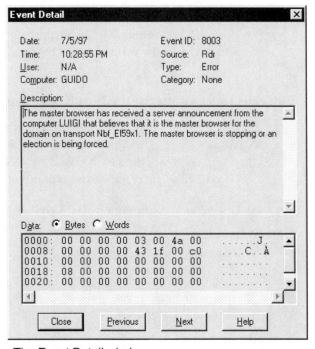

Figure 11-2.   The Event Viewer window

Figure 11-3.   The Event Detail window

I went to look for an error generated last week and the log doesn't go back that far. How can I control the length of time logged events are saved?

By default, a log is 512KB and events are overwritten when they are seven days old. You can control the size of a log file from 64KB on up, and the length of time those events are saved before they are overwritten in the Event Log Settings dialog box, shown here.

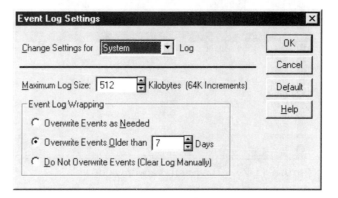

You can save a log to a catalogued log file, and purge the log file manually. By default, when you open the Event Viewer, all three system Event logs are loaded into memory and available to view. If you open a log file other than the three system logs, that log file's name is shown in the title bar of the Event Viewer.

 How do I stop a system when the security log is full?

If you want to bring your system to a halt when the security log is full so that the events can be archived to a catalog file by an administrator, you can make this setting in the Windows NT Registry.

To save all security log entries without overwriting them:

1. Open the Registry Editor (REGEDIT).

2. Locate the following registry key value:

   ```
   HKEY_LOCAL_MACHINE\SYSTEM\CurrentControlSt\
   Control\Lsa\CrashOnAuditFail
   ```

3. Change the value type of the REG_DWORD to one of the following data values:

```
1 - Stop if the audit log is full.
2 - This data value will be set by the operating
system just before the system crashes due to a
full audit log. While the data value is 2, only
the administrator can log onto the computer.
```

4. Close the Registry Editor.

The CrashOnAuditFail entry has the operating system shut down and display a blue screen when the security audit log is full. No additional security or system activities can take place.

 Note: You can archive a log file in three different formats: Log file format, Text file format, and Comma-delimited text file format. The format you select allows you to import and view the log files in a variety of applications.

Where are startup errors logged?

When Windows NT boots up, the CHKDSK (CheckDisk) program runs on the volume that contains system files. Errors that it finds are written to the application log.

If your startup error is a hardware device, that error is written to the system log. If you find a hardware error, you may want to open the Control Panel or any application that manages the device to obtain more information about the device than is available from the system log.

Where are the system logs stored, and what's in them?

The system log files are stored in the C:\WINNT\SYSTEM32\CONFIG folder, where C:\WINNT is the system root folder. There are three system logs:

⇨ *System log.* The SYSEVENT.EVT file stores events generated by system components and device drivers. Any failure of a device or a system component to load at startup is recorded in this log file. Windows NT records events logged by system components. The device manufacturer specifies events logged by the third-party device driver.

⇨ *Security log.* The SECEVENT.EVT file stores logon attempts, both the ones that succeed and the ones that fail. It also records events related to resource access: files, folders, printers, and other objects for which auditing has been turned on.

Note: *Only a system administrator can view security logs. The application and system logs can be viewed by any user.*

⇨   *Application log.* The APPEVENT.EVT file stores events logged by specific applications. The application developer is responsible for specifying the events recorded in this log file.

USING THE PERFORMANCE MONITOR

What kinds of counters can I observe in the Performance Monitor?

Each Windows NT operating system component is classified as an object, and each monitors from two to a dozen built-in performance counters. You can also observe the performance of your microprocessor (CPU), physical disks, and logical disks, and see counters from each of them.

When you open the Performance Monitor, you select a process object to monitor in the Add to Chart dialog box. In the Instance field are shown all of the processes of that type that are currently running. If you click on a specific process, the counters of that type appear in the Performance Monitor window to be graphed or charted over time.

Three performance counters that are of particular importance are those that measure the activity of the microprocessor: the % Processor Time, Interrupts/Sec, and the Processor Queue Length. These counters taken together indicate how efficiently your system is performing.

How do I use the Performance Monitor to view counters?

The Performance Monitor is a graphical tool that plots counters over time in a variety of graph formats that Windows NT calls "charts." When you first open the Performance Monitor, it is blank. You need to specify

⇨   Which computer you want to monitor (you can remotely monitor other computers on the network).

⇨   The names of the counters that you wish to monitor (some, like disk counters, must be turned on manually).

⇨   The type of chart you want to see.

To create a chart in the Performance Monitor:

1. Select the Performance Monitor from the Administrative Tools folder in the Programs submenu of the Start menu.

2. Select the Add to Chart command on the Edit menu to view the Add to Chart dialog box shown in Figure 11-4.

3. Click on the Computer text box and enter the name of the computer you wish to monitor (\\computername); or click the Browse button (…) to specify the computer on the network graphically.

4. Select the Object and Counter that you wish to monitor and study.

5. If you need information about a particular counter, click the Explain button to view online help. The information appears in a drop-down section at the bottom of the Add to Chart dialog box called the Counter Definition section.

6. Select the Color, Scale, Width, and Style desired for the line that you observe in the chart. For multiple counters running, it can be hard to figure out which counter is which without specifying different line styles.

7. Select the Instance of the counter that you wish to chart. For counters that run on different devices (processors, hard drives, logical volumes, and so forth) that occur in a system, you will see an instance for each device.

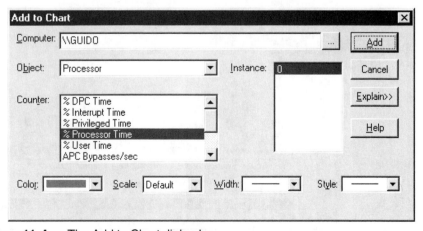

Figure 11-4.   The Add to Chart dialog box

8. Click the Add button and continue specifying counters until you are done; then click the Done button to return to the Performance Monitor.

Figure 11-5 shows you the Performance Monitor window with counters running in it.

❓ How do I log the activities of the Performance Monitor?

To log the counters in the Performance Monitor:

1. Log onto your system as a System Administrator.

2. Select the Performance Monitor from the Administrative Tools folder in the Programs submenu of the Start menu.

3. Select the Data From command from the Options menu, select the Current Activity radio button in the Data From dialog box, and click the OK button.

4. Select the Log command from the View menu.

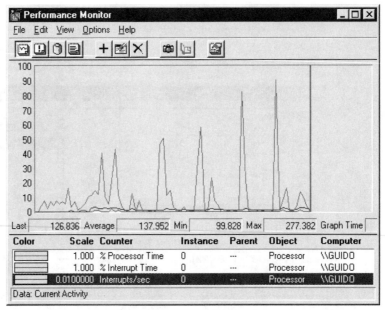

Figure 11-5.   The Performance Monitor window with counters running in it

5. In the Log window (which is empty), select the Add to Log command from the Edit menu to view the Add to Log dialog box shown in Figure 11-6.

6. Select the object whose counters you wish to log in the Objects list, or hold the CTRL key and add any other objects desired by clicking on them; then click the Add button.

7. Select the Log command from the Options menu, and enter the log filename in the File name text box and the Period Update Interval in the Update Time section (the default is 15 sec).

8. Select the Start Log button to initiate logging activity.

To view the data in the log from within the Performance Monitor:

1. In the Performance Monitor Log window, select the Log command from the Options menu.

2. Select the Chart command from the View menu.

3. Select the Data From command from the Options menu and select the log file in the Data From dialog box; then click the OK button.

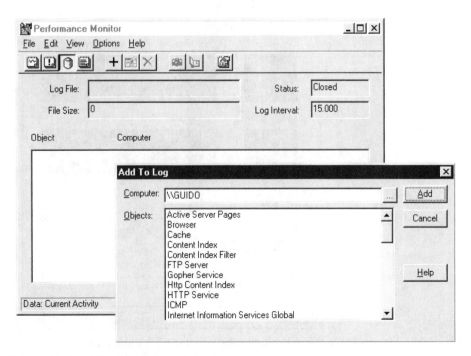

Figure 11-6.   The Add to Log dialog box

4. Click the Add button on the toolbar, and then select the Add to Chart command on the Edit menu.

5. Select from the objects and counters that were previously logged and added; then click the Done button to view the chart of the log file for that counter(s).

? Is there a quick method that I can use to see how my system is performing?

You can use the Task Manager to view some of the performance details for your system. Here's how:

1. Right-click on the Taskbar and select the Task Manager command from the shortcut menu.

2. Click the Performance tab, as shown in Figure 11-7.

The Task Manager shows you CPU usage, memory statistics, open applications, and running services.

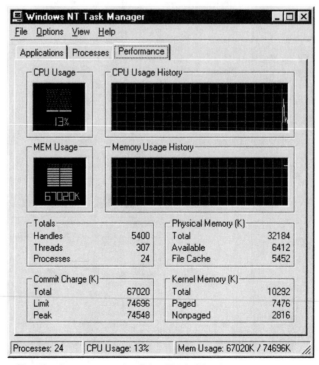

Figure 11-7.   The Performance tab of the Task Manager

? I'm not seeing any disk counters. How do I turn counters on?

Counters are not turned on when you install the operating system, as they slow down low-end workstations and servers but have minimal effect on Pentium computers. There is some suggestion that disk counters can affect multiprocessor (SMP) systems as well.

To turn on disk counters:

1. Select the Command Prompt command from the Programs submenu of the Start menu.

2. Enter the following commands at the command prompt:

```
DISKPERF -Y
EXIT
```

3. Restart your system.

The system starts up with disk counters running and visible in the Performance Monitor. To turn off these counters, perform the above procedure using the –N switch (No).

Note: *DISKPERF takes some other switches that might be of use to you. Use the command itself to determine if counters are active. Use the –YE switch to enable disk counters on mirror or stripe sets and other noncontiguous volumes.*

FINDING BOTTLENECKS

? How can I determine if my hard drive is too slow?

When you see disk activity above 85%, persistent disk queues greater than 2 per disk, and paging in the Memory:Pages Reads/sec and Writes/sec less than 5 per second on average, you should suspect your disk subsystem's performance as a bottleneck. A high disk demand indicates activity but not performance. When you see less than 40 I/O operations per second, you are not fully utilizing the average high-speed disk. Measure the counters Logical Disk:Ave. Disk Queue Length and Memory:Pages/sec for your logical partitions to see if your hard drive is a bottleneck.

Tip: *A considerable portion of the Windows NT Resource kits are devoted to the analysis of counters in the Performance Monitor to find bottlenecks and measure performance.*

How can I determine if my hard drive is failing?

To determine if your hard drive is a system bottleneck, open the Performance Monitor and examine the Disk:Average disksec/transfer counter. If your typical disk access time is greater than 0.3 seconds, you should upgrade or replace your hard disk. A number that large could indicate a problem that could lead to disk failure.

How can I determine if my microprocessor is too slow?

To determine if your microprocessor is a system bottleneck, open the Performance Monitor and examine the counters that are associated with the CPU. Two counters are particularly revealing in this regard:

⇨ *Processor:%Processor Time.* This counter should run between 0% and 80%. Fast Pentium systems and Pentium Pro systems can average around 20% processor utilization. When you are loading applications, you may find processor utilization peak at 100%. If you are typically seeing a value greater than 80%, you should upgrade your processor speed.

⇨ *System:Processor Queue Length.* This counter measures the number of threads being generated that are backing up in the processor queue. A value of 2 or more indicates a CPU bottleneck.

How do I generate a diagnostic report for my system?

The Windows NT Diagnostic program (WINMSD.EXE) lists various hardware devices and operating system components that are referenced in the Windows NT Registry. This program is located in the <systemroot>\System32 folder, where the systemroot is usually C:\WINNT by default. Figure 11-8 shows you this tool.

To create a diagnostic report:

1. Open the Windows NT Diagnostic program.

2. Select the Save Report command from the File menu.

3. Select the All tabs radio button in the Scope section of the Create Report dialog box, as shown in Figure 11-9.

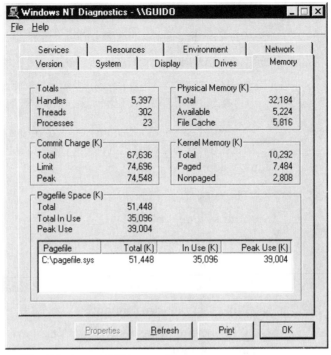

Figure 11-8.   The Windows NT Diagnostic program

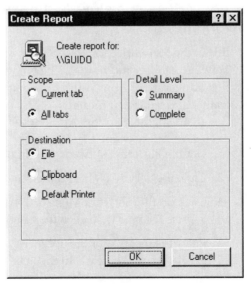

Figure 11-9.   The Create Report dialog box

4. Select the Complete in the Detail Level section.

5. Click on File in the Destination section.

6. Click the OK button.

7. In the Save WinMSD Report dialog box, output the file as C:\MSDRPT.TXT, and then click the OK button.

   Notepad can be used to view this text file.
   This diagnostic program offers you the following information on your system:

   ⇨ The version of your operating sytyem

   ⇨ Your system type

   ⇨ The video display and its device driver

   ⇨ Information about your disk drives

   ⇨ The amount of memory and its current usage

   ⇨ Which services are running

   ⇨ What resources are in use: IRQs, I/O ports, DMA channels, and memory addresses

   ⇨ The nature of your current system and user environment

   ⇨ Network information and user information

The network seems slow. Is there any way to monitor network traffic?

Install the Network Monitor on your system and use it to observe network packets and frames. The Network Monitor captures frames that are sent to or from your local computer, including broadcast frames and multicast frames.
To install the Network Monitor:

1. Double-click the Network icon in the Control Panels folder.

2. Click the Services tab, and then the Add button.

3. Click on the Network Monitor Tools and Agent in the Network Service list box; then click the OK button.

4. Enter the location of the operating system files in the Windows NT Setup dialog box, and then click the Continue button.

5. After Windows NT copies the necessary files, click the Yes button and restart your server.

You must then set a trigger:

1. Log in as an administrator.

2. Select the Network Monitor from the Administrative Tools folder of the Programs submenu on the Start menu.

3. Select Trigger from the Capture menu.

4. In the Capture Trigger dialog box, click on Buffer Space in the Trigger on box and click on 50%.

5. Click on Stop Capture in the Trigger Action box; then click the OK button.

6. Select the Start command from the Capture menu, and click the Run button.

7. Enter the computer name, then click the OK button.

To view captured data in the Network Monitor:

1. Select the Stop command from the Capture menu.

2. Select the Display Captured Data command from the Capture menu.

3. Scroll through the list of captured frames until you see your computer name, and both your server and workstation.

OPTIMIZING DISK STORAGE AND PERFORMANCE

 I have several drives attached to my system bus. How do I optimize bus performance?

You should separate fast and slow devices so that they are not on the same bus. If you are using SCSI-2 and wide SCSI devices, eliminate the slower SCSI-2 devices on the bus and move them to another bus. In that way you will get the best performance out of your wide SCSI devices. Similarly, place slower CD-ROM and DAT drives on a different bus than the one your hard drive is on.

How do I alter the pagefile?

You can change the location of the pagefile, which is placed by default on the same drive that the Windows NT system files are on. By moving the PAGEFILE.SYS file to a faster drive, you can see modest improvement. When you have a RAID 0 disk arrangement, you can create multiple pagefiles and see a dramatic improvement. In RAID 5 (stripe sets with parity), writing parity information will adversely affect performance.

You can also change the size of the page file, adjusting both the initial size and the maximum size. The minimum pagefile you can create is 2MB.

To alter the size of a pagefile:

1. Select the Control Panel command from the Settings submenu of the Start menu.

2. Double-click the System control panel icon.

3. Click the Performance tab.

4. Click the Change button in the Virtual Memory section to view the Virtual Memory dialog box shown in Figure 11-10.

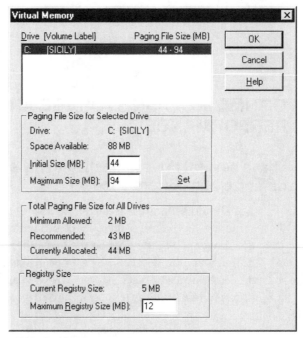

Figure 11-10.   The Virtual Memory dialog box

5. Enter the new Initial Size and Maximum Size, and then click the Set button.

6. Click the OK buttons to close all dialog boxes.

❓ My hard drive is constantly active and my system performance is poor. Is there any way to adjust virtual memory?

When you have a system with low amounts of RAM, Windows NT will swap data in and out to a pagefile to allow a process to complete itself. The constant writing to and from disk is called *thrashing*, and it degrades system performance.

The virtual memory (VM) subsystem in Windows NT is self-optimized, and there isn't a whole lot you can do to improve performance except buy more RAM.

Windows NT requires a pagefile that is the size of system RAM plus 12MB. Most technical studies recommend that a pagefile to RAM size of about 1:2 to 1:3 is more appropriate.

WORKING WITH MEMORY

❓ How can I determine if I need more memory?

Several counters can be used to determine if you need more RAM, and what the optimal amount is. The formula suggested is:

```
Multiply Memory:Pages/s by Logical Disk:Ave.
Disksec/transfer
```

This formula measures the percentage of disk access time that is used in the paging process. For the equation, the logical disk is the one that contains the pagefile. When you see a number greater than 10 percent (0.1) as an average value over time, the system needs more memory.

Use the Process:Working set for each running process on your computer to help you determine how much memory your system needs to work efficiently. Stop the process that has the greatest working set and recheck the Process:Working set counter. When you remove enough processes to bring the counter below 0.1, you can calculate the optimal memory for your system using the following equation:

```
RAM in system + Total memory size required by the
removed working sets
```

PRIORITIZING THREADS AND PROCESSES

How do I change the priorities of processes running on Windows NT?

An application running on Windows NT is a process that occupies an address in memory space. Execution of a process spawns a primary thread, which can generate additional threads of program execution. Each thread is given a priority that governs how effective it is in commanding the attention of the CPU in comparison with other threads that are running. As a CPU gets busier, all threads execute more slowly, but lower-priority threads slow down more than higher-priority ones.

The following priorities have these values:

⇨ *Real time execution.* Priority value 16–31. The highest value allowed is 32.

⇨ *High priority.* Value 13–15.

⇨ *Normal priority.* A foreground application is assigned a value of 9, and a background application is assigned a value of 7.

⇨ *Low or Idle priority.* A value of 0–4 is assigned.

To change the priority of a process:

1. Select the Command Prompt command from the <u>P</u>rograms submenu of the Start menu.

2. Enter the following command line:

```
START ["Window bar title"] [/path of starting
directory] [/LOW | /NORMAL | /HIGH | /REALTIME]
[command/program] [parameters]
```

Changing the priority of processes can have an effect on normal system performance. If you adjust a process too high, it may impact on the performance of your mouse, for example.

Is there an easy way to change the relative priorities of a process?

The Task Manager lets you alter the base priority of a process. It doesn't monitor individual threads, but it allows you to promote or demote an application or service process.

To see the base priority of processes:

1. Press CTRL-SHIFT-ESC to open the Task Manager.

2. Click the Processes tab.

3. Select the Columns command from the View menu.

4. Select Base Priority.

To change the base priority for a process:

1. Click the Process tab.

2. Right-click on a process name to display the shortcut menu.

3. Select the Set Priority command from the shortcut menu, as shown in Figure 11-11.

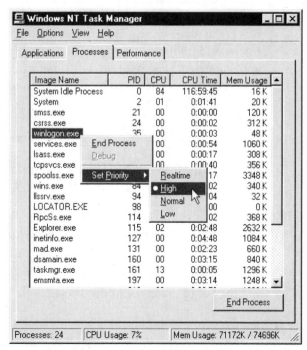

Figure 11-11.   Changing priorities in the shortcut menu of a process within the Task Manager

4. Enter a new base priority: Realtime, High, Normal, or Low.

When you change the priority of a process, Windows NT displays the following message:

```
WARNING: Changing the priority class of this proc-
ess may cause undesirable results including system
instability. Be sure you want to change the prior-
ity class. Changing to RealTime can cause a server
to ignore user requests and devote 100 percent of
its processing power to internal monitoring of the
server.
```

5. Click the Yes button.

6. Close the Task Manager.

Your changes are made when the Task Manager updates your system, and do not require that you restart the process.

? How can I adjust the relative performance of foreground and background processing?

When you click on an application window, you bring it to the foreground. The operating system raises the base priority of that process in order to provide a faster response of window refresh, mouse and pointer movements, and other factors for the user. Other applications or processes run in the background and have lower base priorities. You can change the relative amount of enhancement that a foreground application gets when it is activated from within the System Properties dialog box.

To alter the priority of foreground applications:

1. Select the Control Panel command from the Settings submenu of the Start menu.

2. Double-click the System control panel icon.

3. Click the Performance tab shown in Figure 11-12.

4. In the Application Performance section, drag the slider to the left (Maximum) to boost foreground performance and to the left (None) to retain the normal boost.

Foreground applications boosted to the Maximum experience a priority boost of 2, which would move a normal priority of 7 up to 9.

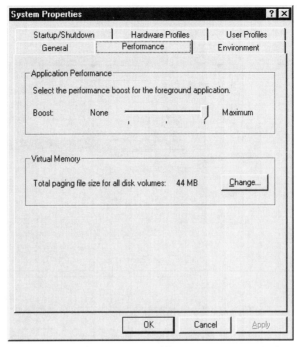

Figure 11-12.   The Performance tab of the System control panel

❓ Is there a way to configure Windows NT Server services?

The Server control panel allows you to optimize server characteristics through an easy dialog box selection.

To optimize Server settings:

1. Double-click the Network control panel icon.

2. Click the Services tab, and then select Server from the Network Services list box.

3. Click the Properties button to view the Server optimization dialog box shown in Figure 11-13.

4. Click the radio button for the server properties you desire.

5. Click the OK button and then close the Network control panel.

The different server settings have the following meanings:

⇨ *Minimize Memory Used.* This minimizes server memory by limiting the number of network connections.

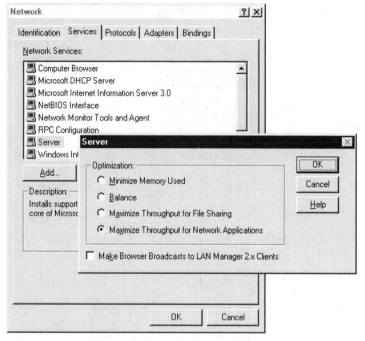

Figure 11-13. The Server optimization dialog box

⇨ *Balance.* The server initially allocates enough memory to establish up to 64 network connections.

⇨ *Maximize Throughput for File Sharing.* This setting initially allocates memory for up to 71,000 network connections.

⇨ *Maximize Throughput for Network Applications.* The server initially allocates memory for an unlimited number of connections and does not reserve as much memory for the system cache as it does with the other settings.

chapter

12 Answers!

Working with the Registry

Answer Topics!

Working with the Registry @ a Glance

⇨ In this chapter you learn **about the Registry**. The central system database file in Windows NT contains all of the machine and user settings that allow your system to boot, your software to load, and your environment to be established. The system is organized in a hierarchical fashion with a top-level set of files or hives, each of which is divided into keys and further subdivided into subkeys. Keys take values that are the actual settings or parameters.

⇨ You **work with keys** using the Registry Editor. Numerous components write data to the Registry: control panel settings, profiles, application installations, and so forth. Each of the various keys stores values relating to its name and location.

⇨ You can **search the Registry** using the Find dialog box of the Registry Editor. When you locate a key or value using the Find dialog box, you can view or modify it depending upon your access privileges.

⇨ You can **modify the Registry** so that none, part, or all of it is accessible to different users and groups. You can also audit the successful and unsuccessful attempts to access the Registry. The Registry Editor even allows you to remotely change a Registry on another computer.

⇨ The **Registry data** is stored in values for each of the different keys. Data is entered in one of six different formats. You can alter the size of the Registry in the Virtual Memory dialog box. The Registry Editor also allows you to export the data in your Registry, or import data that was exported.

⇨ Windows NT comes with several methods for **backing up and restoring the Registry**. Your first line of defense is to create a backup Registry and an Emergency Repair disk. In certain instances you can even directly copy the Registry files. Should you corrupt your Registry, you can reboot to your Last Known Good configuration, which is essentially a backup copy of the Registry from your previous session. Many of the numerous problems associated with a corrupted Registry are described here.

ABOUT THE REGISTRY

What is the Windows NT Registry?

The *Windows NT Registry* is a database of settings and parameters that controls the Windows NT interface and how the operating system works with hardware and software, and stores settings associated with particular users. These features were once part of the various .INI files that were written by the operating system and software applications in releases prior to Windows NT 4.

The Registry is a hierarchical structure where each section is referred to as a *hive,* and each finger of a section is called a *key.* The first key where the hive initiates is called the *primary* key, and each key is composed of *subkeys* that take value entries.

When you install a program or an operating system component like a device driver or service, new subkeys and value entries are written to the Registry. When you uninstall these components properly, these subkeys are removed. The subkeys and value entries store information about hardware settings, driver files, environmental variables that need to be restored— anything the application developer requires reference to.

Most Registry entries are permanent or nonvolatile, but some entries are established during a session as part of a logon or automatic detection of your computer's configuration by the Hardware Recognizer (NTDETECT.COM for Intel computers), which is part of the system boot module. This system for automatic detection is somewhat different for RISC computers, where hardware configuration is stored in ROM and read by the ARC firmware at startup.

Who has access to the Registry?

Only users in the Administrators or Power Users group can access the Registry initially. This group can give additional users privileges to all or part of the Registry. Any other user can see the Registry files, but cannot edit, delete, or copy Registry files.

What's the difference between the Registry of Windows 95 and Windows NT?

Although the Registry in Windows 95 and Windows NT look the same, they are not. Significant differences exist that make them incompatible. First, Windows 95 supports both 16- and 32-bit applications. Also, Windows 95 stores its Registry files in different locations than Windows NT.

When you upgrade from Windows 95 to Windows NT, these differences require that you upgrade and replace not only the operating system and Registry, but all of your applications as well. This is true even if you install the same application to the same directory. As of version 4, Windows NT still doesn't support the Windows 95 plug-and-play standard that automatically detects and configures a computer at startup. The Hardware Abstraction Layer (HAL) on Windows NT cannot accept the configuration information that a Windows 95 computer stores in the Registry.

 Note: Not surprisingly, Microsoft has taken a lot of flak over the fact that both operating systems don't support the same Registry structure. Microsoft appears to want to upgrade Windows 95 to the point that it has the same Registry structure as Windows NT, and that Windows NT v4 supports the common hardware control scheme now used in Windows 95. To this end, Windows 98 supports the same device drivers as does Windows NT.

Where are the Registry files located?

The Registry is found as multiple files (controlled by a single program called REGEDT32.EXE in the SYSTEM32 directory) located at <System Root>\System32\CONFIG. Typically the System Root is installed at C:\WINNT.

Registry data for any individual users are found in the WINNT\PROFILES\<username>\NTUSER.DAT files. Each user with a profile has its own copy of the NTUSER.DAT file that it maintains. Whenever a user logs onto a local computer, a Profile folder for the user is created with an NTUSER.DAT file to hold the user profile. A user who has a roaming profile on the network has the same NTUSER.DAT file on the Domain Controller.

The following files in the CONFIG folder store direct information on Registry hives:

⇨ DEFAULT

⇨ SAM

⇨ SECURITY

⇨ SOFTWARE

⇨ SYSTEM

⇨ USERDIFF

⇨ USERDIFR

⇨ NTUSER.DAT

Several files in the CONFIG directory are auxiliary files for the Registry. These files have the same names as the list above but are .LOG, .EVT, or .SAV files. The .EVT or Event files are viable in the Event Viewer and contain audited events. Log files store changes that can be rolled back. The .SAV files are part of the Last Known Good boot configuration that lets you restore your Registry based on your last booted session. The Last Known Good option is described later in this chapter.

Why do some "made for Windows NT 4" programs still write INI files, and how are INI files related to the Windows NT Registry?

Windows 95 still supports both a Registry and INI files because it is a hybrid 16-bit and 32-bit operating system. However, Windows NT is a full 32-bit operating system that doesn't support older programs that require INI files. Still, some developers write programs that conform to the Win32 specification that store and manage INI files.

In an INI file you will see sections that start with square brackets, as in [section name]. These sections correspond to subkeys in the Registry, where an entire INI file would correspond to a key. Under each section name is a set of statements that set a value to some variable, as in variable = value. These variables and their values are stored in the Registry in a hierarchical display in the subkey.

Multiple versions of subkeys can be stored, each associated with a different user account, thus supporting multiple users. In the INI file, headings can be nested to allow for different values based on a user name, so that only a single INI file is required to support multiple users. However, the Registry allows for essentially infinite nesting of subkeys, as well as for the storage of binary values and executable code. Only text values can be stored in an INI file.

When an MS-DOS program runs in Windows NT, the environment for this program can be set using an AUTOEXEC.BAT and CONFIG.SYS file. These files apply just to the Command Prompt session that calls them. You can also use these environment files to run 16-bit Windows programs.

? I want to examine and modify the Windows NT Registry. What tools are available for that purpose?

Whenever you make a change in a control panel, alter your desktop, or do any of a thousand tasks, you are modifying your Registry. However, you can make these same changes directly in the Registry if you know which subkey to change and what value to enter.

You can use the Registry Editor to view and modify the Windows NT Registry. There are two versions of the Registry Editor: REGEDT32.EXE and REGEDIT.EXE. These programs are intentionally not installed in the Administrative Tools folder where you might expect to find them. This is to discourage casual changes to the Registry. REGEDT32 can be found in the %systemroot%\system32 directory, and the REGEDIT program can be found in the %systemroot% directory.

Tip: *Since editing the Registry is fraught with peril, you might want to select the Read Only Mode command to ensure that you make no changes to the Registry as you wander around.*

To open the Registry Editor, do any of the following:

⇨ Double-click on the program name in the <System Root>\ System32 folder.

⇨ Select the Run command from the Start menu and enter the command REGEDIT or REGEDT32 in the Run dialog box; then click the OK button.

⇨ Open a Command Prompt window and type **START REGEDT32**; then press the ENTER key.

The Registry Editors are tools that let you open, search, and modify entries without restriction in the Windows NT Registry. If you wish to view and modify Registry information relating to services, resources, drivers, memory, display, or network components, you can use the Windows NT Diagnostic program (WINMSD).

The Windows NT Diagnostic program can be opened using any of the following methods:

⇨ Select the Windows Diagnostic program from the Administrative Tools folder on the Programs submenu of the Start menu.

⇨ Double-click on the program name in the <System Root>\ System32 folder.

⇨ Select the Run command from the Start menu and enter the command WINMSD in the Run dialog box; then click the OK button.

⇨ Open a Command Prompt window and type **START REGEDT32**; then press the ENTER key.

Warning: *When you use the Registry Editor to modify the Windows NT Registry, you have direct access to settings, values, and parameters that your system needs to start up and operate. If you delete or modify a required key, you could cause your computer to malfunction. The only recovery method that you can count on in that instance would be to reinstall Windows NT or to use the Repair disk that was described in Chapter 7, "Backing Up and Restoring Your System."*

WORKING WITH KEYS

I want to be able to reverse changes made in the control panels. To which keys do control panels write their settings?

Table 12-1 shows where each control panel makes changes. Some control panels change values in multiple keys, and are listed as such.

The Add/Remove Programs control panel doesn't write to the Registry directly, but opens an installer or uninstaller that creates and deletes Registry entries.

Table 12-1.   Control Panel Relations to Registry Keys

Accessibility Options	HKEY_CURRENT_USER\Control Panel\Accessibility
Add/Remove Software	HKEY_CURRENT_USER\Console\Application Console
Date/Time	HKEY_LOCAL_MACHINE\System\CurrentControlSet\Control\TimeZone Information
Devices	HKEY_LOCAL_MACHINE\System\CurrentControlSet\Services
Display (Machine settings)	HKEY_LOCAL_MACHINE\Hardware\ResourceMap\Video
Display (User settings)	HKEY_CURRENT_USER\Control Panel\Desktop
Fast Find	HKEY_LOCAL_MACHINE\Software\Microsoft\Shared Tools\Fast Find
Fonts	HKEY_LOCAL_MACHINE\Software\Microsoft\Windows NT\CurrentVersion\Fonts
Internet	HKEY_LOCAL_MACHINE\Software\Microsoft\Windows\CurrentVersion\Internet Settings
Keyboard	HKEY_CURRENT_USER\Control Panel\Desktop
Mail	Several places
Modems	HKEY_LOCAL_MACHINE\Software\Microsoft\Windows\CurrentVersion\Unimodem
Mouse	HKEY_CURRENT_USER\Control Panel\Mouse
Multimedia	HKEY_LOCAL_MACHINE\Software\Microsoft\Windows\Multimedia
Network	Several locations
PC Card	HKEY_LOCAL_MACHINE\Hardware\Description\System\PCMCIA PCCARDs
Ports	HKEY_LOCAL_MACHINE\Hardware\ResourceMap
Printers	HKEY_CURRENT_USER\Printers
Regional Settings	HKEY_CURRENT_USER\Control Panel\International
SCSI Adapters	HKEY_LOCAL_MACHINE\Hardware\ResourceMap\ScsiAdapter
Server	Several locations
Services	HKEY_LOCAL_MACHINE\System\CurrentControlSet\Services
Sounds	HKEY_CURRENT_USER\AppEvent\Schemes\Apps\Default
System	Several locations
Tape Devices	HKEY_LOCAL_MACHINE\Hardware\ResourceMap\OtherDrivers\Tape Devices
Telephony	HKEY_LOCAL_MACHINE\Software\Microsoft\Windows\CurrentVersion\Telephony
UPS	HKEY_LOCAL_MACHINE\System\CurrentControlSet\Services\UPS

❓ In what keys do roaming profiles write Registry entries?

A profile can be open and read in any text editor. The information contained in the<USERNAME>\NTUSER.DAT file is stored in the following subkeys of the HKEY_CURRENT_USER:

⇨ AppEvents (sounds)

⇨ Console (Command Prompt and installed applications)

⇨ Control Panel (which control panels are accessible, and their settings)

⇨ Environment (system configuration)

⇨ Printers (Printer connections)

⇨ Software (which software programs are available, and their settings)

❓ When I open the NT Registry, I see the root keys. What do they represent?

At the very top of the Registry are the files or hives that collect all information. The six top-level keys in the Windows Registry are called *root* keys. The top keys shown in the Registry Editor are the *handle* keys that give access to the root keys and in some cases are also root keys. Figure 12-1 shows you these HKEYs. Each tree contains either global information that is applicable to every user of a computer, or individual information that varies based on either user account or user profile.

Note: *With the exception of Figure 12-1, which shows RegEdit, all of the other figures and procedures in this chapter refer to Regedt32.*

The six root keys and their subtrees are

⇨ *HKEY_CLASSES_ROOT.* This subtree stores OLE, file, class, and other associations that allow a program to launch when a data file is opened. Although the HKEY_CLASSES_ROOT is displayed as a root key, it is actually a subkey of HKEY_LOCAL_MACHINE\ Software.

⇨ *HKEY_CURRENT_USER.* All user settings, profiles, environmental variables, interface settings, program groups,

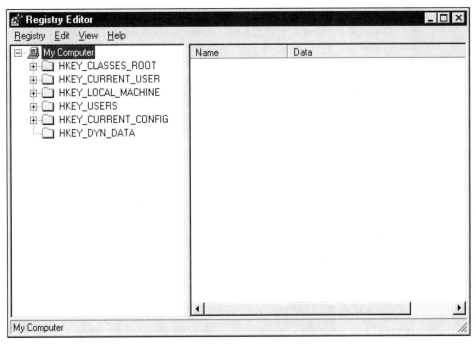

Figure 12-1.   The root keys shown in the Registry Editor

printer connections, application preferences, and network connections for each user are stored in the subkeys of this root key.

⇨ *HKEY_LOCAL_MACHINE.* This subkey contains information that identifies the computer that the Registry is stored on. Information in this key includes settings for hardware like memory, disk drives, network adapters, and peripheral devices. Any software that supports hardware—device drivers, system services, system boot parameters, and other data—is contained in this subkey.

⇨ *HKEY_USERS.* All data on individual user profiles is contained in this subkey. Windows NT stores local profiles in the Registry, and the values are maintained in this subkey.

⇨ *HKEY_CURRENT_CONFIG.* The current configuration for software and any machine values are contained in this key. Among the settings stored in this root key are display device setup and control values required to restore the configuration when the program launches or your computer starts up.

⇨ *HKEY_DYN_DATA.* Transient or dynamic data is stored in this last key in the Windows NT Registry. This root key cannot be modified by the user.

❓ How can I view each root key in its own window?

It can be useful to have a multiwindow view of the Registry's contents. If you need to refer to one value or subkey while changing another in a different subkey, this view will be helpful to you. Luckily the Registry Editor makes this very easy to do.

To view each of the six root keys within its own window:

1. Open the Registry Editor (Regedt32).

2. Select the <u>O</u>pen Local command from the <u>R</u>egistry menu, as shown in Figure 12-2.

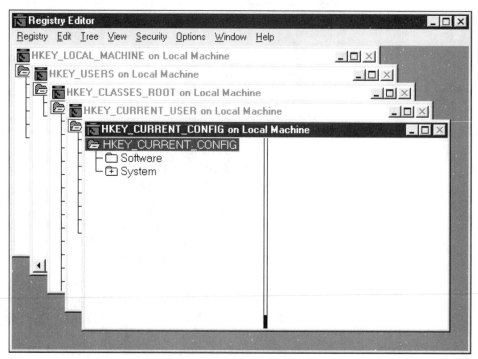

Figure 12-2.   The Registry Editor in the Local view

SEARCHING THE REGISTRY

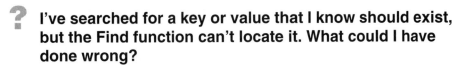

I've searched for a key or value that I know should exist, but the Find function can't locate it. What could I have done wrong?

Since many keys and values have spaces, underscores, or other characters or symbols in their name, don't search for a value or name with the Match Whole Words Only or Match Case options turned on.

How do I find a key or value in the Registry?

To find a subkey name or value:

1. Select the <u>F</u>ind What command from the <u>V</u>iew menu in the Registry Editor to view the Find dialog box shown here:

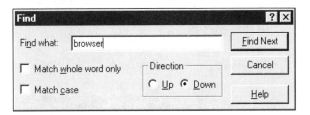

2. Enter the text you wish to search for in the Fi<u>n</u>d What text field.

3. Select any of the following search options:

   ⇨ Match Whole Words Only

   ⇨ Match Case

   ⇨ Search up the tree

   ⇨ Search down the tree

4. Click the Find button.

5. Continue searching by clicking the Find Next button.

MODIFYING THE REGISTRY

How can I audit any access or changes to the Registry?

To audit Registry access or modification:

1. Open the Registry Editor (Regedt32) with administrator privileges.

2. Select the Auditing command from the Security menu to view the Registry Key Auditing dialog box shown in Figure 12-3.

3. Click the Add button to display the Add Users and Groups dialog box.

4. Select a group and then click the Add button.

5. Or click the Members button, select the user, and click the Add button.

6. Continue adding users or groups to the list, and then click the OK button to return to the Registry Key dialog box.

7. Select the events you wish to audit and for which audit messages will be collected in the security and event logs (.EVT files) by clicking on the checkboxes next to their description.

8. Click on the Audit Permission on Existing Subkeys checkbox if you wish to have all subkeys of this key audited.

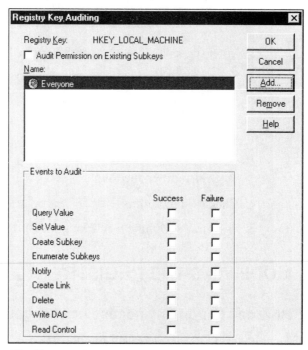

Figure 12-3.   The Registry Key Auditing dialog box

9. Click the OK button.

The following events can be audited:

⇨ *Query Value.* When there is an attempt to read a value entry, a message is generated.

⇨ *Set Value.* Changing a value is audited.

⇨ *Create Subkey.* Any action that creates a subkey on the current key is an audited event.

⇨ *Enumerate Subkeys.* This action lists or identifies a subkey of the current key.

⇨ *Notify.* Any notification event generated in a key of the Registry is logged.

⇨ *Create Link.* A symbolic link to the selected key is an action that triggers an audited event.

⇨ *Delete.* If the specified user or group deletes a Registry object, that action is noted.

⇨ *Write DAC.* If a user tries to modify the security permission of a key by writing to the Access Control List, that is logged by this option.

⇨ *Read Control.* Any attempt to access the Access Control List (ACL) on the selected key is noted.

Warning: *Never remove the SYSTEM as an allowed user in the permissions list. Doing so will prevent a user from changing the Registry with control panels or by installing software. Any changes a user makes in software will not be able to be effected, and the software on your computer will cease to function.*

❓ How can I tell who has permission to view or modify a key, and how can I control these permissions?

Access to the Registry is considered a very high-level privilege, and by default only an Administrator or Power User gets to create, edit, or delete the subkeys in the Registry. There are some keys that set global settings that only an Administrator should be able to access, and many Administrators won't allow a user to have any access to the Registry at all. Still, there are settings that are appropriate to local machines that a network administrator may wish to allow knowledgeable users to modify.

To view permissions for Registry key access:

1. Open the Registry Editor (Regedt32) with Administrator privileges.

2. Click on the key of interest.

3. Select the Permissions command from the Security menu to view the Registry Key Permissions dialog box shown in Figure 12-4.

To add a user or group:

1. Click on the Add button to display the Add Users and Groups dialog box.

2. Select a group and then click the Add button.

3. Or click the Members button, select the user, and click the Add button.

4. Set the privileges desired by selecting the level from the Type of Access list box.

5. Click the OK button.

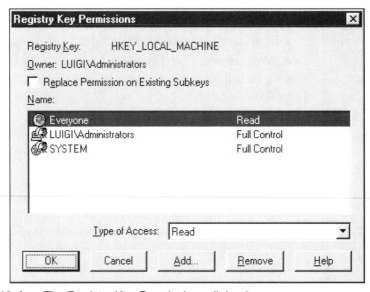

Figure 12-4.   The Registry Key Permissions dialog box

You can set a Special Access from the Special Access dialog box shown in Figure 12-5. In that dialog box, you can control who can Create, Delete, Query, Read, or Set Value for a subkey.

If you wish to set the permissions on all of the subkeys that your active key contains, check the Replace Permissions on Existing Subkeys checkbox in the Permissions dialog box. Or select a user or group and click on Remove if you wish to disallow access to that key and all of its subkeys.

Can I remote access the Registry of another computer on a LAN or through a dial-up connection?

If you have a LAN connection or have established a viable Remote Access link to the network, you can use the Registry Editor to remotely access another computer's Windows NT Registry. The procedure, once properly connected, is not difficult.

To remote access a computer's Registry:

1. Log onto the domain with an appropriate access privilege.

2. Open the Registry Editor (Regedt32).

3. Select the Select Computer command from the Registry menu.

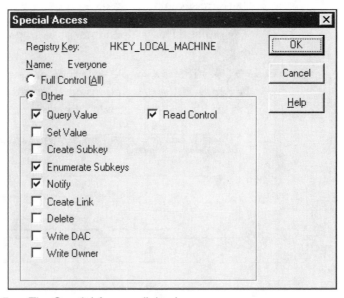

Figure 12-5.   The Special Access dialog box

4. Double-click on the domain in the Select Computer dialog box to view its members.

5. Click on the computer name of interest in the Select Computer list box, and then click the OK button.

The Registry Editor window will display two extra Registry windows, one for the HKEY_USERS and the other for the root key of the HKEY_LOCAL_MACHINE.

Tip: *To load a remote profile (not in use on the remote machine), browse the remote <System Root>\Profiles folder with the Load Hive command on the Registry menu.*

WORKING WITH REGISTRY DATA

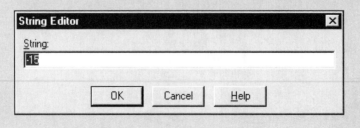

What are the values in the Registry?

The values you see in the right panel of the Registry Editor are the actual settings or parameters that are used to control your computer. All of the keys, subkeys, and so on are the Registry's method for organizing, securing, and protecting this chaos.

There are seven different data types for values:

⇨ *String values.* This is alphanumeric text up to 256 characters long.

⇨ *REG_SZ.* This is a simple text string or a single number. Enter the names, titles, descriptions, instructions, or another entry into the String Editor shown here:

⇨ *REG_MULTI_SZ.* This is a list of items for a single value. If you have a list of devices, services, network protocols, or anything else that requires a multiple entry into a list, you would enter them into the Multi-String Editor shown here:

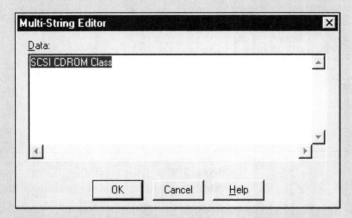

⇨ *REG_EXPAND_SZ.* The expandable string looks identical to the simple text string, but allows for the use of a variable. You enter a variable into the REG_EXPAND_SZ dialog box (which looks identical to the String Editor dialog box), and Windows NT uses that variable and replaces it with text when it is activated. The following are examples of REG_EXPAND_SZ variable entries: %SYSTEMROOT%, %USERNAME%, or %PROCESSORFAMILY%.

⇨ *REG_DWORD.* This is 32-bit data shown as 4 bytes that can be used to perform error control or configuration settings.

⇨ *REG_BINARY.* A binary entry can be any length, and is data that is used by programs in Windows NT. The following illustration shows you the Binary Editor:

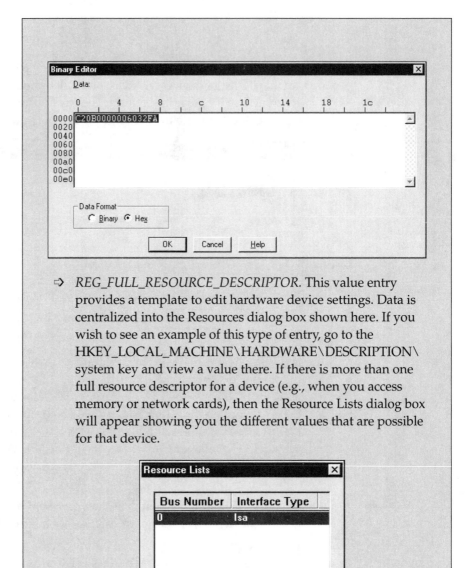

⇨ *REG_FULL_RESOURCE_DESCRIPTOR.* This value entry
provides a template to edit hardware device settings. Data is
centralized into the Resources dialog box shown here. If you
wish to see an example of this type of entry, go to the
HKEY_LOCAL_MACHINE\HARDWARE\DESCRIPTION\
system key and view a value there. If there is more than one
full resource descriptor for a device (e.g., when you access
memory or network cards), then the Resource Lists dialog box
will appear showing you the different values that are possible
for that device.

How big can the Registry become?

To change the maximum Registry size:

1. Double-click on the System icon in the Control Panels folder.

2. Click the Performance tab, and then click the Change button in the Virtual Memory section to view the Virtual Memory dialog box shown in Figure 12-6.

3. Enter a size in the Maximum Registry Size (MB) text box, and then click the OK button.

The actual size of the Registry can be slightly larger than the amount you enter in the System control panel. It is related to the size of your paging file, which is related to the amount of installed RAM in your system.

When the Registry exceeds the size you set, it brings your system to a halt with a STOP error ("Blue Screen of Death"). This problem is very rarely encountered unless you attempt to reduce the size of the Registry artificially. Even on a system heavily loaded with applications and processes, the Registry seldom exceeds 7MB in size.

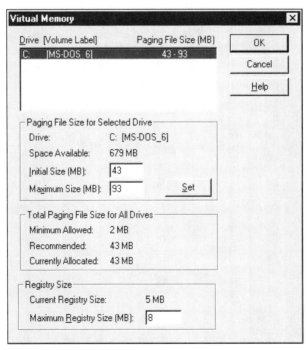

Figure 12-6.   The Virtual Memory dialog box

Keep a maximum Registry size about 2 MB larger than the current size in the Virtual Memory dialog box.

 I want to be able to examine the contents of my Registry in an easy-to-read format. Is there any way to export the data it contains?

You can export the data in the Registry in text form. Doing so will allow you to peruse your settings and check any data or values it contains by using any text editor.

To export data in the Registry as text:

1. Click on the key or subkey that you wish to export in the Registry Editor (Regedt32).

2. Select the Save Subtree As command from the Registry menu.

3. Enter the File name, select a location, and select the text data type in the Save as type list box; then click the OK button.

Figure 12-7 shows you an exported control panel key in the Notepad applet.

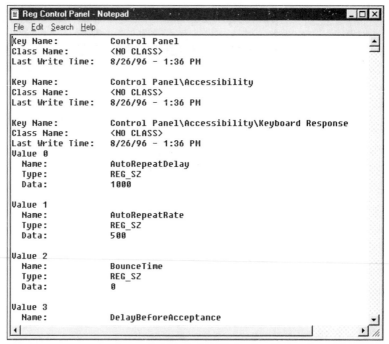

Figure 12-7.   A control panel key as exported text data in the Notepad applet

To export the entire Registry file as data, use the Export Registry File command on the Registry menu. Files exported in this manner are saved with the .REG file extension (but are really text files). A REG file will have the following sections:

⇨ *[keyname].* The HKEY, key, or subkey name.

⇨ *"Valuename"=.* The value name.

⇨ *@=.* The default value for the key.

⇨ *="data".* The string data.

⇨ *="hex".* Binary data in hexadecimal form.

I have a copy of my Registry as a REG file. How do I import a Registry file?

You can use REG files as a backup, to duplicate entries from one user or system to another, or to propagate duplicate changes. Provided you are careful and you know what you are doing, this method can be quick and effective.

To import a REG file:

1. Open the Registry Editor (Regedt32) and select the key to be imported.

2. Select the Import Registry File command on the Registry menu.

3. Select the REG file and click the OK button.

Windows NT will overwrite the entries in the key and subkeys and update your Registry, posting a confirmation dialog box when complete.

BACKING UP AND RESTORING THE REGISTRY

How do I create a backup Registry in case my original gets corrupted?

The Repair Disk utility lets you back up the Registry and repair minor problems that arise. When RDISK.EXE runs, it creates a file that you can store on your hard drive, copy off to a floppy disk or a network location, and so forth. You will also need to create an Emergency Repair Disk (ERD) to hold the system subsection of the Registry, which allows you to boot your computer and work with your backup copy of the Registry. These procedures only have value if you regularly run RDISK and create new ERDs. Chapter 7, "Backing Up and Restoring Your System," describes these procedures in more detail.

Can I back up my Registry files by copying them directly?

If you are running Windows NT, the hives of the Registry are locked and cannot be accessed to be copied. However, if you have a dual boot system or boot your system using MS-DOS or some other operating system, these files are not locked and may be copied directly. You could copy them to another drive or volume.

You will be able to view files on a FAT volume from any other operating system. If the file system is an NTFS volume, then only a Windows NT or Linux system running a disk access utility will be able to view the files, read them, and copy them.

I've mistakenly deleted a key or value in the Registry. What can I do?

If you delete a key or value by accident in the Registry Editor, there is no Undo command to help you recover from this action if you confirmed it. When the Confirm On Delete command on the Options menu is selected (by default), RegEdit will at least post a confirmation dialog box as a safeguard—but it's easy to confirm a mistake.

To recover from a critical deletion:

1. Close the Registry Editor.

2. Immediately restart your computer.

3. Hold down the SPACEBAR key as NT loads and select the Last Known Good option.

Windows NT boots your system using the backup Windows NT Registry, and any changes you made to your system since your last startup will be discarded. But you will be able to recover from any critical error.

Something is wrong with my computer. How do I know if I have a Registry problem?

The following problems are most often related to the Windows NT Registry:

⇨   The Blue Screen of Death.

⇨   A software or hardware component that operated correctly stops working without any physical changes being made to the files or to the device.

⇨   Something stops working after you add new software or hardware and the two are not known to be incompatible.

⇨   Your computer looks or works differently than it once did.

⇨   Your computer won't boot properly or at all.

⇨   Your computer won't shut down correctly.

Of course, there can be other explanations for these problems beyond a corrupted or altered Registry, but most often they are Registry related.

I have a STOP error resulting from a Registry problem. How do I fix it?

The Blue Screen of Death is the most common indication of a STOP error. Try to run the Check Disk program to repair these types of errors associated with disk and file problems. The CHDSK.EXE program is located in the <System Root>\System32 directory.

Exchanging Data Between Applications

Answer Topics!

Exchanging Data Between Applications @ a Glance

⇨ The **Clipboard** is an area of system memory that can be used to transfer information from one document to another. It supports a wide variety of data types, and allows you to move data between the documents of different applications. You can capture a screen to the Clipboard. You can use the ClipBook utility to save the contents of the Clipboard and share it with other users across a network.

⇨ **Object Linking or Embedding**, or OLE, is a system for including an object or data from one application in the document of another application. The source application plays the role of a server, providing display and editing capabilities when the destination document (which is the client) opens or when editing of the object is required. OLE uses a "cut-and-paste" metaphor.

⇨ You can create **compound documents** with OLE by including linked or embedded objects from one application in another. Links can be created, broken, or modified, and you can control when a linked object is updated.

⇨ For a document that doesn't support OLE, you can use the Object Packager utility to package objects. A **package** can be a file, part of a file, or any data object. It can also be a simple command line statement that runs when activated. A package has an iconic representation that you can copy to the Clipboard and paste into your destination document. What happens when you activate the package depends upon what type of object it is.

USING THE CLIPBOARD

What is the Clipboard?

The Clipboard is a reserved section of system memory that can store data. You transfer data to the Clipboard when you select the Copy or Cut commands that are found on nearly all Windows applications' Edit menus. In the former case, you duplicate the selection in memory; in the latter, you remove the selection from the application. The Clipboard can hold only one selection at a time, so moving new data to the Clipboard overwrites the previous contents. Also, the contents of the Clipboard is volatile and is lost when you reboot your system or log on in another Windows session.

To move the contents of the Clipboard to another location, you use the Paste command on the Edit menu of most Windows applications. A copy of the contents is placed at the current location of your selection point or in a location defined by the application—typically the center of a document window. The content of the Clipboard is left untouched by the Paste command. The following illustration shows you the Edit menu of the Notebook applet with the commands of the Clipboard on it: Cut, Copy, and Paste.

Almost universally, Windows applications use the keystrokes CTRL-X for Cut, CTRL-C for Copy, and CTRL-V for Paste. The commands for Paste Special, Paste Link, or other OLE commands vary from application to application, and from data type to data type.

In another metaphor, you can use the Paste Special command (or a similarly named command) to either embed or link the object on the Clipboard into the new location. An embedded object is copied to the location and a link is established between that object and the creator application. Or you can link the object in the document, placing a pointer to the original object in the target location. Object Linking and Embedding (OLE) is described later in this chapter.

The Clipboard is one of the most widely used parts of Windows system software. It is not only useful for transferring data between one document and another, but it will perform some data conversion if necessary. The range of data and objects that can be transferred through the Clipboard is very large and includes text, formatted text, graphics, sound, and video, among others.

❓ I'd like to retain a picture of my screen. How do I capture a screen to the Clipboard?

There are many reasons why you might want to create a screen capture. Screen captures can be used to document software, as wallpaper on your computer, or for printing or display purposes. Windows NT has a handy method for capturing a screen and copying it to the Clipboard as a bitmapped graphic. You can capture the entire screen or just the active window using a built-in system function. Then you can paste the result into Microsoft Paint or another program that supports .BMP files (most programs that handle graphics do).

To copy a picture of the entire screen to the Clipboard, press the PRINT SCREEN key on your keyboard.

To copy the active window to the Clipboard:

1. Open the window or dialog box and adjust its size.

2. Press the ALT-PRINT SCREEN keystroke.

Note: *On some keyboards, the* SHIFT-PRINT SCREEN *keystroke works instead of the* ALT-PRINT SCREEN *keystroke for copying a window.*

Tip: *If you need a more professional screen capture utility that lets you edit, crop, add borders, translate file formats, and organize your screen captures, check out programs like Collage, Tiffany, PixelPop, HotShot, and HiJaak.*

❓ I can't find the ClipBook Viewer in the Accessories folder. How do I open that application?

Some installations don't place the ClipBook Viewer in the Accessories folder. To find and open that application, search for the program file CLIPBRD.EXE using the Find command on the Start menu. You may wish to drag a shortcut of that application to the Accessories folder within the Programs folder of the Start Menu folder. This will make it appear on your Start menu.

I'd like to know the contents of the Clipboard before I overwrite the information or paste it into my document. How do I do that?

Many applications include a Show Clipboard command on one of the menus, often the View or Window menu. For those situations when you are working on the Desktop or in an application that doesn't include that command, Windows NT includes the Clipboard Viewer utility to view the contents of the Clipboard. You can also use the ClipBook Viewer to view the contents of the Clipboard. The Clipboard Viewer and the ClipBook Viewer work similarly. You may find both installed on your system, or just the ClipBook Viewer.

To view the contents of the Clipboard:

1. Select the Clipboard Viewer from the Accessories folder on the Programs submenu of the Start menu. If you are using the Clipboard Viewer, no other steps are required; the contents of the Clipboard opens automatically.

2. Double-click on the Clipboard icon found in the bottom left of the window.

3. Or select the Clipboard command from the Window menu.

The contents of the Clipboard appears in a window in the viewer. Figure 13-1 shows a graphic image in the ClipBook Viewer.

Text will always display correctly, but you may see a distorted image. Also, any information that relates to OLE is not shown in the Viewer.

If the image in the Viewer window doesn't look correct, you may wish to change the format of the image by selecting a command from the View menu. The format changes the display of an image, but has no effect on the actual contents of the Clipboard itself.

 I would like to copy MS-DOS information to a Windows document. How do I do that?

You can copy text or graphics from a DOS program into a Windows document. If you are running the DOS program full screen, you will need to switch that program into a Command Prompt window.

Text and graphics that you copy to the Clipboard are treated differently depending on the video mode that the DOS window is in. If the DOS application is running in text mode, the data is transferred

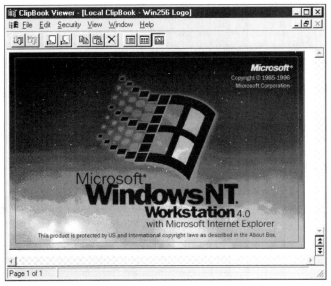

Figure 13-1.   A graphic image displayed in the ClipBook Viewer

as text to the Clipboard and can be pasted into a text editor or word processor like Notepad or WordPad, respectively. If the DOS application is running in graphics mode, the information is placed on the Clipboard as a bitmapped graphic and can be pasted into a graphics program like Microsoft Paint.

Tip   *If you get information in one form and want it in another, try changing the video display of your MS-DOS program. The MS-DOS program manual should explain how this is done.*

To copy information from an MS-DOS program:

1. Start the program and open the document you desire.

2. If the document isn't in a window, press the ALT-ENTER keystroke to switch out of full-screen mode into a windowed environment.

3. Click on the MS-DOS icon at the top-left corner of the window to open the window menu, or press the ALT-SPACEBAR keystroke.

4. Select the Mar_k_ command from the _E_dit submenu on the window
    menu, as shown here. If you change your mind, press the ESC or
    ENTER key with nothing selected on your screen.

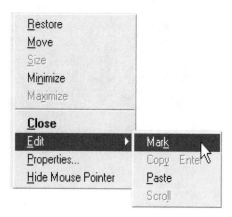

5. Move your cursor to highlight the information, data, or object that
    you wish to copy to the Clipboard, and then release the mouse
    button. The word "Select" appears in the title bar.

6. Press the ENTER key to move the information onto the Clipboard.

    You can't cut information from a DOS box, only copy it to the
    Clipboard.

❓ How can I tell what formats the Clipboard is using for the data it contains?

The View menu in the ClipBook Viewer will list all of the different
data formats in use when you open to a page. If you want to view the
format of the current contents of the Clipboard, paste a new page and
open the View menu. For simple data like a bitmapped graphic, you
might only see Bitmap listed in the View menu. For complex data, you
might see a wide variety of data types.

If you select a different format for the view in the ClipBook
viewer, it changes the appearance of the data in the window, but has
no effect on the underlying data stored in the file. If you paste the data
into another application, that application decides which format in
which to import the data into its document.

Table 13-1 lists some of the common formats for data copied to the
Clipboard.

Table 13-1. OLE Component Files

Data Format	Notes
Text	Unformatted text in ANSI standard characters.
OEM Text	Unformatted characters in the extended ASCII character set (used also by MS-DOS applications).
Rich Text Format	Text with embedded codes for formatting, font, paragraph, and other style information. RTF is a common interchange file format.
Bitmap	A graphic in the form of a set of pixels. Windows uses the .BMP file format, the native file format of Microsoft Paint, for data of this type.
Picture	A picture is an object description of a drawing. The native format of a picture in Windows is the Windows Metafile (WMF). A metafile is one that can contain multiple object descriptions. WMF can contain bitmapped objects in addition to drawings.
DIB	A Device Independent Bitmap, a newer version of a bitmap that contains information about the colors used and the resolution of the creator device or application. This extra information makes it easier to reproduce a bitmapped image correctly.
BIFF, BIFF3, CSV, DIF, Sylk, and Wk1	These formats are used by database and spreadsheet applications to exchange information.
Link, OwnerLink, ObjectLink	These formats contains OLE links between an object and a server application.
Unicode Text	This is a 16-bit format for specifying text and symbols in a wide variety of supported international languages.

I know that I can't paste graphics from the Clipboard into an MS-DOS document. Is there a workaround?

Although you can't paste graphics into an MS-DOS document from the keyboard, you can paste graphics into a program like Microsoft Paint or Corel Draw. Save the graphic in a file that your MS-DOS application can read. Most will read a .BMP or .PCX file.

I want to paste text on the Clipboard into an MS-DOS document. How do I do that?

You can paste data into an MS-DOS document, even though it would seem intuitively that you couldn't. You are limited to pasting text into a DOS box. Graphics would require matching carefully or translating the video resolution and color depth, and so are not supported.

To paste text on the Clipboard into an MS-DOS document:

1. Open the MS-DOS application and document in a window. Press the ALT-ENTER keystroke to toggle from full screen to window environment, if necessary.

2. Move the cursor in the window to the position where you want the text to be inserted.

3. Press the ALT-SPACEBAR keystroke to open the System menu, or click on the MS-DOS icon.

4. Select the Paste command from the Edit menu, as shown here:

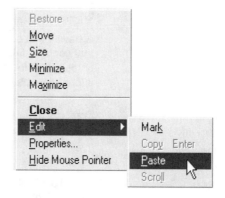

The text appears to the right of the cursor. Pasting into a DOS window works by filling a keyboard buffer from the Clipboard.

Note: *Simply clicking the MS-DOS icon and using Edit/Paste does not work, so follow the instructions above carefully.*

Why do programs display a dialog box about the contents of a private Clipboard when I exit them?

Many large programs implement their own internal or private Clipboards to manage proprietary data types and large amounts of data. Programs like Word and Photoshop fall into this category. In general, older 16-bit applications are more likely to work this way. These programs generally make the copied data available to the Windows NT system Clipboard, but not always. This is one of the reasons why you see a message when you exit a program of this type asking you if you want to save any large amounts of data on the Clipboard.

What methods can I use to save the contents of my Clipboard so that it isn't lost?

There are three methods you can use to save the contents of the Clipboard:

⇨ Paste the contents into a document and save that document to disk.

⇨ Save the data as a Clipboard file (.CLP) so that you can open and view the data at a later time, or share that file over the network.

⇨ Save the data as a page in the ClipBook utility so that you can view it later or even share it over a network with another user.

Note: The .CLP file format is a proprietary format. It hides many pieces of information relating to the Clipboard contents: formatting, the link to the creator application, and so forth. Your view of the Clipboard may be distorted, but when you actually paste the contents into a destination document and print it, the data should view or print properly.

In the first instance, when you attempt to paste the contents of the Clipboard into a document, the target application examines the data type and picks the format that it best supports. If there is no format that the data can be accepted in, the Paste command is grayed out and the data can't be pasted. If you want to save the data as a .CLP file, you can use either the Clipboard Viewer or the ClipBook Viewer.

To save a Clipboard file:

1. Open either the ClipBook Viewer or the Clipboard Viewer and display the contents of the Clipboard in the window.

2. Select the Save As command from the File menu to view the Save As dialog box shown in Figure 13-2.

3. Enter the name of the file in the File name text box, select the file location from the Folders list box, and select Clipboard Files (*.CLP) from the Save as type list box. Then click the OK button.

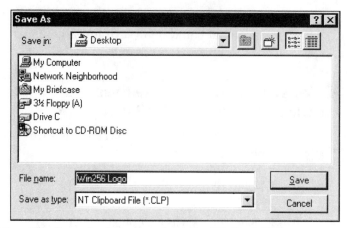

Figure 13-2.   The Save As dialog box from the ClipBook Viewer

Shown here is an icon for a .CLP file. A file saved in the Clipboard file type can be opened using the Open command on the File menu of the ClipBook Viewer.

While it is convenient and easy to save .CLP files, if you use a lot of these files, you can have trouble keeping track of them. ClipBook allows you to store up to 127 different items (one to a page), create a thumbnail representation of each page, and name each page. You can also share any or all of your pages with other users over the network.

To save an item as a ClipBook page:

1. Select the ClipBook Viewer from the Accessories folder on the Programs submenu of the Start menu.

2. Select the Paste command from the Edit menu.

3. In the Paste dialog box that appears (shown here), enter a Page name.

4. Select the <u>S</u>hare item now checkbox (optional).

5. Click the OK button.

When you want to paste the contents of a page from the ClipBook into your document, turn to that page and select the Copy command on the Edit menu. Then select the <u>P</u>aste command in your document.

I want to be able to share the contents of my Clipboard with other users across a network. How do I do that?

To share the contents of your Clipboard, first copy the Clipboard to a page in the ClipBook. Then set the page so that it can be shared.
To share the contents of your Clipboard:

1. Select the ClipBook Viewer from the Accessories folder on the <u>P</u>rograms submenu of the Start menu.

2. Select the Local ClipBook from the <u>W</u>indow menu.

3. Select the Copy command from the Edit menu to copy the Clipboard to a ClipBook page.

Note: *There are three ways to view pages in the ClipBook: Table of Contents, Thumbnails, or Full Page.*

4. Or double-click on the thumbnail (see Figure 13-3) of the item you wish to share to switch to that page in the ClipBook.

5. Select the Share command from the <u>F</u>ile menu.

6. Click on the <u>S</u>tart Application on Connect checkbox in the ClipBook Page Properties dialog box as shown here:

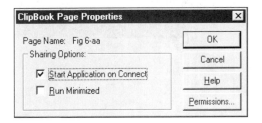

7. To limit access to a page (Full Access is the default), click on the Permissions button to view the ClipBook Page Permissions dialog box shown in Figure 13-4.

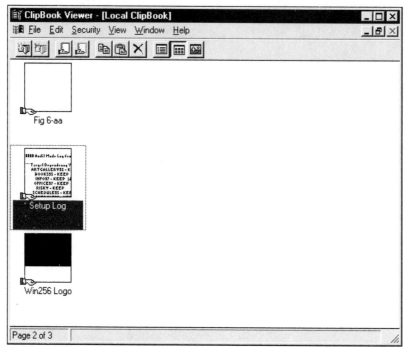

Figure 13-3.   The Thumbnail view of the ClipBook Viewer

8. Select the name of the group or member from the Name list box, and then select the level of access from the Type of Access list box.

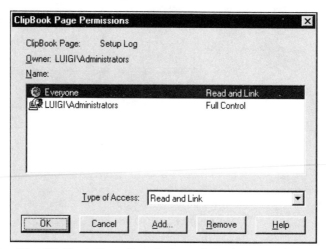

Figure 13-4.   The ClipBook Page Permissions dialog box

9. If you wish to audit access to the ClipBook, click on the Auditing button and set the options desired in the ClipBook Page Auditing dialog box shown in Figure 13-5.

10. Click the OK button twice to return to the ClipBook Viewer; then select the Exit command from the File menu.

The purpose of the ClipBook Page Properties option is to allow a user to run the application necessary to use the data on the ClipBook page. You don't need this option if the data is text, formatted text, or a simple bitmapped image. But for anything more complex, and just to be on the safe side, it is a good idea to enable the application for remotely connected users.

If you want to share another computer's ClipBook page, use the Connect command on the File menu in the ClipBook Viewer to open the remote ClipBook, and then enter your password if one is required. When you are done, select the Disconnect command on the File menu to end your access.

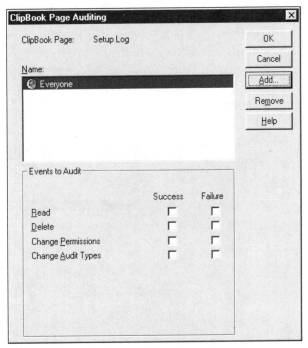

Figure 13-5.   The ClipBook Page Auditing dialog box

OBJECT LINKING AND EMBEDDING

What is OLE?

Object Linking and Embedding, or OLE, now in version 2.0, is a means of sharing data between applications and having that data serviced by the creator application in the document of the application that is using the data. OLE uses the terms *client* for the container of the data, and *server* for the application that can manage or modify the data. OLE is an outgrowth of older messaging technology in Windows, Dynamic Data Exchange (DDE), Network DDE, and the original OLE specification. Recently, Microsoft has specified OLE for Internet use and dubbed the technology ActiveX.

OLE uses the "cut-and-paste" metaphor. When you Cut or Copy an object in one application's document and open another application's document, you will see a Paste Special command (or something similar) in the other application's Edit menu. If you use the Paste Special command, a dialog box opens asking if you wish to embed the object or link to the object. The following illustration shows you the Paste Special dialog box from Word 97. Embedding puts a copy of the object in your document, while linking places a pointer to the original data file. The registration of the object's data type (as seen within the Windows NT Explorer) is the connection between the object and the server application.

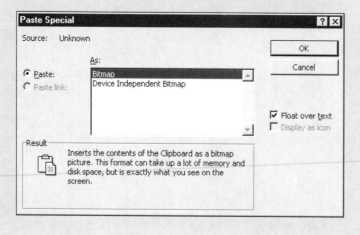

It is the task of the server application to provide display capabilities for the object. When you double-click on the object in your document, the server application opens and provides the editing capabilities. In some instances, the object opens in another window of the server application. Newer technology called "editing-in-place" opens the server application within the window of the client application, temporarily replacing the client application's menus and toolbars until you click outside of the object to deselect it. The next illustration shows you an Excel spreadsheet object within Word being edited in place.

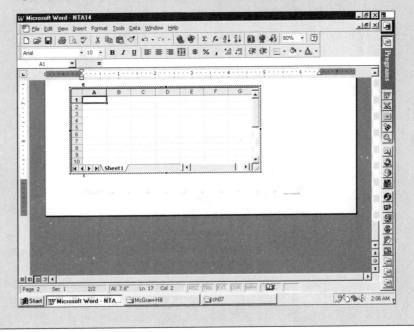

My OLE object doesn't work. What are some possible explanations for this problem?

There can be many reasons why a linked or embedded object might not be displayed or updated properly. Here are some common ones:

⇨ *The OLE data file is corrupted.* This happens often when an older OLE object overwrites a newer one, and the owner application can't properly handle the newer object.

⇨ *Neither application is an OLE server.* OLE depends on a client/server system. One application must provide the services necessary to display and modify an OLE object.

⇨ *The Registry entry for that object is either incorrect or corrupted.* Sometimes the Registry incorrectly specifies the linkage.

⇨ *Your current network doesn't fully support OLE2, or requires special configuration to do so.* Examples in this category include Artisoft LANtastic, Banyan Vines, and others.

⇨ *An important OLE DLL file is either missing or corrupted.*

What files on my system are responsible for providing OLE services?

Most of the files that support OLE are dynamic link libraries, with one notable exception: OLE2.REG. You will find these files in the <SYSTEM ROOT>\WINNT\SYSTEM folder. Table 13-2 shows the main OLE component files.

Table 13-2. OLE Component Files

File Name	Purpose
OLESRV.DLL	Supports the server routines.
OLECLI.DLL	Supports the client routines.
OLE32.DLL	The 32-bit routines for the base OLE code. Most of these programs have counterparts with 32 in their names that serve this function.
OLE2NLS.DLL	This provides National Language Support (NLS) so that OLE can work with data in languages other than English.
OLE2DISP.DLL	The display routines for objects.
OLE2CONV.DLL	A set of generic routines that convert one object into the client's native format.
OLE2.REG	A Registry file that you can import into your Registry to install OLE2. Since applications install OLE2 as needed, this file is useful as a backup should your Registry get corrupted.
OLE2.DLL	The central set of routines supporting OLE2.
MFCOLEUI.DLL	The Microsoft Foundation Classes provide a C++ interface for OLE that allows programmers to write OLE code more easily into their application.
MCIOLE.DLL	The routines for handling sound objects.

❓ Where in the Windows NT Registry is OLE information maintained?

Not all Windows NT applications support OLE. Those that do have their information stored in the Windows NT Registry in the HKEY_CLASSES_ROOT key. Figure 13-6 shows you that subkey of the HKEY_LOCAL_MACHINE key in the Registry Editor.

COMPOUND DOCUMENTS

❓ I want to create a new link between an object and an OLE server to make use of a new program. How do I do that?

You can cancel or delete a link between an OLE object and its server application by selecting the object and then selecting the command in the client application that manages links. In WordPad, for example, the command is the Links command on the Edit menu. Figure 13-7 shows you the Links dialog box from WordPad. If you click on the Break Link button, that link is broken. An orphaned data object can still be displayed, viewed, or played if the client application is capable of doing so. Otherwise, only an icon is displayed.

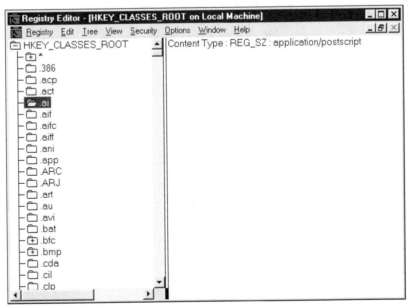

Figure 13-6.   The HKEY_CLASSES_ROOT key in the Windows NT Registry

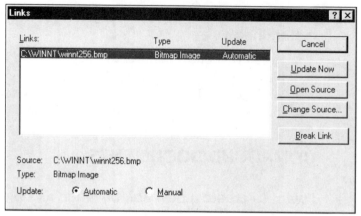

Figure 13-7.   The Links dialog box

To edit the source application for a linked object in WordPad, click on the Change Source button in the Links dialog box and specify the application that you wish to be the new server application.

? A linked object in my document isn't updating or can't be displayed. How do I fix that?

You can reestablish a broken link or control how linked objects are updated from within the Links dialog box. The Links command typically is found on the Edit menu. All linked objects are updated whenever you open a destination document. You can suppress automatic updates and change to a manual update at the time you specify.

To fix a link or control link update:

1. In the destination document, select the Links command from the Edit menu.

2. Click on the link you want to modify in the Links list box of the Links dialog box.

3. Click on the Update Now button to force a link object to be refreshed.

4. Or click on the Manual radio button to defer updates of that link until you click on the Update Now button at some later date.

5. Click on the Close button in the title bar to close the dialog box.

PACKAGING OBJECTS

 What are the built-in OLE object types that I see?

Table 13-3 shows you the various OLE object types that are there after you install Windows NT. The server application responsible for the OLE object type is also shown. As you install additional applications into Windows NT, you will see additional OLE object types appear in dialog boxes showing the kind of object you can insert into a document.

Can I embed a program that runs from the command line in a document?

You can package a command line statement using the Object Packager, and copy that package into a destination document.

1. Select the Object Packager command from the Accessories folder on the Programs submenu of the Start menu.

2. Select the Command Line command on the Edit menu to open the Command dialog box shown here.

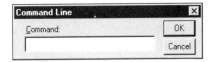

Table 13-3. Built-in OLE Object Types and their Associations

OLE Object Type	Server Application
Bitmapped Image	Microsoft Paint
Image Document	Imaging
Media Clip	Media Player
MIDI Sequence	Media Player
Package	Object Packager
Paintbrush Picture	Microsoft Paint
Video Clip	Media Player
Wave Sound	Sound Recorder
WordPad Document	WordPad

3. Enter the command with any associated parameters or switches, and then click the OK button.

4. Click the Insert Icon button and select the icon you desire.

5. Select the Copy Package command from the Edit menu to place the package on the Clipboard.

6. Open the destination document, position the cursor where the object will go; then select the Paste command from the Edit menu.

When the recipient of your package double-clicks on the icon for the command line statement, the statement is run.

? Is there any way that I can include an OLE object in a document that doesn't support OLE?

To include an OLE object within an application that doesn't support OLE, you create a package and insert it within the destination document. Microsoft includes the Object Packager application in Windows NT for this purpose.

Packaging creates an iconic representation of the data object that you can drop into your document from the Desktop or using the Windows NT Explorer. When the viewer double-clicks on the icon, the package activates. What happens next depends on the particular data type. A video clip would run in a window, or a sound would play. If the data is a spreadsheet, word processing document, or other data type, the creator application opens to display the data.

To create a package from a file:

1. Select the Object Packager command from the Accessories folder on the Programs submenu of the Start menu.

2. Click on the Content window of the Object Packager, as shown here.

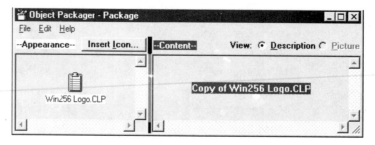

3. Select the Import command from the File menu.

4. Select the file you want to package in the Import window.

5. Select the Copy Package command from the <u>E</u>dit menu to place the package on the Clipboard.

6. Open the destination document and position the cursor where the object will go; then select the <u>P</u>aste command from the <u>E</u>dit menu.

Figure 13-8 shows you a package inside WordPad.

The Object Packager is also capable of creating a package from an object that isn't a complete data file. You can select the data, copy it to the Clipboard, and then paste it into the Object Packager. From there the procedure follows along as above.

 Tip: *To find out what kind of object an embedded, linked, or package object is in a destination document, right-click on the object and select the Properties command from the shortcut menu.*

? Is there a way of creating a permanent copy of an object without going through the Clipboard or the Object Packager?

You can create a document scrap using an application that supports this feature.

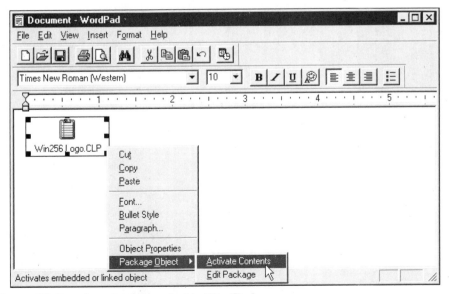

Figure 13-8. A package icon inside WordPad

To create a scrap file:

1. Select the object within your document or application.

2. Drag your selection to the Desktop.

A scrap file is created that contains the selected information. Shown here is the icon for a scrap file. If you double-click on the scrap file icon, the creator application opens, displaying the contents of the scrap file.

Answer Topics!

Networking Issues @ a Glance

⇨ When you install a **network interface adapter** card (NIC) in Windows NT, you must create a network binding for that card. This binding assigns a network address to the card so that other computers can communicate with that card. This system allows Windows NT to support multiple NICs in the same computer for different purposes.

⇨ Windows NT provides a rich range of **network services**. You can manage security on Windows NT using the User Manager for Domains, establishing users and groups as well as machine accounts. Through a users logon, applications that use the NT security scheme can have resource requests validated by Windows NT Server.

⇨ You can install different **network protocols** on Windows NT Server or Workstation and have them run singly or in a protocol stack. These protocols are used in servicing different clients or accessing different resources.

⇨ You can install and manage multiple **modems** in Windows NT. From within the Modems control panel, you can call up the Install New Modem wizard or configure the properties of an existing modem. Modems use the new Unimodem driver interface in Windows NT that also supports telephony applications.

⇨ Many network problems are cable related. This is particularly true when you have just installed new hardware or reconfigured your network. **Cabling issues** are best corrected by isolating the segment or connection responsible.

⇨ You can create **shares** so that other users on a network can access files or folders. These shares are protected by the Windows NT security scheme.

⇨ Windows NT can serve as a **remote access** server or client. Using RAS, clients can call into a network and log on as if they were a local node on the network. You can connect to a RAS server by using the PPTP protocol and connecting through your local Internet Service Provider. A PPTP connection is encrypted and secure, and replaces a long-distance phone call to a RAS server with a local dial-up connection.

⇨ Windows **NT Server and NetWare** can coexist on the same network. To have Windows NT and NetWare communicate with one another, the IPX/SPX protocol should be installed and properly configured on Windows NT. You should also install the Gateway Services for NetWare on NT.

NETWORK INTERFACE CARD ISSUES

I've just gotten a newer, faster, better network adapter for my computer. How do I install a network interface card?

Network interface cards (NICs), like most networking components in Windows NT, are installed using the Network control panel. In most cases, you will find that Windows NT knows about your NIC and lets you assign the appropriate software. For NICs that Windows NT doesn't know about, it's handy to have the manufacturer's installation instructions about as you do the installation.

Prior to installation, make sure that you know what IRQ and Base I/O address are used by your card. When installing multiple cards, determine that there is no conflict between these settings and other NIC cards or any other expansion cards in your system. You may need to adjust these settings on your card through either software or hardware DIP switches or jumpers on the card.

The following procedure is for the installation of your computer's first NIC.

To install a NIC, do the following:

1. Open your computer case and install your NIC card.

Warning: Make certain that your NIC card is firmly seated in the hardware slot in your computer. All of the connectors should mate with the contacts in the slot, and the card should be solidly placed into the slot. Try wiggling the card around to make sure it isn't loose, as this problem is difficult to diagnose otherwise. You should also be aware that NICs have a somewhat higher failure rate than most other components. So it is possible to buy a new and unused NIC that doesn't function properly.

2. Select the Control Panel command from the Settings submenu on the Start menu.

3. Double-click the Network icon, and then click the Adapters tab as shown in Figure 14-1.

4. Click the Add button to view the Select Network Adapter dialog box as shown in Figure 14-2.

5. If you see your adapter on the list, select it and click the OK button.

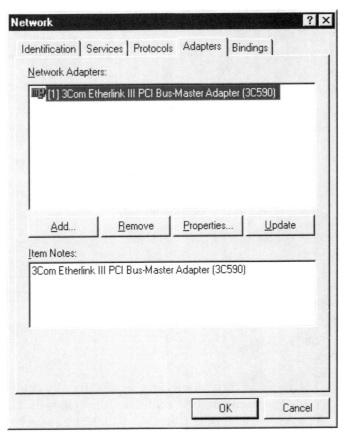

Figure 14-1.   The Adapters tab of the Network control panel

6. Or click the Have Disk button and copy the NIC driver file from your NIC vendor's installation disk.

7. Some NIC cards require that additional configuration information such as the IRQ Level and I/O Port Address be entered or confirmed. Try to obtain this information, or you may have to enter some different combinations until you find one that works properly. Click the OK button to continue.

8. Confirm the location of the files supplied by the Windows NT installation disk (if you don't use another disk), and click the Continue button; then click the Close button to add the network binding for your NIC.

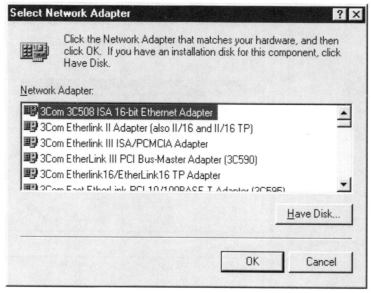

Figure 14-2.   The Select Network Adapter dialog box

9. Some protocols may require that you enter the protocol
   configuration information that binds the NIC to a specific
   network address (like TCP/IP, for example). Enter this
   information and restart your computer.

❓ What can I do if Setup doesn't recognize my network adapter?

Setup is very good at recognizing NIC cards. Hundreds are supported
directly or through emulation of another NIC card. If your card isn't
in the list of network adapters, click the Have Disk button, insert the
installation disk that came with your NIC card, and install the driver
for Windows NT from that disk using the OEMSETUP.INF file on that
disk. If you don't have an installation disk, check your NIC manual to
see if another driver may be used as a substitute.

NETWORK SERVICES

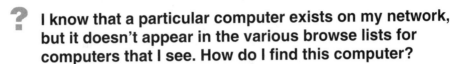

I know that a particular computer exists on my network, but it doesn't appear in the various browse lists for computers that I see. How do I find this computer?

Often Windows NT networks have problems browsing a network correctly. The reasons are many and varied, and not always easy to ascertain. If you know the name of the computer, use the Find command on the Start menu to locate the computer. Create a shortcut from the Find window and use that to access your computer.

To find a missing computer on the network:

1. Select the Computer command from the Find submenu of the Start menu.

2. Enter the name of the computer in the <u>N</u>amed text box, as shown in Figure 14-3.

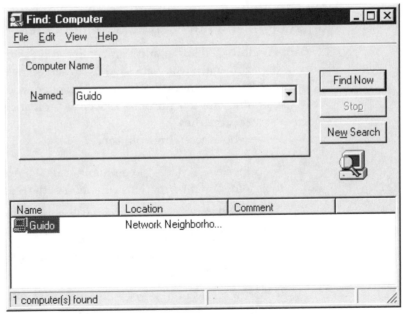

Figure 14-3.   The Find Computer dialog box with a returned search

3. Click the Find now button.

4. Right-click and drag the computer from the Find dialog box onto your desktop to create a shortcut to that computer.

5. Select the Create Shortcut(s) Here command from the shortcut menu.

Should you have difficulties finding or connecting to that computer, try using the shortcut you just created to open that computer.

If you wish to search for specific files on a computer, map the drive and use the following path:

```
\mapped drive letter\folder (optional)\filename
```

Or enter the path in UNC form as:

```
\\computername\drive\folder
```

How can I tell who is connected to my server or workstation, and how can I disconnect them?

Both Windows NT Server and Workstation come with the Server control panel, which lists connected users and allows you to disconnect them. Windows NT Server also offers you the Server Manager utility for this purpose, as well as for managing shares and other server properties.

To see who is accessing your server:

1. Select the Server Manager command from the Administrative Tools folder on the Programs submenu of the Start menu.

2. Double-click on the server name that you wish to check to see the Properties dialog box for that server, as shown in Figure 14-4.

3. Click the Users button to view the User Sessions dialog box shown in Figure 14-5.

4. To close a connection, select that user in the Connected Users list box, and then click the Disconnect button.

5. Click the Close button, and then close the Server Manager.

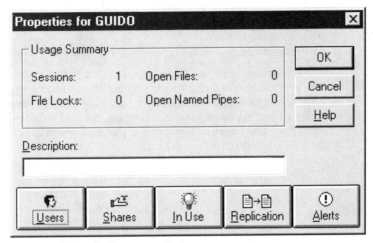

Figure 14-4.   The Server Property window

? I could not log on to the domain. What are some possible explanations?

Logon problems are among the most common network problems. Several different logon error messages can appear, and they can be attributable to different causes. Use Table 14-1 to ascertain which problem applies, and to check for potential solutions.

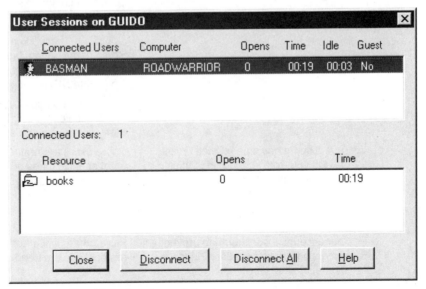

Figure 14-5.   The User Sessions dialog box

Table 14-1.   Typical Logon Problems

Error Message	Possible Cause
The system could not log you on. Make sure your username and domain name are correct, and then type your password again. Letters in passwords must be typed using the correct case. Make sure that the CAPS LOCK key is not accidentally on.	You may have entered an incorrect domain name or username. Check to see that you haven't accidentally pressed the CAPS LOCK key, as passwords are case sensitive in Windows NT.
	The password is wrong. If you have forgotten the password, get your system administrator to delete or reassign you a password.
	Your account or changes to your account are too new to be reflected in the BDC that is validating your logon request. Synchronize domain controllers.
A domain controller for your domain could not be contacted. You have been logged on using cached account information. Changes made to your profile since you last logged on may not be available.	Several different possible explanations exist for this error. Check that the domain controller is on, and online.
	Try promoting a BDC to a PDC.
	Check your network protocol settings. For example, an invalid TCP/IP address or subnet mask can prevent access to your domain controller.
	Check your network cable.
	Check your network interface card. Some cards have a fault light that indicates if they aren't seated properly. Check the NIC's settings.
	Restart the computer. Or try restarting the domain controller. This can solve many spurious logon and network errors.
Your account has time restrictions that prevent you from logging on at this time. Please try again later.	Some users are restricted from logging on at specific times during the day. Either consult your system administrator, or log on as an administrator and modify the account's logon hours.
Your account is configured to prevent you from using this workstation. Please try another workstation.	Have an administrator change the restriction in the Logon To restrictions.

We don't have e-mail set up on our computer, but I would like to send a message to another computer. How can I do that?

Windows NT has an application called Chat that you can use to send a message to another computer on the network. It isn't secure communication and it doesn't have many features, but it's perfect for simple, quick messaging sent and received in real time.

To use Chat:

1. Select the Chat command from the Accessories folder on the Programs submenu of the Start menu.

2. Click the Chat session button to view the Select Computer dialog box.

3. Double-click on the computer you wish to send a message to. A Chat window will open on the other computer, and the other user initiates the chat by clicking on the pick-up icon.

4. Enter your message into the top pane; you will see a response in the bottom pane.

5. Click the Disconnect icon to close the Chat window.

How can I change the name of my computer?

1. Select the Control Panel command from the Settings submenu on the Start menu.

2. Double-click the Network icon, and then click the Identification tab.

3. Click the Change button to view the Identification Changes dialog box.

4. Delete the name of the computer and enter the new name you wish.

5. Click the OK button in the alert box that warns you about name changes in a domain; then click the OK button to close the Identification Changes dialog box.

6. Close the Network control panel.

The old machine account must be deleted from the domain in the Server Manager for Domains on the Windows NT Server, and a new machine account for the computer with its new name should be created there prior to your next logon.

❓ My Primary Domain Controller has gone down or is offline. How do I promote a Backup Domain Controller?

If your PDC is no longer available, the BDC will continue to validate user requests for access to network resources. However, you will not be able to perform any administrative duties on domain account information. To do that, you need to promote your BDC to a PDC. Promotion makes the Security Account Manager database (SAM) on the BDC the master SAM for the domain.

To promote a BDC to a PDC:

1. Log on to the domain as an administrator.

2. Select the Server Manager from the Administrative Tools folder on the <u>P</u>rograms submenu of the Start menu.

3. Highlight the BDC in the Server Manager.

4. Select Promote to Primary Domain <u>C</u>ontroller from the <u>C</u>omputer menu.

5. Click Yes when you see the following message:

```
Promoting <Server> to Primary may take a few minutes.
Promoting <Server> will also close client connections to
<Server> and to the current domain controller (if any).
Press 'Help' for details if either machine is a Remote Ac-
cess server.
Do you want to make the Change?
```

6. If the PDC is already offline, click OK when the following message appears:

```
Cannot find the Primary for <domain name>. Continuing with
the promotion may result in errors when <domain name>'s old
Primary comes back online. Do you want to continue with
the promotion?
```

7. A status dialog box appears that shows the following messages (if the PDC is online):

```
Synchronizing <BDC Servername> with its primary domain controller
Stopping Net Logon Service on <BDC Servername>
Stopping Net Logon Service on <PDC Servername>
Changing <BDC Servername's> role to Backup
```

```
Changing <PDC Servername's> role to Primary
Starting Net Logon service on <BDC Servername> *(now the PDC)
Starting Net Logon service on <BDC Servername> *(now the BDC)
```

8. Close the Server Manager window.

The BDC is then promoted to the PDC. When (if) the previous PDC comes back online, it becomes a BDC.

If you wish to promote the demoted PDC from its role as BDC to PDC again, do the following:

1. Select the PDC in the Server Manager window.

2. Select the Demote to Backup Domain Controller command from the Computer menu, and then click Yes in the confirming dialog box.

3. Start the Net Logon service on the former PDC that was now demoted back to a BDC.

4. Select the BDC that was the original PDC, and then select the Promote to Primary Domain Controller command from the Computer menu.

5. Click Yes in the confirmation dialog box.

Your original BDC is demoted back to the BDC from its previous role as PDC and the original PCD is promoted to become the PDC once again from its previous role of BDC.

? I've just made a number of important domain account and group changes. How do I ensure that these changes are synchronized throughout the domain?

On a Windows NT network, domain changes are synchronized every five minutes by default. You can change the interval between synchronization events in the Windows NT Registry.

To manually synchronize domain changes to other domain controllers:

1. Log on to the server as an administrator.

2. Select the Synchronize Entire Domain command on the Computer menu.

3. Click the Yes button in the confirmation dialog box to begin resynchronization.

4. Click OK in the second alert box.

There is no confirmation of a successful synchronization in the domain. However, you can open the Event Log on a BDC and on the PDC to see if the synchronization was successful.
To verify synchronization:

1. Select the Event Viewer in the Administrative Tools folder of the Programs submenu on the Start menu.

2. Select the System command from the Log menu.

3. Select the most recent NETLOGON event under Source.

4. Select Detail on the View menu.

5. Read the details of the event, and then click Next until you see the confirmation of the synchronization event.

6. Close the Event Viewer.

? I want to join a domain so that I can better manage passwords and network resources. How do I do that?

To change a workgroup to a domain:

1. Select the Control Panel command from the Settings submenu on the Start menu.

2. Double-click the Network icon, and then click the Identification tab.

3. Click the Change button to view the Identification Changes dialog box.

4. Click the Domain radio button, and then enter the name of the domain that the workstation will join in the Domain text box.

5. Click on the Create a Computer Account in the Domain checkbox.

6. Enter a User Name and Password of an existing user account capable of creating user accounts and machine names, into those two text boxes. Click the OK button.

7. Click the Close button in the Network control panel, and then restart your computer.

When you next log on at your workstation, select the domain in the From list box and enter your username and password.

INSTALLING AND WORKING WITH NETWORK PROTOCOLS

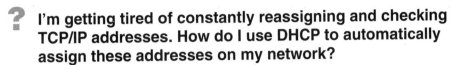 **I'm getting tired of constantly reassigning and checking TCP/IP addresses. How do I use DHCP to automatically assign these addresses on my network?**

The Dynamic Host Configuration Protocol or DHCP is a service that runs on Windows NT Server that can assign available TCP/IP addresses to computers at logon from a range of addresses that you specify. Addresses are assigned based on a "lease," and when that lease nears the end of its allotted time, a client will poll the service for a new address.

To install and configure DHCP:

1. Double-click the Network icon in the Control Panel folder.

2. Click the Services tab, and then the Add button.

3. Select the DHCP Server from the Network Services list, and then click the OK button.

4. Check the location of the Windows NT operating system files; then click the Continue button.

5. A dialog box appears telling you that the DHCP server will require a static TCP/IP address for the adapters on this server. Click the OK button, and then the Close button to continue and restart your system.

6. After restarting, select the DHCP Manager from the Administrative Tools folder on the Programs submenu of the Start menu.

7. In the DHCP Manager window shown in Figure 14-6, select Local Machine in the DHCP Servers list.

8. Select the Create from the Scope menu.

9. In the Create Scope dialog box shown in Figure 14-7, enter the Start Address and End Address for the range, and the Subnet Mask, into the text boxes.

10. If there is an excluded range of addresses, enter them into the Exclusion Range section, or add individual addresses into the Excluded Addresses list box.

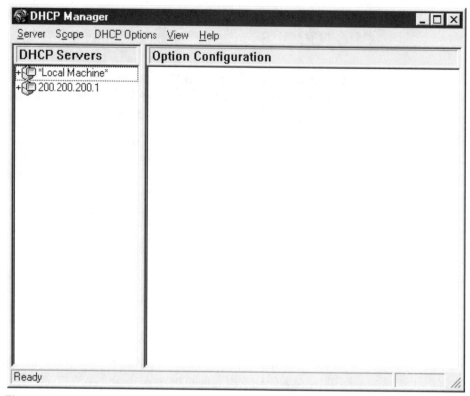

Figure 14-6.   The DHCP Manager window

11. Set the Lease Duration using either the Unlimited radio button or the Limited radio button and the Day(s), Hour(s), and Minute(s) spinners.

12. Click the OK button to create the scope, click Yes to activate it, and then close the DHCP Manager.

Once you have set up the DHCP server, go to your client computers and open the TCP/IP Properties dialog box from within the Network control panel's Protocols tab. Set the Obtain An IP Address From a DHCP Server option on.

? There's a network problem that requires that I know a specific computer's TCP/IP address. Is there any way to determine which DHCP address a client has been assigned?

To determine which computer has which assigned address from the DHCP service, look inside the DHCP Manager.

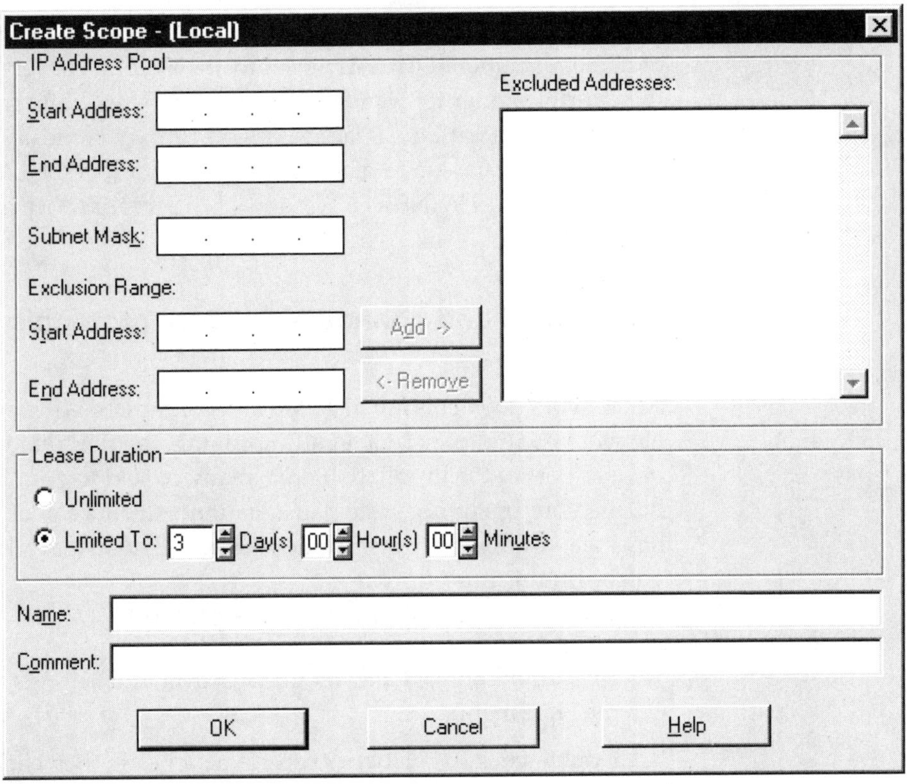

Figure 14-7.   The Create Scope dialog box

To find an associated computer name and TCP/IP address:

1. Select the DHCP Manager from the Administrative Tools folder on the Programs submenu of the Start menu.

2. Double-click on the Local Machine icon.

3. Select the TCP/IP address for the appropriate DHCP Server.

4. Select the Active Leases command from the Scope menu to view the Active Leases dialog box.

In the Client list box are both the TCP/IP address and the name of the computer associated with that address.

? How do I associate friendly names with IP addresses?

The older system of association maintains a LMHOSTS text file where names are matched to their IP addresses. For a static system of IP addresses, you can manually edit this file on the server.

Dynamic TCP/IP address assignment requires a different system of name resolution. DHCP is normally installed in concert with WINS, the Windows Internet Naming Service. WINS associates friendly Internet names with the IP addresses that are dynamically assigned. It frees you from having to manage this association in the LMHOSTS text file. You add WINS as a Windows NT Server service just as you added DHCP.

How do I install and configure network protocols in Windows NT?

All network protocols are installed and configured within the Network control panel. Generally speaking, the files that you need to have as part of the installation are already copied to your hard drive during your operating system installation. Still, it's a good idea to have the Windows NT distribution disks (CD-ROM) available when you begin this procedure.

To install and configure a network protocol:

1. Select the Control Panels command from the Settings submenu on the Start menu.

2. Double-click the Network control panel icon; then click the Protocols tab as shown in Figure 14-8.

3. Click the Add button to view the Select Network Protocols dialog box shown in Figure 14-9.

4. Select the protocol you desire from the Network Protocols list, and then click the Continue button.

5. Windows NT copies the files and adds the protocol. If additional settings (like network addresses or subnet masks for TCP/IP) are required, a configuration dialog box will appear asking for those settings.

6. Click the Close button and restart your computer.

NetBEUI is probably the easiest protocol to install, as it requires the fewest additional settings. When you select the NetBEUI protocol, you will notice that the Properties button in the Protocols tab is grayed out. NetBEUI uses the name of your computer as its machine identification.

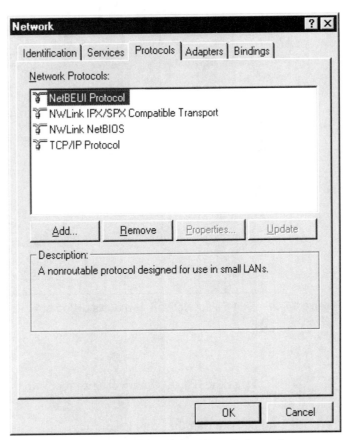

Figure 14-8.   The Protocols tab of the Network control panel

If you need to communicate with a Novell NetWare network, you will probably want to install the IPX/SPX protocol. This protocol *isn't* required to communicate with a NetWare server, but it is helpful and convenient for that application. IPX/SPX will require some additional configuration details once you have restarted your computer after installation.

To configure IPX/SPX:

1. Open the Network control panel.

2. Select the NWLink IPX/SPX Compatible Transport from the Network Protocol list box; then click the Properties button to view the NWLink IPX/SPX Properties dialog box (see Figure 14-10).

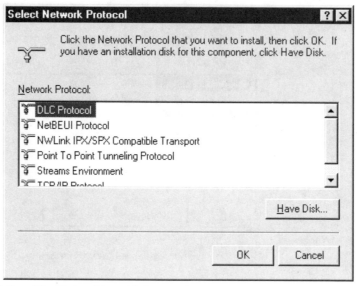

Figure 14-9.   The Select Network Protocols dialog box

3. Enter the IPX/SPX network number into the Internal Network Number text box.

4. Select either the Auto Frame Type Detection or Manual Frame Type Detection radio button

5. For manual detection, click the Add button and enter the frame type. NetWare uses either 802.2 or 802.3 as its frame type.

6. Click the OK button, and then the Close button to return to the Desktop.

7. Restart your computer.

Of the three common protocols, TCP/IP is the most complicated to configure. It is also becoming the de facto standard for Windows NT networks, and it is not unusual to find networks set up with only this protocol running. You will need at a minimum the IP address for your computer, as well as the subnet mask for the portion of the network that you are on. If your network has a gateway, you will need the hexadecimal address for that computer as well.

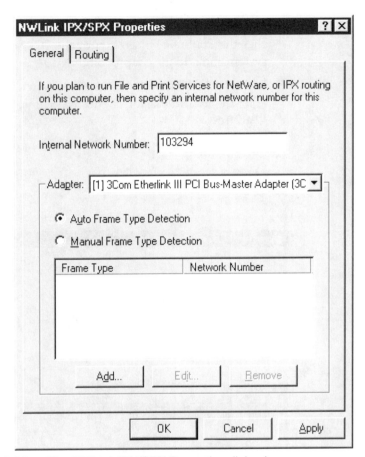

Figure 14-10.   The NWLink IPX/SPX Properties dialog box

To configure TCP/IP:

1. Open the Network control panel (as described above), click the Protocols tab, and click the Add button.

2. Select the TCP/IP Protocol from the Network Protocols list in the Select Network Protocols dialog box.

3. A dialog box appears asking if you have a DHCP server that automatically assigns your computer a TCP/IP address. Click the Yes button to continue the installation if a DHCP server is present, and you will not be required to enter a TCP/IP address for your computer. Otherwise, click the No button.

4. If the Windows NT operating system files are correctly shown, click the Continue button to copy the TCP/IP protocol to your system and add the adapter binding.

5. In the TCP/IP Properties dialog box shown in Figure 14-11, enter the IP Address, the Subnet Mask, and the Default Gateway IP address.

6. Click the OK button twice and restart your computer.

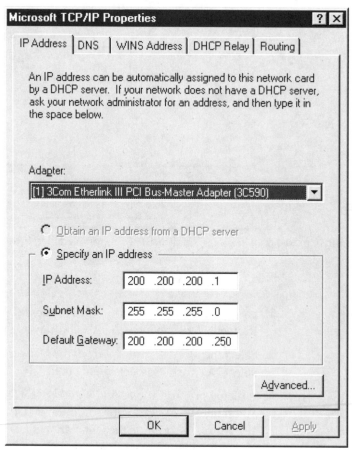

Figure 14-11. The TCP/IP Properties dialog box

? I have several network protocols installed on my computer, but I primarily use one of them. Is there any way to improve the performance of one network protocol over another?

When Windows NT communicates over a network, it first checks for communication using the top protocol listed in the Network dialog box on the Bindings tab. Then it proceeds down the list.

To improve a protocol's performance:

1. Select the <u>C</u>ontrol Panel command from the <u>S</u>ettings submenu on the Start menu.

2. Double-click the Network icon, and then click the Protocols tab.

3. Click on the protocol you wish to promote, and then drag it up to the top of the list.

4. Or use the Move Up button to promote the protocol.

5. Click the OK button.

? TCP/IP has been installed on my computer, but I can't seem to browse network resources using my Internet browser. How do I check that TCP/IP was properly installed?

Try using the PING utility to send and receive a reply and to check network TCP/IP addresses.

To PING another computer:

1. Select the Command Prompt command from the <u>P</u>rograms submenu on the Start menu.

2. Enter the command:

```
PING ###.###.###.###
```

Note: *###.###.###.### is a valid TCP/IP address of a computer on your network (or any valid TCP/IP address if you have an Internet connection). You can also use PING with a host name, such as PING <servername>, to see if that computer responds. Doing so helps determine whether the DHCP service has been correctly set up.*

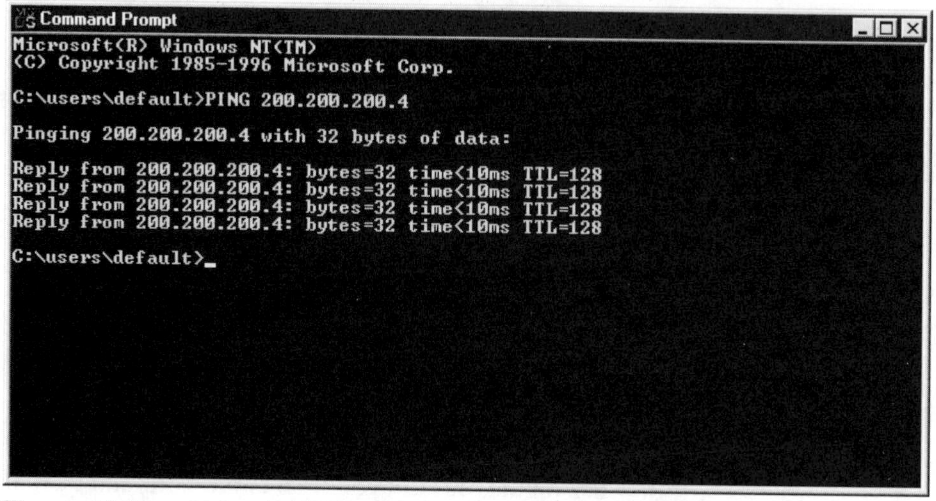

```
Command Prompt                                              _ □ ×
Microsoft(R) Windows NT(TM)
(C) Copyright 1985-1996 Microsoft Corp.

C:\users\default>PING 200.200.200.4

Pinging 200.200.200.4 with 32 bytes of data:

Reply from 200.200.200.4: bytes=32 time<10ms TTL=128
Reply from 200.200.200.4: bytes=32 time<10ms TTL=128
Reply from 200.200.200.4: bytes=32 time<10ms TTL=128
Reply from 200.200.200.4: bytes=32 time<10ms TTL=128

C:\users\default>_
```

Figure 14-12.   Using the PING command to check a TCP/IP connection

3. Check to see if a correct response is generated from the computer you ping'ed, an example of which is shown in Figure 14-12.

MANAGING MODEMS

How do I add a modem to Windows NT?

You add a modem to Windows NT through the Modems control panel. Before configuring the modem driver, shut down your computer and install the modem. For an internal modem, seat the modem in an expansion slot. For an external modem, plug the modem's serial cable into the serial port at the back of the computer and turn the modem on.

To install a new modem:

1. Double-click the Modems control panel icon.

2. Windows NT will detect a new modem and launch the Install New Modem wizard.

3. If not, click the Add button to initiate the wizard.

4. Allow Windows NT to auto-detect the modem type. (You can manually specify a modem, if you like.) When the correct modem is listed, click the next button and verify port selections.

5. Continue the installation until it is finished.

   You do not have to restart your computer to use the new modem. If you want to remove a modem, select that modem in the Modems control panel and click the Remove button.

❓ My modem doesn't function correctly after installation. What could be wrong, and how can I fix this problem?

Common problems are

- ⇨ The modem is not turned on.
- ⇨ The phone line is not operating
- ⇨ A program has interfered with a modem setting.

The first two issues are easily verified. See if the modem lights are on, and if there is a dial tone on your phone line. Check any cabling to see if it is seated properly.

You may see the message "Modem will not initialize" in a communications program. Some older communications software will change a modem's setting. First, try restarting your computer. If that doesn't work, try removing and reinstalling the modem in the Modems control panel.

Many modems are not properly configured by the Add Modem wizard. Try opening the Advanced Properties dialog box for that modem and enter an initialization string that is appropriate to your modem. Click the Properties button on the General tab of the Modems control panel, and then the Advanced button to view this dialog box. Consult your modem's documentation to see what the appropriate initialization string is for your modem.

DIAGNOSING CABLING ISSUES

❓ My computer can't connect to the network. What can be wrong?

Many, but not all network connection problems are cable related. You may see messages that indicate that no domain server could be contacted, or other messages that aren't obviously hardware specific. If you have changed any of your cabling or hardware connections, suspect these issues first.

For some networks like Token Ring networks, a single broken cable or improperly seated connector can bring the entire network down. For other network configurations like a star or bus topology, only a single branch or computer may be affected. The key to finding and managing these problems is to isolate individual network components in a logical fashion. Try first to determine which cable segments are at issue. Disconnect the cable and reconnect segments and connectors one at a time; eventually this will locate the problem.

SHARING FILES AND FOLDERS

? How can I run an application on another computer?

Create a share for the volume that contains that application. On the client, map that share as a network drive. Find the application-executable file and run the program. You can also create a shortcut to that program on your local computer and use that shortcut to launch the application.

? How do I share a folder across the network?

You can share a folder on either a FAT or NTFS volume so that others can view it. In the first step you create the share; then you configure the share permissions.

To share a folder:

1. Right-click on the folder you wish to share in the Windows NT Explorer or on the Desktop, and select the Sharing command from the shortcut menu.

2. On the Sharing tab of the folder Properties dialog box (see Figure 14-13), select the Share As radio button and modify the name of the share from the default of the folder name (optional) in the Share Name text box.

3. Click on the number of connected users desired in the User Limit section, either the Maximum Allowed or the Allow radio button with a number entered into the Users spinner.

4. Click the Permissions button. Initially the Everyone group has full control of a folder.

5. Select the permission level you require, add or remove groups as appropriate, and then click the two OK buttons.

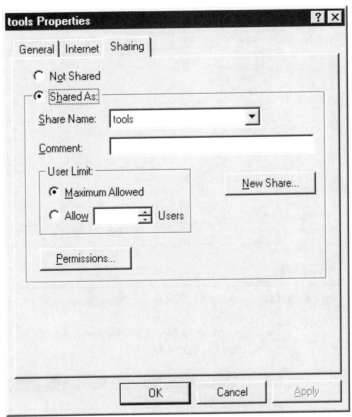

Figure 14-13.   The Sharing tab of the folder Properties dialog box

There's a volume or directory on another computer that I use all the time. Is there a convenient method for viewing a remote volume?

You can map a shared directory on another computer so that it appears as if it is a disk drive on your own system. A mapped drive appears in the My Computer window or under My Computer in the Windows NT Explorer as if it were a local drive. Figure 14-14 shows you a mapped drive in an Open dialog box.

To map a drive:

1. Double-click on Network Neighborhood on the Desktop.

2. Right-click on the share drive you wish to map, or open that drive and right-click on the shared directory.

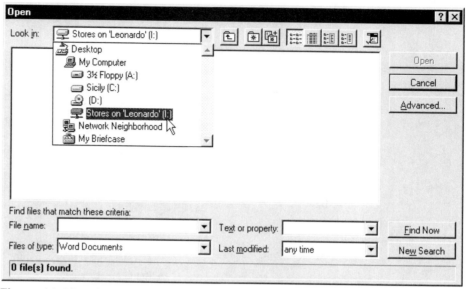

Figure 14-14.   A mapped drive in an Open dialog box

3. Select <u>M</u>ap Network Drive command from the Shortcut menu, as shown in Figure 14-15.

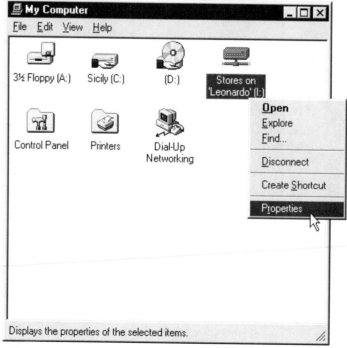

Figure 14-15.   A network folder's shortcut menu

4. Select a drive letter from the Drive list box of the Map Network Drive dialog box, as shown in Figure 14-16.

5. To have this volume automatically mounted when your computer boots, click the Reconnect at logon checkbox.

6. Click the OK button.

Shown here is a mapped volume icon.

Stores on
'Leonardo' (I:)

To remove a mapped drive, right-click on that drive and select the Disconnect command.

The Windows NT Explorer also allows you to map a drive using the Map Network Drive command on the Tools menu.

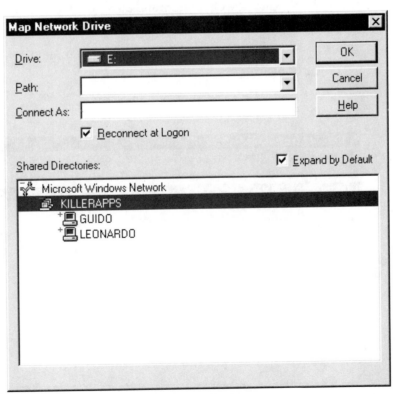

Figure 14-16.   The Map Network Drive dialog box

REMOTE ACCESS SERVICES

 I can't connect to the RAS Server using my valid account name and password. Why is that?

You need to be assigned permission to connect to a RAS Server, either through your personal user account or through your membership in a group of users who have this privilege.

To assign RAS access:

1. Select the Remote Access Admin command in the Administrative Tools folder on the Programs submenu of the Start menu.

2. Select the Permissions command from the Users menu in the Remote Access Admin window as shown in Figure 14-17.

3. In the Remote Access Permissions dialog box shown in Figure 14-18, select the user in the Users list box and check on the Grant dialin permission to user checkbox.

4. Click the OK button, and then close the Remote Access Admin utility.

You can also set dial-in permissions through the User Manager for Domains.

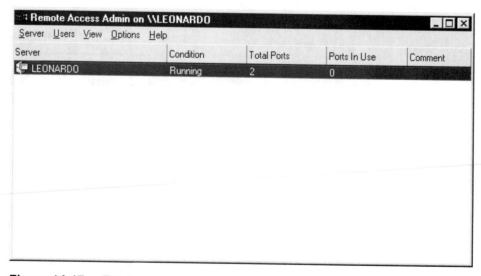

Figure 14-17.   The Remote Access Admin window

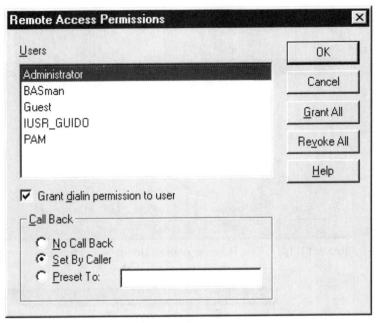

Figure 14-18.   The Remote Access Permissions dialog box

? I've connected to a Remote Access Server, but I can't see other computers on the network. What's wrong?

When the RAS service is configured, you can set an option that limits the RAS connection to the server, or that allows access to your entire network.

To allow full network access, do the following:

1. Double-click the Network control panel icon.

2. Click the Service tab, select the Remote Access Service and click the Properties button to view the Remote Access Setup dialog box shown in Figure 14-19.

3. Click the Network button to view the Network Configuration dialog box shown in Figure 14-20.

4. Click the Configure button next to the network protocol that you wish to network enable; then set the Entire network radio button in the RAS Server <Network Protocol> Configuration dialog box. Figure 14-21 shows you the TCP/IP version of this dialog box.

5. Click the OK buttons to close all dialog boxes.

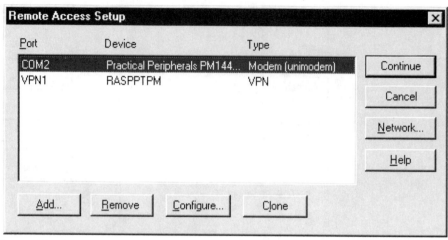

Figure 14-19.   The Remote Access Setup dialog box

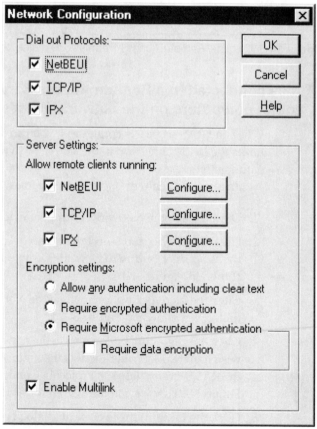

Figure 14-20.   The Network Configuration dialog box

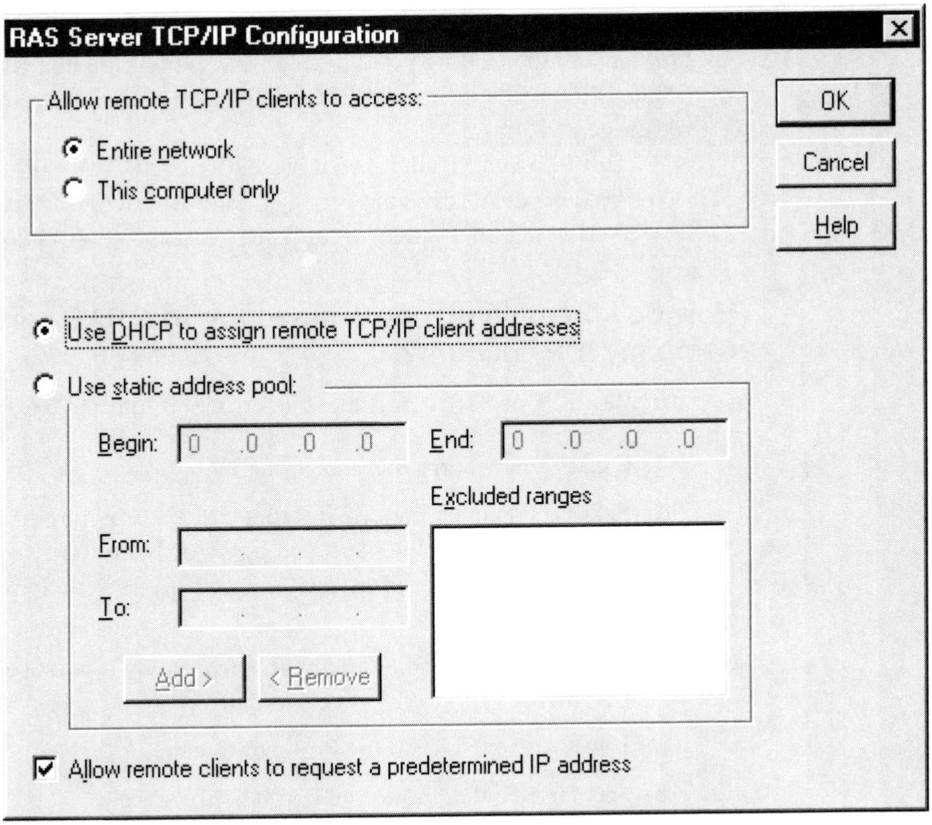

RAS Server TCP/IP Configuration   ☒

Allow remote TCP/IP clients to access:

   ⦿ Entire network

   ○ This computer only

OK

Cancel

Help

⦿ Use DHCP to assign remote TCP/IP client addresses

○ Use static address pool:

   Begin: [0   .0   .0   .0]   End: [0   .0   .0   .0]

                              Excluded ranges

   From: [ ]

   To: [ ]

     [Add >]   [< Remove]

☑ Allow remote clients to request a predetermined IP address

Figure 14-21.   The RAS Server TCP/IP Configuration dialog box

❓ I want to use the Remote Access service on a client. How do I install the client software?

RAS client software for Windows NT Server or Workstation installs using the Network control panel. The service is directly supported by the operating system. There is also support for the Point-to-Point Transfer Protocol (PPTP) for a Virtual Private Network connection over the Internet when you install that additional protocol.

For Windows 3.1, Windows for Workgroups, and MS-DOS, special software is required to install a RAS client. These clients do not support the PPP protocol, and they may require that you install the NetBEUI transport protocol as their network access protocol.

Windows 95's Remote Access client software can also be installed from the Network control panel. In the original release, the client software does not allow for the use of the Point-to-Point Transfer

Protocol (PPTP). If you wish to use PPTP with Windows 95, download and install the Dial-up Networking (DUN) upgrade that is available from Microsoft's Web site. PPTP will be part of the next release of Windows 98.

Third-party PPP clients that use either the TCP/IP, IPX/SPX, or NetBEUI protocols can gain access to Microsoft RAS services. The RAS server negotiates a logon and authenticates these clients.

? How do I create a dial-up connection to a RAS server using my ISP account?

Create a PPP or SLIP connection. To create an Internet RAS connection:

1. Create a new entry in your phonebook.

2. Select the I am calling the Internet checkbox in the Server screen of the wizard. Enable plain text passwords, and The non-Windows NT server I am calling expects... options, if necessary on that screen.

3. Enter a phone number and enable telephony if you use that feature.

4. Select PPP or SLIP on the Protocol screen.

5. Set a login behavior on the Login Script screen.

6. Supply your computer's IP address, as well as the IP addresses of the name (DNS and WINS) servers. If they are automatically assigned, leave "0.0.0.0" in the text boxes.

7. When you reach the end and view the Dial-Up Networking dialog box, use the Edit entry and modem properties command on the More... button menu to edit the Server tab. There you should check whether your ISP allows for Enable PPP LCP extensions. Select the Enable software compression.

8. Since it is hidden, and crucial, check the TCP/IP Settings dialog box to see if your addresses are correctly entered. Also check with your ISP to see if you can leave IP header compression enabled. Most ISPs don't support this feature, so if you are unsure, turn it off. Also leave the Use default gateway on remote network turned on unless otherwise instructed.

9. Return to the Security tab and enable the authentication and encryption policy that your ISP supports.

10. OK your way out of all of the dialog boxes.

After you have configured your phonebook entry for your ISP account, you should test it to see if it works correctly. If you can browse files and download them from your Internet browser, chances are that the connection works correctly. If not, alter a property or two and see if you can establish a valid connection. Since about half the properties refer to the connection and half to the method of data transport, you should be able to quickly isolate an incorrect parameter.

You may wish to call your ISP to get help. Many ISPs' support desks will walk you through this process. Ask for an NT support specialist.

NT AND NETWARE

Why can't I connect to a Novell server on my network?

Make sure that you have installed the IPX/SPX protocol on your computer, and that the frame type is correct for the type of NetWare server you wish to connect to. NetWare servers default to use Ethernet 802.2. You'll have to manually add Ethernet 802.3 if this protocol is required.

One common reason why you can't connect to a Novell server is that the CSNW of GSNW (Client Services for NetWare of the Gateway Service for NetWare) may not be installed or configured properly. You must install CSNW on each client to allow NT clients to access a NetWare printer. To create a Novell print server used by NT clients, you will need to install the GSNW on Windows NT Server. This software is installed using the Network control panel, and managed through the GSNW control panel.

NetWare clients requiring access to an NT network printer, and Microsoft Network clients who wish to print to NetWare PServers must use the File and Print Services for NetWare (FPNW). FPNW is sold separately from Windows NT, and allows access to Novell's directory services.

I want to run Windows NT and NetWare together on a network. How do I install and configure the Gateway Services for NetWare?

To install and configure NetWare Gateway Services:

1. Select the Control Panel command from the Settings submenu on the Start menu.

2. Double-click on the Network icon, and then click the Services tab.

3. Click the Add button and select the Gateway (And Client) Services for NetWare service from the Network Services list box.

4. Click the OK button, verify the Windows NT operating system files location, and click OK.

5. After the service is copied, click the Close button and restart your computer.

When you install the Gateway service, Windows NT checks to see if the IPX/SPX protocol is installed, and installs that protocol if it is not installed. The NetWare Gateway control panel is added to your computer, and provides the means to configure NetWare volumes as Windows NT shares.

Any user who logs on will be asked to select their desired server, or the tree and context they wish to connect to. For NetWare 2 or 3, the server is set. For NetWare 4, servers run in the Bindary Emulation mode. NetWare 4 NDS configuration uses tree and context.

The entered user account and password for Windows NT are used to authenticate account validation on NetWare. NetWare 2 and 3 do not automatically synchronize passwords, and must be manually maintained. NT passwords are automatically maintained with NetWare 4.

How do I gain access to a Novell NetWare network using a RAS server?

To access a Novell NetWare network, you will need to run a client NetWare redirector. Install this redirector as a service in the Network control panel Services tab as the Client Service for NetWare. On the server, you must have the Gateway Service for NetWare installed. As long as RAS Server has GSNW or CSNW, client enables IPX/SPX, and they have a valid Netware account, they should get through to Netware Resources.

chapter

15 Answers!

Internet and Intranet Support

Answer Topics!

Internet and Intranet Support
@ a Glance

⇨ You can **install the Internet Information Server** (IIS) on either Windows NT Server or Workstation. Installation can provide a WWW, Gopher, or FTP service running on your computer.

⇨ You can set up IIS to filter incoming users based on their location, authenticate them based on their password, and control their access to both services and content. When **setting up Internet/Intranet services,** you will find that IIS provides numerous important features like multi-homing and virtual servers.

⇨ Many networks rely on TCP/IP networking as their main and often their only networking protocol. This protocol underlies both the Internet and Intranet communication. Windows NT comes with several utilities to test correct **TCP/IP addressing**.

⇨ You can use the **DHCP and WINS** services to dynamically assign IP addresses from a pool of available addresses, and to associate those addresses with friendly computer names, respectively. Setting up these services frees a network administrator from the tedium of having to manage frequently changing text files with these configurations.

⇨ You can use the **Internet Explorer** to browse Internet/Intranet content, open HTML files, download files, and launch news and mail services. The browser is installed with the Windows NT operating system and will be an integral part of future versions of the OS.

INSTALLING MICROSOFT INTERNET INFORMATION SERVER

? **What is the difference between installing IIS on Windows NT Server or Workstation?**

The software for IIS installs on each version of the operating system identically, and is in fact identical software. Briefly during beta of Windows NT Workstation 4, Microsoft hardwired a maximum of ten simultaneous connections for the workstation version. However, this limit was removed and the restriction was left only in the licensing agreement. Still, there are good reasons to use IIS on Workstation for low transaction volumes and install IIS on production servers running on Windows NT Server. One good reason is that it provides a working design environment. Another reason that you might want to have a workstation Web server is that it distributes the task of supplying Web content around your network.

 ## What are the meanings of some of the common error messages that appear with IIS?

Table 15-1 lists some common error messages for IIS 2.0 and their possible explanations.

Table 15-1. Common IIS Error Messages

Port Number	Description
Unable to connect to target machine.	The computer could be unavailable. This is an RPC error that occurs when attempting to access the IIS API. The system error generated is EPT_S_NOT_REGISTERED or RPC_S_SERVER_UNAVAILABLE.
Unable to create directory.	The directory name and path entered into the New Directory Name text box could not be created. You entered an invalid path or tried to create a file that already exists.
The alias you have given is invalid for a non-home directory.	You tried to assign the home directory alias "/" to a non-home directory.
The service configuration DLL 'filename' failed to load correctly.	The DLL is missing or corrupt. Reinstall IIS again.
Invalid server name.	You entered a server name that doesn't exist. Check the syntax or spelling and attempt to connect again.
No administerable services found.	The particular service (WWW, Gopher, or FTP) has not been installed on this IIS server.
A home directory already exists for this service. Creating a new home directory will cause the existing directory to no longer be a home directory. An alias will be created for the existing home directory.	You get this warning message when you try to add a home directory that already exists to IIS. Only one home directory per virtual root is allowed. This is not an error event, and is not logged as such.
More than 1 home directory was found. An automatic alias will be generated instead.	IIS has found a duplicate directory entry in the Registry.

? **I realize that I need to have Web services running on my computer. How do I install Microsoft Internet Information Server?**

When you install Windows NT Server or Workstation version 4, you are prompted to install the Internet Information Server version 2 as part of the original setup. If you don't choose to install IIS at that time, a shortcut to install IIS is added to your desktop.

To install IIS after the operating system is installed:

1. Double-click on the Install Internet Information Server shortcut.

2. Verify the location of the system files, and then click the OK button in the Setup dialog box.

3. In the IIS Installation Options dialog box that appears (Figure 15-1), select the desired components and then click the OK button.

4. Click the OK button in the dialog box that appears asking you to create the C:\WINNT\SYSTEM32\INETSRV directory.

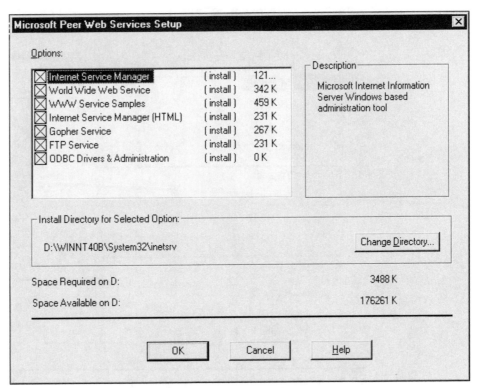

Figure 15-1.   The IIS Installation Options dialog box

5. Accept or change the locations of the default directories in the Publishing Directories dialog box shown in Figure 15-2; then click the OK button and Yes in the confirming dialog box.

6. Click OK to dismiss the Internet domain name warning dialog box.

7. If you selected the ODBC Drivers and Administration option, then select the driver you require and click the OK button in the next dialog box.

8. Click the OK button to complete the installation.

You will need to restart your computer, but when you do you will find that the documentation in HTML form has been copied to your computer.

If you wish any component of IIS to start up when your server boots, open the Services control panel and set that service's boot option.

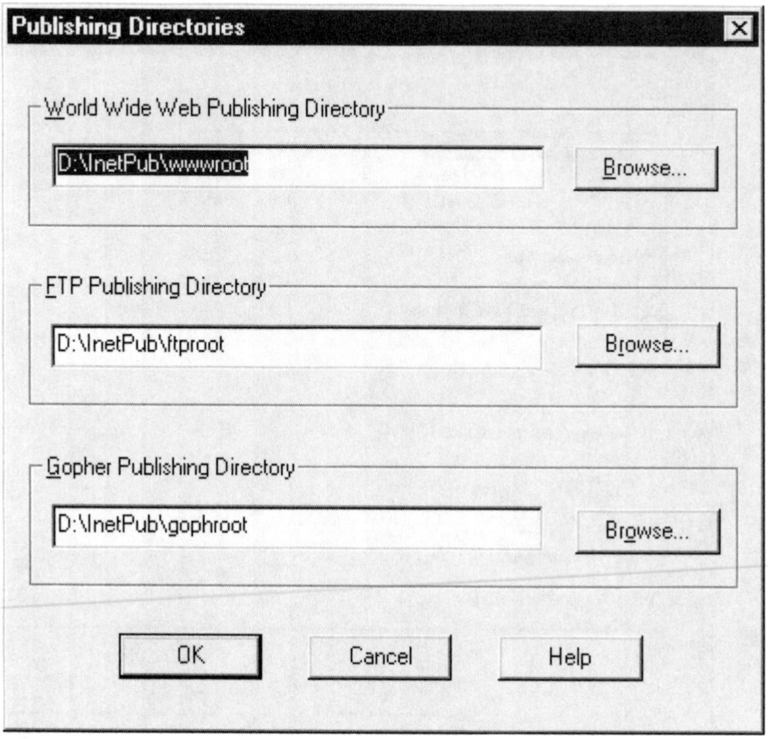

Figure 15-2.   The Publishing Directories dialog box

Additionally, you will want to add the IUSR_COMPUTERNAME username to the list of user accounts in the User Manager for Domains. This account should be set up to allow anonymous user access to an Internet service when you desire it. FTP services typically create a PUB or Public folder that an anonymous user (using the actual name "ANONYMOUS", any username, or no username with no entered password) can access.

❓ I want to check whether an Internet service is active, and determine its properties. How do I do that?

You use the Internet Service Manager to control the various Internet services that you install with IIS. This utility will show you what computers are running what services, and the status of these services. You can start, stop, and pause services using this utility, as well as control other important properties. The Service Manager is contained in the Microsoft Internet Server (Common) folder in the Programs submenu on the Start menu. Figure 15-3 shows you the Service Manager in Services view.

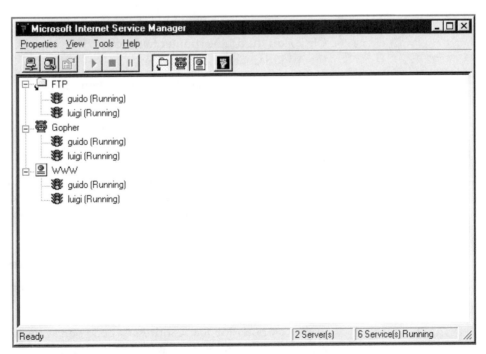

Figure 15-3.   The Internet Service Manager in Services view

SETTING UP INTERNET/INTRANET SERVICES

 I'm setting up a WWW service, and I want to determine my server's bandwidth. How can I monitor Web performance?

Use the Performance Monitor to determine the activity of counters related to the HTTP service. First, reset all counters by stopping and then restarting your WWW service in the Internet Service Manager. Then add the appropriate counters to the Performance Monitor and start an HTTP session.

To add HTTP counters to the Performance Monitor:

1. Select the Performance Monitor command from the Administrative Tools folder on the Programs submenu of the Start menu.

2. Select the Add to Chart command on the Edit menu.

3. Select HTTP Service from the Object list box.

4. Click on the Counter list box and select the Bytes Total per second counter.

5. Set the scale from Default to 1.0.

6. Click Add to add the counter to the chart; then click Done to close the Add to Chart dialog box.

7. Select the Chart command from the Options menu to open the Chart Options dialog box.

8. Set the Vertical Maximum to 100 and click on Horizontal Grid.

9. Click the OK button.

To test your counters, run an internal session using the Microsoft Internet Explorer. Leave the Performance Monitor open and running on your screen before you start the following task.

To test an HTTP session:

1. Double-click the icon for the Microsoft Internet Explorer.

2. Enter into the URL text box either your server's IP address:

   ###.###.###.###

   or the computer loopback address (when you use the same computer for your browser and Web server):

127.0.0.1

The home page then comes into view.

3. Refresh the page, and then click on a link on that page.

4. Switch to the Performance Monitor and check the bytes total that was transferred.

The bytes total over time will give you the prediction for the bandwidth of your Web service.

How can I limit users browsing my Web site to only a single directory?

Unless you specifically want users to be able to examine your entire file structure, limit what a user can see by disabling directory browsing. Directory browsing can be disabled on the Directories tab of the WWW Service Properties dialog box, as shown in Figure 15-4.

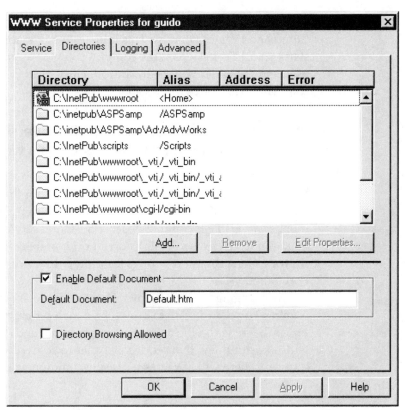

Figure 15-4.   The Directories tab of the WWW Service property sheet

❓ Is there a way of providing information to users who access my FTP site?

You can add a welcome and exit message to users who connect to your FTP site so that they know what server they have connected to, the content of that server, and how to use the resources it contains. You add these messages using the Internet Service Manager.

To create a welcome and exit message:

1. Select the Internet Service Manager from the Microsoft Internet Server folder on the Programs submenu of the Start menu.

2. Double-click on the FTP service.

3. Click the Messages tab of the FTP Service property sheet.

4. Enter the welcome message into the Welcome message box, and the exit message into the Exit message box.

5. Click the OK button to close the FTP Service property sheet.

If you want to test these messages, enter FTP 127.0.0.1 into the Command Prompt window. This initiates the IP loopback address and starts your FTP session on the computer. Log on as an anonymous user, and then after you see the introductory message, enter the command BYE to exit the session.

❓ I want to control the access of my IIS servers so that they aren't visible in normal use. Is there a way to hide IIS servers?

When you install IIS, you set the port numbers for the different services to their common default options. For example, the port number for HTTP is commonly set to 80. Other services also take what is referred to as a "Well-Known Port Number." Table 15-2 shows you the common settings for different services' Well-Known Port Numbers.

By changing the Well-Known Port Service to another port number, you deny access to browsers, e-mail programs, and any other utility that relies on the default setting to locate and communicate with a host running that service. In order to access the server and that service, a client will have to specifically communicate with the new

Table 15-2.   Well-Known Port Numbers

Port Number	Process	Description
1	TCPMUX	TCP Port Service Multiplexer
5	RJE	Remote Job Entry
20	FTP-DATA	File Transfer Protocol—Data
21	FTP	File Transfer Protocol—Control
23	TELNET	Telnet
25	SMTP	Simple Mail Transfer Protocol
42	NAMESERV	Host Name Server
49	LOGIN	Login Host Protocol
53	DOMAIN	Domain Name Server
69	TFTP	Trivial File Transfer Protocol
70	GOPHER	Gopher
80	HTTP	HTTP
103	X400	X.400
110	POP3	Post Office Protocol v3
137	NETBIOS-NS	NETBIOS Name Service
138	NETBIOS-DG	NETBIOS Datagram Service
139	NETBIOS-SS	NETBIOS Session Service
156	SQLSRV	SQL Service
179	BPG	Border Gateway Protocol

port number for that service. As a typical example, here is how you change the HTTP port.

To change the default port of an HTTP server:

1. Select the Internet Service Manager from the Internet Information Server (Common) folder on the Programs submenu on the Start menu.

2. Double-click on the WWW service to open the property sheet.

3. Enter a new port number such as 5200 in the TCP Port text box as shown here; then click the OK button.

WWW Service Properties for guido

Service | Directories | Logging | Advanced

TCP Port: 80

Connection Timeout: 900 seconds

Maximum Connections: 100000

4. Click OK to dismiss the dialog box asking you to restart the service.

5. Start and then stop the WWW service in the Service Manager. (You do not have to restart your computer to set the port number.)

If you want to verify that the port number has been reset, you can use a browser like the Microsoft Internet Explorer to request that a page be served up from the new port number.

To query your WWW service at the new port setting:

1. Double-click the icon for the Microsoft Internet Explorer on your Desktop.

2. Enter the following into the Address text box:

```
http://###.###.###.###:5200/
```

The number placeholders represent the IP address for your WWW server. The default page for your WWW service should be displayed.

3. To verify that port number 80 is no longer active, enter the following into the Address text box:

```
http:/// - ##.###.###.###:80/
```

You will receive an error message.

How can I limit access to my Web server?

You can control whether anyone accesses your Internet services by allowing or disallowing anonymous logon on the Service tab of the Service property sheet. Figure 15-5 shows you the WWW Service

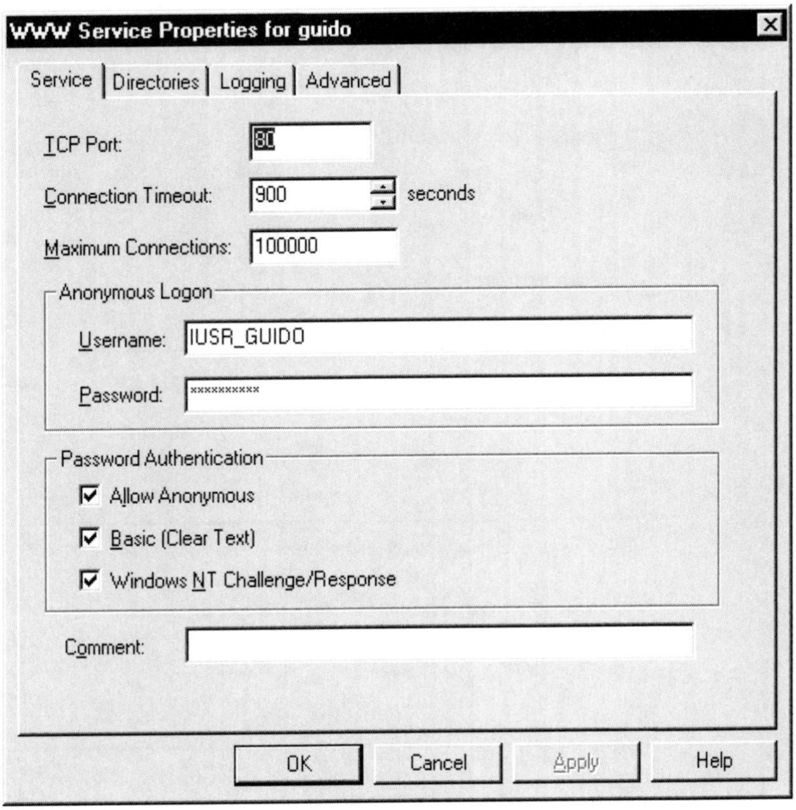

Figure 15-5.   The WWW Service property sheet

property sheet that appears when you double-click on the WWW service in the IIS Service Manager. FTP and Gopher services offer similar options.

If you allow anonymous access, you can control what that group of users are allowed to access. The IUSR_COMPUTERNAME account that is created during installation of IIS is part of the Guest group, and can be further modified.

Other options allow you to authenticate passwords using the Windows NT Challenge Response login mechanism. Users of this type will be known to your domain server, or be validated through the services of a domain server in a trusted domain.

You can further limit access to your Web server using the client's IP address as the filter. To configure IIS to grant or deny service to a computer based on its IP address, or a range of computers that might be found on a network, open the Advanced tab of the WWW Service

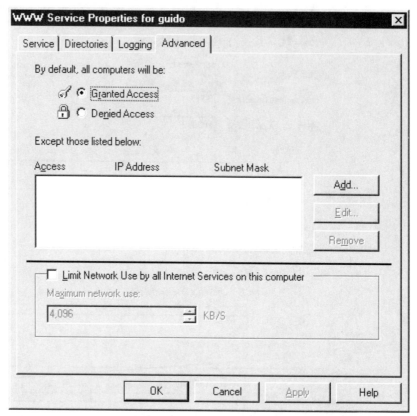

Figure 15-6.   The Advanced tab of the WWW Service Properties sheet

Properties sheet by double-clicking on the WWW service in the IIS Service Manager. Figure 15-6 shows you this dialog box.

❓ I want to monitor who is accessing my FTP site, and what activity is taking place?

There are two basic tools for monitoring FTP activity: the NETSTAT utility and the Windows NT Performance Monitor. NETSTAT can show you static information listing the status of connections. The Performance Monitor shows you events happening in real time.

NETSTAT displays the following information: the protocol in use (TCP or UDP), local and foreign addresses using friendly names, the port number in use on the local computer, and the status of the connection.

The Performance Monitor can be used to check the status of a user, file transfers in progress, and throughput in bytes sent or received. Other counters can measure connection attempts, current number of users and connections and their types, files sent or received, logon attempts, and maximum and total numbers of users and connections.

You will need to add some of the counters that the Internet Information Server installed on your computer before you can begin to track this information, and add those counters to your log chart. Here is how you do that:

To add FTP counters:

1. Open the Internet Service Manger and stop and restart the FTP service.

2. Select the Performance Monitor command from the Administrative Tools folder on the Programs submenu of the Start menu.

3. Select the Add to Chart command from the Edit menu.

4. Select the FTP Server object in the Object lib box of the Add to Chart dialog box.

5. Select the Connection Attempts and Logon Attempts (as an example) in the Counter box.

6. Click Add, and then Done to dismiss the Add to Chart dialog box.

7. Select the Chart command from the Options menu to view the Chart Options dialog box.

8. Set the parameters you desire for the chart, its height and the grid; then click the OK button.

You can keep the Performance Monitor open as you check FTP access. If you want to test these counters, enter **FTP 127.0.0.1** in the Command Prompt window to start the IP loopback address and begin a session on your local computer. Log on as anonymous and access the FTP site. Type **BYE** into the Command Prompt window. Your activities should appear in the Performance Monitor.

 Note: *These procedures can also be used to monitor WWW and Gopher services.*

I've run out of disk space on my Web server. How do I manage larger amounts of content in virtual directories?

You can create a virtual directory with IIS that appears as if it is local on your Web server, but which can be located remotely on one or more volumes. To set up a virtual directory, you must create and share the directory and set the appropriate permissions so that the users you desire can access them through the Web server.

Note: Virtual directories can only be created using a WWW service.

You complete the setup of a virtual directory by specifying the location of the virtual directory in the Directories tab of WWW Service property of the IIS Service Manager. If the virtual directory is local on your computer, you will need to supply the location of the directory, its name, and the alias name you will use to identify that virtual directory. With a remote directory you will need to supply the UNC name for the directory that will be part of the virtual directory.

 I want to run two or more domains on the same virtual server. How do I do that?

You can configure IIS to perform what is called *multi-homing,* allowing a single server to service the incoming requests for two or more domains. A multi-homed server is how ISPs service clients without having to buy one server for each domain. The process involved requires that you map an IP address to the default directory for each domain.

Note: Only WWW services can be multi-homed.

To create a multi-homed Web service:

1. Create the directory that will contain all of the other domains' directories and share it with full permissions.

2. Open the Directories tab of the WWW Service Properties dialog box in the IIS Service Manager by double-clicking on the WWW service.

3. Click the Add button to view the Directory Properties dialog box, as shown in Figure 15-7.

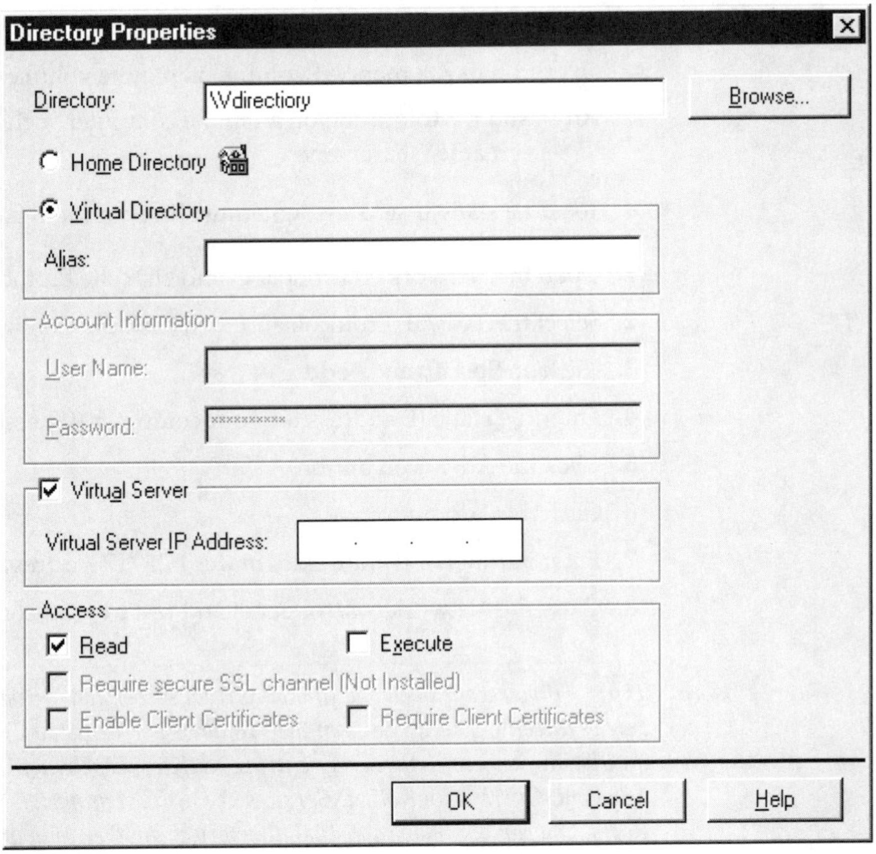

Figure 15-7. The Directory Properties dialog box

4. Assign the default directory in the Directory text box using a valid UNC name for the home directory.

5. Click the Home Directory radio button.

6. Click the Virtual Server checkbox and enter the address in the Virtual Server IP Address text box.

7. Click the OK button.

When you close the Directory Property dialog box, you see the virtual directory listed in the Directories tab of the WWW Service Properties dialog box. You will now want to add additional static IP addresses to your virtual server.

The following addresses represent valid locations for a virtual server:

⇨ Any directory on a local drive of the computer running IIS

⇨ D:\ through Z:\ mapped volume on remote volumes

⇨ Any valid UNC location on a remote computer such as \\servername\sharename

To add a static IP address, you must first bind it to your NIC:

1. Open the Network control panel and click the Protocols tab.

2. Select the TCP/IP Protocol, and then click the Configure button.

3. Click on Specify an IP address.

4. Enter the static IP address for your computer (if necessary).

5. Click the Advanced button.

6. Click the Add button.

7. Enter additional IP addresses in the TCP/IP Address dialog box.

8. Close the Network control panel and restart your computer.

Tip: If you want to add additional virtual server and virtual directory entries directly, you can do so in the Windows NT Registry. The following multistring key stores the server entries: \HKEY_LOCAL_MACHINE \System\CurrentControlSet\Services\W3SVC\Parameters\Virtual Roots. You can also move a virtual directory to another computer by copying the Virtual Roots key and restoring this key on the destination computer.

SETTING TCP/IP ADDRESSING

I'm setting up my network and I want to register a domain. How do I do that?

If you are connected to the Internet through an Internet Service Provider (ISP), that ISP can help you register your domain. Some ISPs tack on additional charges for handling this service, while others do not. To register a domain directly with InterNIC, contact them at the following location:

Network Solutions
InterNIC Registration Services
505 Huntmar Park Drive
Herndon VA 22070 USA
Tel: (800)444-4345 or (703)742-4777
e-mail: HOSTMASTER@INTERNIC.NET

The current charge for registering a domain is $50.00 U.S. per year.

? I need to enter the IP address of my computer into setup dialog boxes. Is there an easy way to find this information?

You can determine the static IP address of a computer by looking in the Network control panel for the assignment. If your computer is dynamically assigned using a DHCP (Dynamic Host Configuration Protocol) server, you will need another method. One quick way to determine your current IP address (even those only assigned for a single session) is to use the IPCONFIG command.

To determine your computer's IP address:

1. Select the Command Prompt command from the <u>P</u>rograms submenu of the Start menu.

2. Enter the command:

   `IPCONFIG/?`

   and press the ENTER key. Figure 15-8 shows you the Help screen that appears with all of the IPCONFIG options.

3. Enter the following:

   `IPCONFIG/ALL`

   You will see your computer's IP address attributes listed, as shown in Figure 15-9.

? My company runs a WAN or an internetwork of connected LANs. How can I determine the path of a packet from my computer to another?

Different factors determine how a packet is routed using the TCP/IP protocol. In some instances a routing table is used, and that

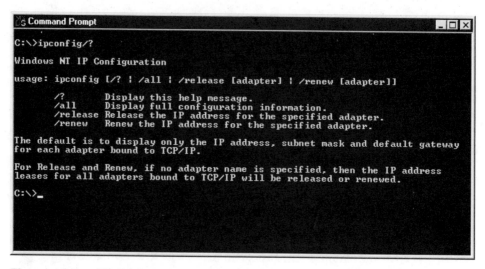

Figure 15-8. The Help screen for the IPCONFIG command

information is static. Routers on a network may use static assignments, or may sense network traffic loads and route your packet appropriately. In any case, you can determine the path that an IP packet travels to another computer using the TRACERT command.

To determine the path an IP packet travels:

1. Select the Command Prompt command from the Programs submenu of the Start menu.

```
Command Prompt                                              _ □ ✕
C:\>ipconfig

Windows NT IP Configuration

Ethernet adapter El59x1:

        IP Address. . . . . . . . . : 200.200.200.1
        Subnet Mask . . . . . . . . : 255.255.255.0
        Default Gateway . . . . . . : 200.200.200.250

C:\>
```

Figure 15-9. A returned IP address from the IPCONFIG command

2. Enter the command:

TRACERT

and press the ENTER key. Figure 15-10 shows you the Help screen that appears with all of the TRACERT options.

3. Enter the address of a known host on the Internet or on your Intranet. For example, enter either:

TRACERT www.microsoft.com (for the Internet)
TRACERT servername (for an Intranet)

or the IP address itself, as in TRACERT 200.200.200.1.

4. Repeat step 3 to get additional paths, if desired.

A list of hops appears that shows each of the paths taken to the destination host. Figure 15-11 shows this result: an Internet connection tracing the path to Microsoft's home page.

? How can I tell if my Internet or intranet connection has an adequate response time?

To test the response of a known IP address:

1. Select the Command Prompt command from the Programs submenu of the Start menu.

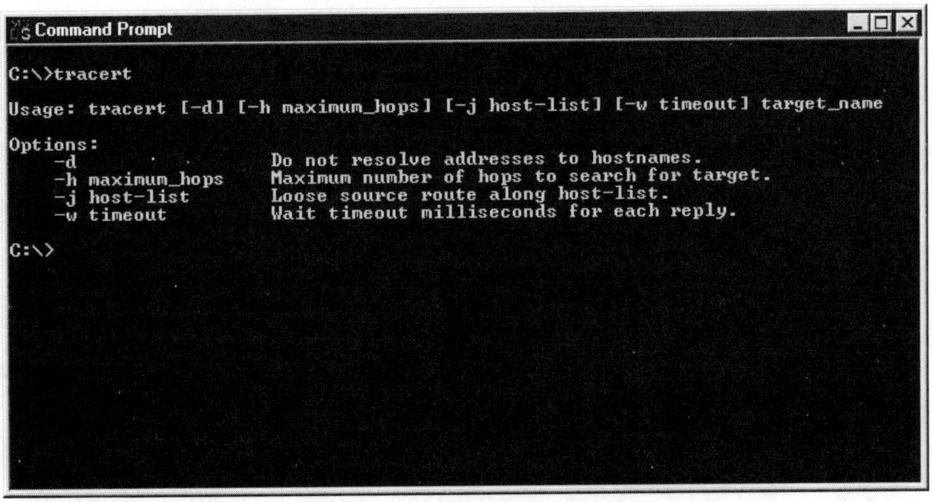

```
C:\>tracert

Usage: tracert [-d] [-h maximum_hops] [-j host-list] [-w timeout] target_name

Options:
    -d                   Do not resolve addresses to hostnames.
    -h maximum_hops      Maximum number of hops to search for target.
    -j host-list         Loose source route along host-list.
    -w timeout           Wait timeout milliseconds for each reply.

C:\>
```

Figure 15-10.   The Help screen for the TRACERT command

```
Command Prompt                                                    _ □ X

C:\>tracert www.tiac.net

Tracing route to www.tiac.net [199.0.65.125]
over a maximum of 30 hops:

  1    *        *        *        Request timed out.
  2   300 ms   311 ms   310 ms   core-ether1-0.bedfo.MA.tiac.net [207.60.16.1]
  3   330 ms   351 ms   330 ms   web.tiac.net [199.0.65.125]

Trace complete.

C:\>
```

Figure 15-11.   The hops to my ISP's Web server using the TRACERT command

2. Enter the command **PING**, and then press the ENTER key. Figure 15-12 shows you the Help screen that appears with all of the PING options.

3. Enter the address of a known host on the Internet or on your Intranet. For example, enter either:

```
PING http://www.microsoft.com (for the Internet)
PING servername (for an Intranet)
```

or the IP address itself, as in PING 200.200.200.1.

```
Command Prompt                                                    _ □ X

C:\>ping

Usage: ping [-t] [-a] [-n count] [-l size] [-f] [-i TTL] [-v TOS]
            [-r count] [-s count] [[-j host-list] ¦ [-k host-list]]
            [-w timeout] destination-list

Options:
    -t              Ping the specifed host until interrupted.
    -a              Resolve addresses to hostnames.
    -n count        Number of echo requests to send.
    -l size         Send buffer size.
    -f              Set Don't Fragment flag in packet.
    -i TTL          Time To Live.
    -v TOS          Type Of Service.
    -r count        Record route for count hops.
    -s count        Timestamp for count hops.
    -j host-list    Loose source route along host-list.
    -k host-list    Strict source route along host-list.
    -w timeout      Timeout in milliseconds to wait for each reply.


C:\>
```

Figure 15-12.   The Help screen for the PING command

4. Repeat step 3 to get additional response times.

The time it takes for a frame to reach the host you specified and be returned is shown for four attempts. Figure 15-13 shows this result for a small network.

DHCP AND WINS

? **How can I tell which DHCP client is using which TCP/IP address?**

If you are trying to locate the source of a network problem, you will need to be able to associate an IP address with the computer that is broadcasting the faulty packets. You can use the DHCP Manager to find out who has what assignment.

To determine which computer has which TCP/IP assignment, do the following:

1. Select the DHCP Manager command from the Administrative Tools folder on the Programs submenu of the Start menu.

2. Double-click the Local Machine icon.

3. Select the TCP/IP address that you are trying to locate.

4. Select the Active Lease command from the Scope menu.

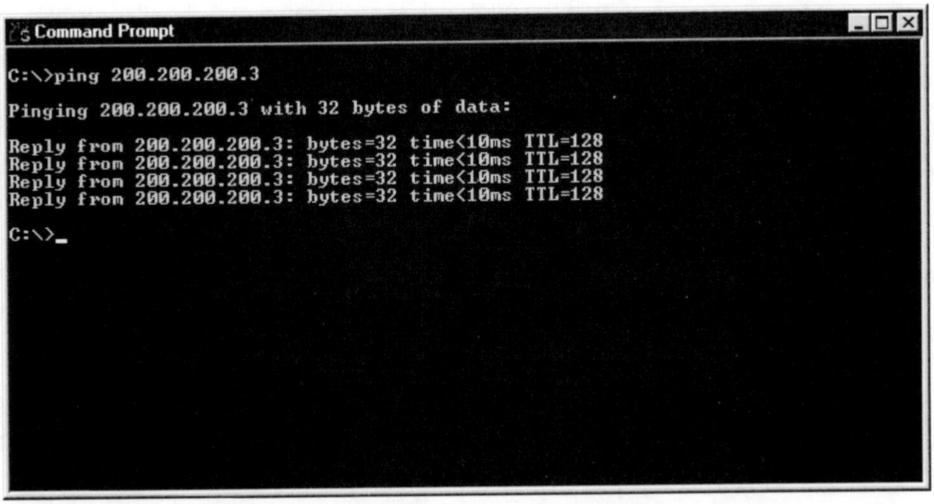

```
Command Prompt                                        _ □ ×
C:\>ping 200.200.200.3

Pinging 200.200.200.3 with 32 bytes of data:

Reply from 200.200.200.3: bytes=32 time<10ms TTL=128
Reply from 200.200.200.3: bytes=32 time<10ms TTL=128
Reply from 200.200.200.3: bytes=32 time<10ms TTL=128
Reply from 200.200.200.3: bytes=32 time<10ms TTL=128

C:\>_
```

Figure 15-13.   The results of a PING

5. The Active Leases dialog box appears with a list of Client IP addresses and the name of the computer that is currently assigned that address.

? I want to use friendly names on my network and not have to worry about IP address assignments. How can I do this?

The service that manages friendly names is the Windows Internet Name Service. This service is often installed along with the DHCP service on a network. DHCP assigns an IP address from a pool, and WINS matches the NetBIOS name, or so-called friendly name, that you have assigned to your computer to that address.

To install WINS:

1. Double-click the Network control panel icon.

2. Click the Services tab; then click the Add button.

3. Select the Windows Internet Name Service from the Network Services list in the Select Network Service dialog box; then click the OK button.

4. Confirm the location of the operating system files, and then click the Continue button.

5. Click Close and restart your system.

You will need to configure a client to use WINS, as follows:

1. Open the Network control panel of a client computer (or even an NT Server that is a WINS service client).

2. Click the Protocols tab, select the TCP/IP protocol, and click the Properties button.

3. Select the WINS Address tab, and enter the TCP/IP address of the primary WINS server that you just created.

4. Click the OK button.

5. Close the Network control panel and restart your system.

Since WINS and DHCP free a network administrator from managing cumbersome text files that configure the network clients and servers, they are well worth the effort to install and use.

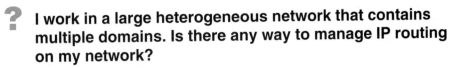 I work in a large heterogeneous network that contains multiple domains. Is there any way to manage IP routing on my network?

Consider installing the DNS or Domain Naming Service on one of your computers. That service can help route requests for IP services on your network. Many small networks do not install this service, relying instead on the DNS server that is installed on their ISP's server. DNS is installed through the Services tab of the Network control panel.

Once installed, DNS adds the DNS Server Management tool to the Administrative Tools folder. Use this tool to create zones and a zone file. A zone is a domain name.

How do I manage a large number of IP address changes or allocations?

If you have a network of users whose computers are reconfigured on a regular basis, or if you require doling out IP addresses on a need-to-have basis, you can install the Dynamic Host Configuration Protocol (DHCP) on Windows NT Server. This service assigns an IP address to a computer at logon, and gives out that address for a lease duration that you set.

DHCP manages IP addresses on the server without your having to create a set of static addresses that are logged into an LMHOST file. The DHCP server requires a static address, but another computer on the network that uses this service has a volatile IP address. You are still given the option of assigning static IP addresses to other computers on the network, and can exclude those static addresses from the range of allowed addresses in the DHCP pool.

As an example of a situation where DHCP is quite useful, consider a network where there are few assignable IP addresses and many clients. Any client needing Internet access can be assigned an IP address as needed. For remote users logging into the network using a RAS client and the PPP protocol, the RAS server makes use of a DHCP service (it is actually a mini-DHCP server) to assign an allowed address to the remote client.

To install the DHCP service:

1. Double-click the Network control panel icon.
2. Click the Services tab; then click the Add button.

3. Select the DHCP Server from the Services list, and click OK.

4. Confirm the location of the operating system files, and then click the Continue button.

5. A message appears indicating that this computer will require a static TCP/IP address for its network adapters. Click OK, and then Close.

6. Restart your system.

When your system starts up, you will need to configure the DHCP service using the DHCP Manager. Open this utility from the Administrative Tools folder on the Programs submenu of the Start menu. You will need to create a scope of allowed IP addresses.

To create a scope in the DHCP Manager:

1. Click on the Local Machine in the DHCP Servers list box.

2. Select the Create on the Scope menu.

3. In the Create Scope dialog box shown in Figure 15-14, enter the start and end TCP/IP addresses and the value of the subnet mask.

4. Enter any excluded addresses or any excluded range by clicking the Add button and adding them to the Excluded Addresses list box. Any static address on the network should be in the excluded list, as well as any other addresses managed by a different DHCP server.

5. Assign a lease duration.

6. Click the OK button and then close the DHCP Manager.

With the DHCP service running, you will need to configure clients to use the service:

1. Open the Network control panel of a client computer (or even an NT Server that is a DHCP service client).

2. Click the Protocols tab, select the TCP/IP protocol, and click the Properties button.

3. Select the Obtain An IP Address From A DHCP Server radio button.

4. Dismiss the message box that indicates that the DHCP assignment will take precedence over the assignment on the property pages.

5. Close the Network control panel and restart your system.

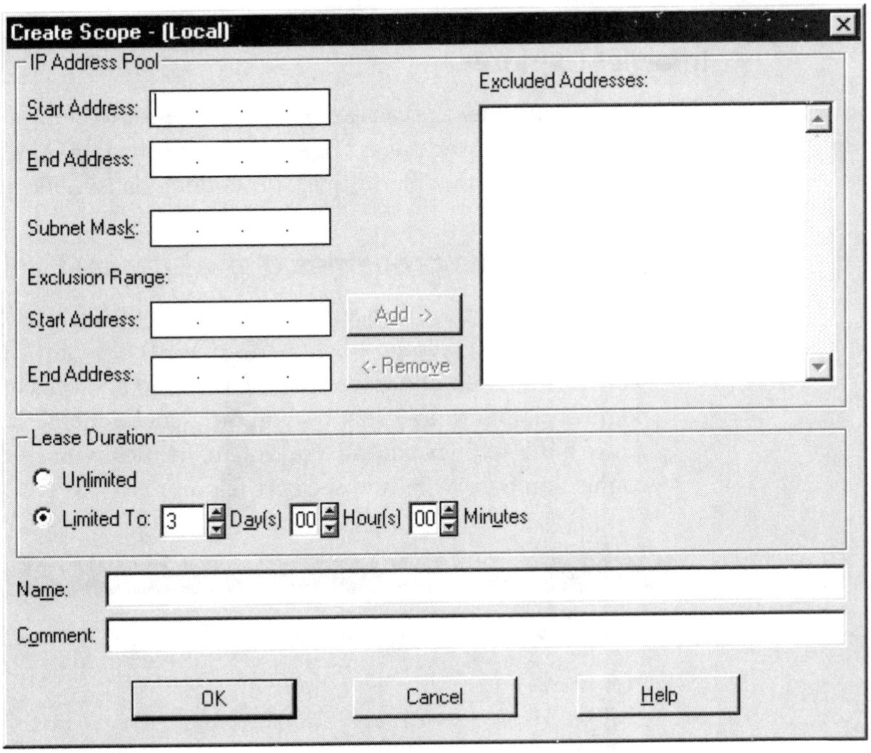

Figure 15-14.   The Create Scope dialog box

You may notice a brief message box during startup that indicates that an address was allocated.

USING THE INTERNET EXPLORER

How do I make the Internet Explorer my default browser?

When you double-click on an HTML file, your default browser will open to show you the contents of that file. You can manually register the HTM file extension as being associated with Internet Explorer through the File Type tab on the Options dialog box that is opened from the View menu of the Windows NT Explorer. If you open the Microsoft Internet Explorer and attempt to open an HTML file, Windows will post a dialog box (this can be suppressed) that allows you to make this association directly and thereby make the Internet Explorer your default browser.

❓ How can I improve the performance of the Internet Explorer?

You can increase the cache size of the browser to help store recently used pieces of Web pages. This cache stores text, HTM files, graphics, and so forth, and will improve subsequent visits to like pages.

❓ How do I alter the properties of the Internet Explorer?

A number of settings are available to you in the Properties dialog box of the Internet Explorer. To view this dialog box, right-click on the icon for the Internet Explorer on the Desktop and select the Properties command. Figure 15-15 shows you the General tab of this dialog box. Among the settings you can control are the behavior of links, toolbars, connection to servers, and security features.

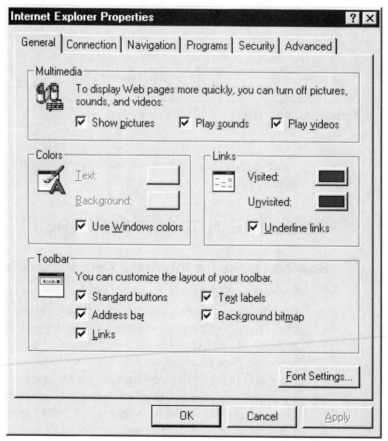

Figure 15-15.   The General tab of the Internet Explorer Properties dialog box

? **How do I work with helper applications, Netscape Plug-ins, and ActiveX components with the Internet Explorer?**

In order to increase the functionality of the Internet Explorer, you can specify applications or applets that can serve as helper applications. To do so, specify the association of a file type with that application. For example, associate the Portable Document Format (PDF) file type with the Adobe Acrobat Reader. Many helper applications (like Acrobat) will make this association for you during their installation. When MSIE attempts to download a PDF file, it will hand the file off to the application that is registered for that file type.

If you have a Netscape Plug-in that you wish to use with MSIE, install that plug-in into the Netscape Navigator folder. When you install MSIE, it will automatically copy the plug-in to its folder. For an existing copy of MSIE, copy the plug-ins from

```
C:\program files\netscape\navigator\program\plugins
```

to

```
c:\program files\plus!\microsoft internet\plugins
```

Any ActiveX component that is required by a Web page is automatically downloaded and made available to MSIE. The specification requires that the component be available from the server if required.

? **Where can I find out about upgrades and new developments concerning the Internet Explorer?**

Microsoft is upgrading the Internet Explorer and adding various components like Internet News and Mail, NetMeeting, ActiveX components, and so forth at a much faster rate than the various operating systems are being revised. You will find the latest version of the software at the following Web location:

```
http://www.microsoft.com/ie
```

and the latest download at:

```
http://www.microsoft.com/ie/download
```

Make sure that you obtain the 32-bit version of this program meant for Windows NT. Version 3.0 was current for Windows NT 4, with version 4.0 (Nashville) currently in beta and scheduled for release with Windows 98 (Memphis) and Windows NT 5.0.

How can I tell if I entered a valid URL address?

When you enter a Uniform Resource Locator address into your browser, you might expect that resource to appear on your screen. URLs are not case sensitive, but are very sensitive to the syntax that is used to create them. An incorrectly entered address might give the appearance of a valid address that doesn't exist or can't be located. Therefore, it is important to know the rules used to compose URLs.

A valid URL takes the form:

```
Access method://protocol.hostname.type/directory
```

An access method can be http (hypertext transfer protocol) for the World Wide Web protocol, as in the example http://www.microsoft.com/NT. Here the access method is how the resource is accessed, the protocol describes what is returned from the resource, and the hostname is where the resource is located. The domain name is microsoft, and the domain type is com, short for commercial. You can also create subdomains, which appear in the following form: http://www.marketing.microsoft.com. If the servername is called "marketing" in microsoft.com, then the previous URL is an example of a Fully Qualified Domain Name (FQDN).

The following are valid domain types in addition to com:

edu	U.S. educational institutions
gov	U.S. government organizations
mil	U.S. military organizations
net	a network service provider
org	U.S. organizations that don't fall into any of the preceding categories

International domains take a domain type indicative of their origin such as: au, for Australian; uk, for United Kingdom; de, for

German; hu, for Hungarian; and so forth. A domain type is actually a top-level domain in the Domain Name System, managed as part of the distributed database of valid domains.

A registered domain maps to an Internet address or a set of addresses of the type ###.###.###.###, where ### are numbers from 0 to 255. The Domain Name System (DNS) is a database that manages the worldwide assignments of friendly names to IP addresses. For information on domain names and their assignments, contact the Network Information Center (InterNIC) at: http://www.internic.net/.

Other access methods and URLs are possible on the Internet. The Internet Information Server embraces two other types of access: FTP and Gopher. FTP (file transfer protocol) lets you access a directory of files and either upload or download them from your computer.

Gopher service is similar in many respects to the WWW service in that it manages content in a hypertext manner across all of the servers in Gopherspace. A central index lets you efficiently search for content, but there is no Gopher browser that displays active content as a Web browser would.

In either of these URLs, when you don't enter a specific document or resource, the default document is used or a listing of a directory's contents is displayed.

There are many changes in the works that will affect how we use URLs in the future. It is likely that there will be additional domain types created to lessen the crowding that the popular .COM domain type has experienced. Also, in development as part of RFC 1630 is a system that will allow a resource to be tracked using a Uniform Resource Identifier (URI) to locate that resource should it be moved. A Uniform Resource Characteristic (URC) may be applied to a site or resource that will list information like author, keywords, dates, ownership, and other information. Another scheme called a Uniform Resource Name (URN) may be applied to resources that are replicated across mirrored sites.

Note: *Information on Internet proposals and conventions in progress may be found at http://merlin.cnri.reston.va.us/.*

Index